The
MIND
and
MOOD
of
BLACK AMERICA

20th CENTURY THOUGHT

THE DORSEY SERIES IN AMERICAN HISTORY

EDITOR   IRVIN G. WYLLIE   *University of Wisconsin, Parkside Campus*

The
MIND
and
MOOD
of
BLACK AMERICA

20th CENTURY THOUGHT

S. P. FULLINWIDER
Arizona State University

1969

The Dorsey Press, Homewood, Illinois

IRWIN-DORSEY LIMITED, Georgetown, Ontario

First Printing, March, 1969
Second Printing, September, 1969
Third Printing, April, 1970

Library of Congress Catalog Card No. 69–19985

Printed in the United States of America

For
my Mother,
my Wife,
and the little one

Preface

This is a study in the history of ideas; specifically, ideas held by black Americans. It is not an attempt to restate the patterns the Negro's formal ideas have taken. What is attempted is to get behind the formal ideas to their origins in myth and social necessity. This will help put some of the formal ideas into new perspective and, perhaps, give them some clarity; but the purpose is to study myth itself, its origins, and its influence in structuring the patterns those ideas have taken.

Myth grows out of psychological need; when it is tested against reality, ideology results. Both inner need and outer reality must therefore be considered. In several ways the Negro's myths are not unique—fairly close parallels can be drawn with myths historically associated with Americans of the more general sort, with Jews, and perhaps others. They are defensive myths, myths associated with an uprooted people in search of identity. They are myths that assert moral superiority—a feeling, for instance, deeply rooted in the American consciousness. Just why the American people as a whole feel so strongly about moral superiority is a question, but it is fairly easy to understand that same feeling in an oppressed people. Oppression robs one of status; the feeling of moral superiority gives it back. Oppression makes for a good deal of repressed hostility; the statement of moral superiority is a means of expressing aggression.

Myth, though it may express truths, is by definition an irrational thing. It is an extension of the emotions; it takes from reality only those facts which reinforce it. So there must of necessity be a constant warfare between myth and reality. In the present case—that of the black man in America—it has taken the form of a dialogue (perhaps a dialectic) between the myth makers and the sociological imagination. Myth has constantly dragged Negro ideology in the direction of the irrational. The sociological imagination has constantly worked to pull it back. In the end (the late

1960's) a compromise was made. The world was divided into *society* (America as the sociologist sees it) and a mystical *community;* these stand side by side but are separate. Society remains the province of the sociological imagination; the mystical community of "soul brothers" the province of myth. The most recent of the Negro's idea patterns—"black power"—managed to embrace both the rational and the mythological by using this device.

The myth to be discussed in this study has evolved over the years from its first full development at the turn of the century to the present. The inner needs shaping the myth have remained relatively constant, but the outer realities—the shift from the rural community to the big-city ghetto with relatively more freedom of expression—have changed a good deal; so also have the thought patterns of not only American culture but western civilization. Myth was forced to accommodate these changes. Basically, the myth has stated that the Negro is *more human* (more loving, higher morality, less depersonalized by industrial society, and the like) than the white man. This "more human" core of the myth has not changed over the years, but the way in which it has been explained has changed. At first it was dressed in the garb of Christianity, indicating that the black man was more Christlike than the white man (this was carried forward by Martin Luther King, Jr.). But later on, Christ was replaced by the con man as the social ideal. With the con man as the new ideal, the myth took on an outlaw aspect and a transvaluation occurred—the con man is one who defies social convention. Also productive of change in the myth's form was the tendency of black intellectuals and writers during the 1920's to turn away from the aristocratic patterns that characterized the thought of the earlier intellectuals to the thought patterns (the "blues") of the masses. The aristocratic ideal of rationalism was then replaced by a reverence for emotion. The new reverence for emotion combined with the substitution of values to reinforce the tendency of myth, itself, to drag Negro ideology towards the irrational. For these reasons Negro ideology has been under constant pressure to break away from its original demands for social reform (which included everything from simple civil rights to demands for far-reaching structural change) to a separatist position which would be only too happy to blot out the whole white world.

My deep gratitude goes to my teacher, Merle Curti, whose faith in the efficacy of scholarship and rootedness in the humanist tradition have been as beacon lights in the darkness. My thanks go also to Edmund David Cronon and J. Saunders Redding for their critical and valuable comments on the manuscript. Research would have been impossible without the kindness and fortitude of Mrs. Dorothy Porter, librarian, and Mrs. Ethel V. Ellis, cataloguer, of the Negro Collection at Howard University, and of Arna Bontemps at the Fisk University Library. Cindy Stump, ASU journalist extraordinary, directed her considerable talents to the final typing of the manuscript. My mother undertook the awful burden of feeding me during long months of research. My wife put in long hours of editing; wherever the book is readable, the fault is hers.

Tempe, Arizona   S. P. FULLINWIDER
February, 1969

Table of contents

I

From hope to hatred

As the United States entered the final quarter of the 19th century the land was crawling with activity. The great sectional bloodletting was a thing of the past. Two armies had marched home again, one in triumph, one in defeat. The North, having just dealt out the victor's brand of justice in a halfheartedly administered program that we call Reconstruction, now turned its wholehearted attention to ushering in the Gilded Age. Industrial capitalism had come of age—a brawling infant giant that demanded the rapt attention and adulation of everyone. With bands of steel reaching across the West to the Pacific, with steamships coming into their own and oil gushing from the ground, there was too much to fight, swindle, and connive about to pay much attention to the recently emancipated black man. A great new myth was in the making—"from rags to riches"—and there were new cultural heroes to adore—"captains of industry." The spirit, which in antebellum times was at best equal partners with a more humane tradition, had lately captured the minds and hearts of a victorious people.

The southern portion of the nation—the defeated portion—felt the new spirit and was torn between its call and a deep sense of loss. In the tense decade that led to secession the South managed to work itself into a frenzy of fear and hatred. Fear of the dynamite lurking in its slave population, hatred of anyone or anything that might light the fuse. Civil War and Reconstruction followed. The South drank her cup of gall—in bitterness and defeat she faced the future.

1

With the freedmen it was otherwise—this was the season of hope. When young Booker T. Washington packed his scant belongings and in blind faith left the coalfields of West Virginia in search of the magic thing called education he was simply following the example being set by thousands. Anyone who could laborously work his way over the printed page was in danger of being drafted into service as a schoolteacher. Any shelter, no matter how small or ramshackle, was subject to being made a schoolhouse. A tiny black schoolboy, R. R. Wright, became an instant celebrity when he told an important visitor to his boxcar schoolhouse (who wanted a message to the children of the North): "Tell them we are rising." In that season of hope he had expressed the feelings of the black multitude.

It is true that the Redeemers and Ku Klux Klan had their day—the Negro knew what it meant to be the victim of terrorism. Yet, there was hope—hope in the intentions of the "good" whites of the South; hope that they would reach out to the lowly freedman and help him climb the ladder that led to civilization and culture. There were the Wade Hamptons and the L. Q. C. Lamars of the South; men who fit the myth of paternalism; men who offered hope. But far more important, there was the memory of the Civil War and the fact of Emancipation; obviously part of a divine plan that was unfolding in a universe rigidly bound by the government of moral law.

The divine plan idea was central in the thought of those who proclaimed themselves spokesmen for the black race—it perfectly explained the situation of the Negro in white civilization. Africa, as the plan had it, had long since been cast into darkness for some unnamed sin, but God had relented and had seen fit to send a few chosen people into bondage, there to be initiated into Christianity and Christian civilization. The ultimate mission of this chosen people was to relight the torch of civilization and true religion in benighted Africa. There was nothing in this theory that would conflict with what the spokesmen of the race knew of science. They believed without question that no race is innately superior to any other; but they admitted that the African environment had delayed their race's social and cultural development, that given his American environment the Negro would quickly regain lost ground. Culture, they said, is not carried in the blood; it is learned. The Negro would quickly learn it in America.

The black race's spokesmen at this time were also thoroughly convinced that Western culture represented the quintessence of advanced culture. Furthermore, as it seemed to them, Western culture embodied the principles of Christianity. Indeed, that was what made it the most advanced culture in the world. This is an important consideration regarding what the spokesmen thought about the subject of culture. They judged culture and civilization according to the degree to which (in their minds) it embodied Christian principles. A civilization might well be industrially advanced and yet be among the most backward of cultures. Should the day come (as it would) when the Negro doubted the white man's Christian spirit he would become profoundly disillusioned with Western civilization itself. To understand the mind of the black race's spokesmen during the 1880's and 1890's it is necessary to realize that it judged by the measure of Christianity.

Strangely in contrast with the Negro spokesman's beliefs about race and culture was a set of stereotypes which he held concerning the white and Negro races. Though he believed that American civilization represented culture at its most advanced and most Christian stage, he thought in terms of stereotypes that were entirely inconsistent with such a belief. When he thought of the Negro race it was in terms of a meek and humble, patient and forgiving, kindly and compassionate race—a race which had all the characteristics of the gentle Christ. When he thought of the white race, he thought of it as a race of vigorous, hard, unsentimental, even cruel people—quite the opposite of the Christ-like image he held of his own people. This inconsistency was not of great importance so long as a mood of hope and optimism prevailed. The stereotypes grew in importance as the mood changed. This chapter will trace the mood and show something of the consequences of the change.

The Negro's first efforts in America toward scholarship were, in large part, shaped by his reaction to the literature of white racial apologists—a literature that was growing in volume and influence during the last two decades of the 19th century. It was a literature which encompassed such pseudoscientific inanities as John H. Van Evrie's *White Supremacy and Negro Subordination; or, Negroes a Subordinate Race* (1867), in which the claim was made that because of the sloping angle of the Negro's head any attempt to educate him would lower his center of gravity and render him incapable of walking upright. It was a literature which at times was cloaked in the sort of theological garb given it by the Rev. G. C. H. Hasskarl in his *The Missing Link: Has the Negro a Soul?* (1898). "The Negro," wrote Hasskarl, "is a separate and distinct species of the *genus homo* from Adam and Eve. . . . He is inevitably a beast and as a beast entered the ark." The beast, or brute, motif was becoming popular. In his *The Negro a Beast; or, In the Image of God* (1900), Charles Carroll identified the Negro as a "beast, created with articulate speech, that he may be of service to the white man." Thomas Dixon popularized this kind of stereotype in his triology of the Reconstruction. Such blatant prejudice, however, was of less concern to the Negro spokesmen than prejudice wrapped in the paraphernalia of statistics and data alleged to be of scientific value. Of such nature was Josiah Nott's *Types of Mankind*, published in 1854. This work (for many years highly regarded) had attempted to prove a multiple thesis: that culture is a racial product; that there has never in all history been a Negro culture of merit; that racial traits are not affected by environment; and that the several races were created separately, and moreover, were created at their present level of intellectual and moral efficiency. Similarly imposing with thickets of facts and seeming objectivity was a work by a Prudential Life Insurance statistician, Frederick L. Hoffman. His *Race Traits and Tendencies of the American Negro* (1896) tried to show that tuberculosis, venereal disease, scrofula, and the like, would presently make an end of the Negro race. Parenthetically he added that the source of this disastrous trend could be traced to the Negro's innate immorality.

Thus, as the 20th century approached, the spokesmen for the Negro race in America found themselves fighting a swelling tide of racism ranging from those of pretentious erudition to the crudities of the red-neck demagogue. Energies that might have been turned to constructive channels were dissipated in a futile attempt to bring a modicum of reason into the picture. In defense of their race, Negro writers produced works that ranged from admixtures of biblical scholarship and doubtful anthropology to what was, in one case, quite respectable history. Always it was defensive, but usually it struck a note of faith, both in God and in the ultimate victory of reason. This was the season of hope.

The first and foremost of the objectives of these early works was to demonstrate the Negro's potential equality with the white man. This task was approached in three ways (often in the same work): through the Scriptures; by a historical demonstration of the greatness to which Negroes have at times risen; and, by the argument that culture is a product of environment. The standard scriptural argument for proving the equality of races was given by a Raleigh, North Carolina lawyer, businessman and school principal, Edward A. Johnson, in his *A Short History of the Negro Race in America* (1891), a book otherwise devoted to the historical approach. White racists had got much mileage out of the supposed curse laid upon Ham by Noah. By their reckoning Ham, at the moment of the curse, ceased to be a brother of Shem and Japeth, and so the races sired by the three were never to meet on the plane of equality. Not true, wrote Johnson: Noah was in a drunken stupor at the critical moment and so could not have been giving voice to God's will. With this fact demonstrated Johnson needed only to go on to cite biblical evidence of brotherhood. Ham was the father of Canaan and Cush from whom the Canaanites and the Babylonians were descended. To Ham's progeny may also be traced the origins of Egypt.[1] And so it went.

Johnson's scriptural argument was merely a prelude to the main body of his work, and of only tangential importance in his thought. By the 1880's, the scriptural argument was being relegated to the background because the main battlefield was quickly shifting to the area of (what was then considered) science. It was to history and anthropology that the writers turned their attention. The best history written by a Negro during this period was a work by George Washington Williams, a Civil War veteran who survived battle wounds to become the first Negro to graduate from Newton Theological Seminary. Williams was a man of extraordinary vitality and ability. If he never quite achieved fame it was perhaps because he wanted to experience life in too many ways. For him the pulpit was but a stepping-stone to politics. In his spare time he studied law under Alfonso Taft and eventually got himself elected to the Ohio legislature. Once thoroughly involved in Ohio politics he went from appointive office to appointive office until

---

1 Edward A. Johnson, *A Short History of the Negro Race in America, from 1619 to 1890. With a Short Introduction as to the Origin of the Race; Also a Short Sketch of Liberia* (Chicago, 1891), pp. 14, 9–10.

he was at last made minister to Haiti. From minister Williams went to the writing of history. What caused this sudden descent no one can say with certainty. Perhaps a calm and logical temper guided him—having explored the upper limits to which American society was prepared to let a Negro climb he turned to rational persuasion in the hope of further extending those limits. Voluminous research—years of hunting down documents—went into his two-volume work, *History of the Negro Race in America, from 1619 to 1880* (1883), a massive effort which, because of an unfortunately turgid style, was panned by reviewers.

Williams dutifully introduced the scriptural argument into the preface of his work, and thereafter ignored it. Turning to the "light of philosophy, ethnology, and Egyptology," he went on to demonstrate the past greatness of his race. From the "venerable Negroes" up the Nile Egypt borrowed her "light," Greece her Homeric mythology, Rome her law. "Thus the flow of civilization has been from the East—the place of light—to the west. . . ."[2]

William T. Alexander, a Negro historian whose life has been completely obscured by time, described a once great continent known to the ancients as Atlantis (destroyed by earthquake) from which the Negro race controlled the world. Citing Heroditus, he noted that the majority of Egyptians had, in that past age, been black with curly hair. The Negro, in other words, had once stood at the very pinnacle of civilization. This was a thesis echoed and reechoed. Rufus L. Perry, in his *The Cushite, or the Descendants of Ham* (1893), placed the cradle of Western culture in Ethiopia. Perry traced the origins of that land back to Ham and then proceeded to prove it to be the mother of the Negro race as now constituted.[3]

Welcome as such arguments concerning the distant past might be, the writers and historians of the Negro race in the 1880's and 1890's realized that the much more important problem was to account for the apparent disparity between the races in modern times in terms other than innate racial characteristics. Their ap-

---

[2] George Washington Williams, *History of the Negro Race in America, from 1619 to 1880*, Vol. I (New York: G. P. Putnam's Sons, 1883), pp. vi, 22.

[3] William T. Alexander, *History of the Colored Race in America* (Kansas City, Mo.: Palmento Publishing Co., 1888), pp. 22–26; Rufus L. Perry, *The Cushite, or the Descendants of Ham* (Springfield, Mass.: Wiley and Co., 1893), pp. vii–x.

proach to this aspect of the problem was twofold: they pointed out, in the first place, that great Negroes had arisen in America despite the vast handicap of race, and they attempted to show, in the second place, that culture and personality are products of environment and not of innate race traits. Their discussions of race bring out two underlying assumptions which are more important for present purposes than their conclusions. First is their unquestioned acceptance of Western culture and civilization as the most advanced of its time—advanced in the sense of being what a civilization *should* be. The second assumption was that the Negro had fallen far behind the standards set by Western civilization and culture, and must hasten to catch up.

"The present condition of the African," wrote Edward A. Johnson in 1891, "is the result of the fall of the Egyptian empire, which was in accord with the Bible prophecy of all nations who forgot God and worshipped idols." The Africans fell because they transgressed against God, but also because of African environmental conditions—the climate. "Long years spent in the most debilitating climate on earth and violation of divine law," he wrote, "made the African what he was when the slave trade commenced in the 16th century." The assumptions in these passages are: first, that the African is backward compared to the European; second, that the African became morally debased over the years; and third, that environment (physical) and God, rather than innate race traits, account for the African's predicament. William T. Alexander agreed on all counts but the one concerning morality. It was his opinion that the African, though a semibarbarian, had become a "child of nature."[4]

George Washington Williams agreed with Johnson's theory that the Negro's fall away from civilized conditions must be accounted for by the tropical environment and by God's wrath: "But, again, what was the cause of the Negro's fall from his high state of civilization? It was forgetfulness of God, idolatry! 'Righteousness exalteth a nation; but sin is a reproach to any people.' " Beyond that however, as Williams thought, we find the destructive influence of the "miasmatic districts" of Africa which changed the Negro's complexion, stature and intellectual vigor until all that remained

---

[4] Johnson, *op. cit.*, pp. 10, 11; Alexander, *op. cit.*, pp. 9, 23.

of the once-proud race was a species of man that closely resembles the slum and criminal classes of England, who have likewise been debased by their environment. Williams also agreed with Johnson about the race's moral debasement, and he was not ambiguous on the subject of its great need of civilization and Christianity.[5]

There was, then, a unanimity among the historians concerning their race's backwardness, but also a unanimity about its ability to match the white race in civilization and culture. Outside forces— God and the physical environment—accounted for their race's adverse condition. Unanimity, however, did not extend to full acceptance of the idea that white civilization was morally advanced beyond the Negro race. We saw that Alexander had doubts on that score. Rufus L. Perry, writing in 1893, entertained no doubts at all. "The moral character of the thoughtful Cushite and his keen sense of right, seems to be peculiarly fundamental," wrote Perry, ". . . In this ethical trait he is admittedly ahead of his predatory white brother." When confronted with the problem of race in America Perry struck a new note. The others saw its solution in the civilization and acculturation of the Negro race. Perry accepted this as one viable solution, but added that the same effect would be accomplished if the white man were to become Christianized.[6]

Perry's dissent is important as a hint of things to come. He was making explicit an opinion which is implicit in the writings of the others—that the Negro is actually in advance of Western civilization when it comes to morality. This belief as yet (except in Perry's case) existed only at the level of stereotype and had not begun to influence formal thought. These early spokesmen loudly and earnestly declaimed against racism and brought all their knowledge to bear against it. They were trying to prove the Negro race's potential equality with the white race—given time, hard work, and exposure to civilization and Christianity. But deeply imbedded in their concepts was a potentially reverse racism. According to the stereotypes these men held the Negro was more like Christ than the white man.

In his *Short History*, Johnson wrote this about the Negro in slavery: "The negro being largely endowed by nature with af-

5 Williams, *op. cit.*, Vol. I, pp. 24, 47–49.
6 Perry, *op. cit.*, pp. 146, 155–56.

fection, affability, and a forgiving spirit, generally won for himself good treatment. Then too, the master had some soul. . . ." In that short passage Johnson laid bare his true opinion of the relative merits of the two races—the almost reverent description of the Negro's nature, the grudging admission that the white man has a soul. Williams, likewise, demonstrates the logical inconsistency lurking in the background of his thought. In the following passage he tried to have it both ways: the Negro is rapidly advancing, and the Negro is already quite perfect: "Every year since the close of the Rebellion the Negro had been taking on better and purer traits of character. Possessed of an impressible nature, a discriminating sense of the beautiful, and a deep, pure taste for music, his progress has been phenomenal. Strong in his attachments, gentle in manners, confiding, hopeful, enduring in affection, and benevolent to a fault, there is no limit to the outcome of his character." This kind of inconsistency—the idea that the Negro has a perfect nature together with the idea that he still has some distance to go to catch up with the white man—could exist only in a milieu of optimism and the absence of bitterness. Williams concluded his two-volume work with an expression of faith that race prejudice against the Negro will end when the Negro has attained education, character, and wealth. It is, he concluded, all part of God's great plan.[7]

One of the best windows into the thought of those Negro intellectuals who came to maturity of mind during the 1880's and 1890's is provided by the ideas of Alexander Crummell. This New York-born graduate of Cambridge University played an important role in the intellectual development of the Negro race in America. For 22 years he held a prestigious ministerial post at St. Luke's Protestant Episcopal Church in Washington, but beyond this he gathered around him the leading Negro intellectuals (not the least of whom was W. E. B. Du Bois) into the American Negro Academy, which he founded in March, 1897. Within the tightly knit groups of Negro intellectuals forming in Washington and Boston this man of sweet disposition and large erudition became a venerated figure holding a position not unlike that of the elder Channing among the Transcendentalists of an earlier time.

On March 7, of the year 1897, Alexander Crummell stood be-

---

[7] Johnson, *op. cit.*, pp. 143–44; Williams, *op. cit.*, Vol. III, pp. 548–49.

fore the Academy and unburdened himself on the subject closest to his heart—the chief need of the Negro race. This need, he said, is civilization—civilization such as the great spirits of Western culture—Plato, Socrates, Aristotle, and Euclid—had created for Europe and America. Until such time as the Negro race produces such men it will remain a benighted race. "Who," he asked, "are to be the agents to lift up this people of ours to the grand plane of civilization? Who are to bring them up to the height of noble thought, grand civility, a chaste and elevating culture, refinement, and the impulses of irrepressible progress?"[8]

That Crummell considered Western civilization the paragon of man's highest attainments is abundantly clear. He went further. It is, he thought, the embodiment of the Christian spirit—God's instrument for the spread of Christianity. He went so far in this direction at one time as to proclaim that European imperialism in Africa was a grand and benevolent thing. Here, surely, was a man who believed wholeheartedly in Western civilization and who longed for the Negro to rise to the greatness of its example. He could give the white man almost unlimited praise: "No civilization on this continent," he wrote, "will be worth a cent which lacks a large infusion of the large common sense, the strong practicality, the fine intelligence, the lofty culture, the freedom-loving spirit, and the restless aspirations of the people of the North." He had unbounded faith in the future of the Negro in the hands of such people. And why not? The age, to this minister of the Gospel, was infused with the spirit of benevolence. One need only look at the facts—the recent emancipation of the slaves, for example—to realize that the world is ruled by a "moral government."[9]

In general, Crummell voiced the prevailing attitudes of optimism and faith. But underneath this sort of effusion, rushing to the surface at odd and unexpected times, is the mix-up of stereotypes which potentially constitute a complete reversal of attitudes.

---

[8] Alexander Crummell, "Civilization the Primal Need of the Race," *Occasional Papers*, III (Washington, D.C.: American Negro Academy, 1898), pp. 3–7.

[9] Alexander Crummell, "The Greatness of Christ," *The Greatness of Christ, and Other Sermons* (New York: Thomas Whittaker, 1882), pp. 8–11, 16–17; Alexander Crummell, "Address before the American Geographical Society," *Africa and America: Addresses and Discourses* (Springfield, Mass.: Wiley and Co., 1891), pp. 309–15; Alexander Crummell, "A Defense of the Negro Race in America from the Assaults and Charges of Rev. J. L. Tucker, D.D. of Jackson, Mississippi," *Africa and America: Addresses and Discourses* (Springfield, Mass.: Wiley and Co., 1891), p. 122.

Looking toward the South and at the race he so strongly believed would one day rise, he saw a "low, degraded, miserable, almost beastly . . ." people. The elevation of this Negro race, he stated sadly, would be "hard, serious, long-continued, painful, plodding work." But on the other hand, not so fast: "The negro, however, is brave as well as gentle; courageous as well as amiable; a gallant soldier as well as a patient sufferer and an enduring martyr. The quiet and submissive qualities of the race have been, not seldom, the butt of ridicule and the sneer of the jester."[10]

If Crummell could see his people as imbruted, he could also see them as Christ-like. He loved to quote (and did so in print three times) a statement concerning the Christ-like qualities of the Negro made by William Ellery Channing: "We are holding in bondage one of the best races of the human family. . . . His nature is affectionate, easily touched; and hence he is more open to religious impressions than the white man. . . . When I cast my eyes over the Southern region, the land of bowie knives, lynch law and duels . . . can I hesitate in deciding to which of the races in that land Christianity is most adapted, and in which its noblest disciples are most likely to be reared?"[11]

So long as Negro spokesmen and intellectuals had Crummell's optimism their admiration of American civilization and their faith that the Negro would soon master its techniques remained their dominant faith. But the invidious comparison between the "Christ-like" Negro and the brutal white man was always there in latent form. It was a comparison that, after a long period of frustrated hope and the onslaught of desperation, would turn into a rather virulent racism. The Christ-like image of the Negro was to serve as the vehicle for racial prejudice.

---

10 Alexander Crummell, "The Social Principle among a People, and Its Bearing on their Processes and Development," *The Greatness of Christ, and Other Sermons* (New York: Thomas Whittaker, 1882), pp. 304, 301; Alexander Crummell, "Incidents of Hope for the Negro Race in America," Thanksgiving Day sermon, Nov. 26th, 1895, to St. Luke's Church, Washington, D.C. (Washington, D.C.: John H. Wills, 1895), pp. 10–11.

11 Crummell, Thanksgiving Day Sermon, *ibid.*, p. 10. For a discussion of the Black Christ myth among whites prior to the Civil War, see Kenneth S. Lynn, *Mark Twain and Southwestern Humor* (Boston: Little, Brown and Co., 1959), pp. 105–111. According to Lynn this was the most potent myth of the Negro held by white Americans.

II

In the year 1911, a young teacher of languages at the American Missionary Association College in Talladega, Alabama, sat down to write the first chapters of an autobiography, *The Heir of Slaves.* William Pickens, the subject of this work, thought back to his early childhood in Pendleton, South Carolina, and paused for a moment in wonderment. Those had been happy years—years free from the ravishes of racial antagonism. His father, as he recalled, had worked for the head man ("town councillor") of the village, and the two men had been boon companions, running the town together. "Race antagonism," wrote Pickens, "seemed not to touch our world." In those dimly remembered days—it was of the early 1880's that he wrote—there had been a curious Christmas ritual. The younger Negro men of the town would capture the sheriff and throw him in jail saying, " 'there is no law on Christmas,' " and then, "one of them would put on the badge and strut around town getting applause and laughter." Looking back in 1911, Pickens wryly commented that such behavior now would bring the militia from four states.[12]

The world of the southern Negro had changed in those short years. The same phenomenon was witnessed by one of the most astute minds the Negro race in America has produced, James Weldon Johnson. In his autobiography, *Along This Way* (1933), Johnson told of his boyhood in Jacksonville, Florida—a small village in those years of the 1870's and 1880's. When he was growing up there, he recalled, many of the town policemen, town councilmen, and justices of the peace were Negroes. Johnson, who was born in 1871, was describing a period which must have lasted some years beyond the Compromise of 1877 and subsequent withdrawal of federal troops from the South. As he, himself, makes clear, this was a time when the well-to-do "Redeemers" still controlled the politics of the South. Johnson believed, and was probably right in his belief, that the change for the worse came when the aristocratic families with names like L'Engle, Hartridge, and

---

[12] William Pickens, *The Heir of Slaves: An Autobiography* (New York: The Pilgrim Press, 1911), pp. 16–17.

Daniels were driven from power by the rising poor whites and their leaders, poor or otherwise.[13]

The key to the thought of Negro spokesmen during the 1890's and early years of this century is a shift from an outlook of hope to one of bitterness. They were witnessing a social revolution take place in the South and, with each turn of the wheel, they watched their own race become more deeply submerged in the quagmire of caste. What has been called the "revolution of the red-necks" in Mississippi and Tillmanism in South Carolina, what Thomas E. Watson and Hoke Smith represented in Georgia, was happening to the Negro. Jim Crow was happening to the Negro. Tennessee began it in 1881 with a law segregating first-class accommodations on railroads. Louisiana, Alabama, Arkansas, Georgia, and Kentucky had, by 1894, followed Tennessee's example. It took the people of South Carolina until 1898 to make up their minds; then came North Carolina and Virginia. Soon the practice was broadened to include mandatory segregation in waiting rooms, theaters, boardinghouses, water fountains, ticket windows, streetcars, penitentiaries, county jails, convict camps, institutions for the blind and deaf, hospitals for the insane, and, in Atlanta, Georgia, courtroom Bibles. Disfranchisement was happening to the Negro. Begun with the Mississippi constitution of 1890, the process was completed by Oklahoma in 1910. The provisions were ingenious: residence requirements, poll taxes, literacy tests, grandfather clauses—all were effective. Best of all, however, was the white primary. In 1896, some 130,344 Negroes were registered to vote in Louisiana. By 1900, after two years of the new constitution, only 5,320 Negroes were registered in that state. Alabama figures are equally impressive—only 3,000 Negroes there registered to vote after the new constitution went into effect in 1901.

Probably most distressing was the new sense of race hatred. The Reconstruction and "redemption" periods had their quotas of terrorism, but there had always been some party or faction to support the Negro's cause: the Republicans, or the Populists or the Bourbons, depending on time and place. But the 1890's and the dawn of the 20th century brought into power in the South a group of demagogues whose only appeal (at least, so it seemed

[13] James Weldon Johnson, *Along This Way: The Autobiography of James Weldon Johnson* (New York: The Viking Press, Inc., 1933), p. 45.

to the Negro, despite much talk about progressive measures) was to race prejudice. Hatred seemed to suddenly overshadow everything. There was, for instance, a spate of race riots to occupy the Negro's thoughts. Riots broke out in Greenwood, South Carolina, and Wilmington, North Carolina, in 1898; Statesboro, Georgia, and Springfield, Ohio, in 1904; Atlanta, Georgia, Greensburg, Indiana, and Brownsville, Texas, in 1906. Then, lynching was (or seemed to be) becoming something of a sport—a holiday affair— in some of the southern states. The 30-year period covered by the NAACP publication, *Thirty Years of Lynching in the United States, 1889-1918*, witnessed the mob-murder of some 3,224 persons, about three fourths of whom were Negroes—the vast majority of cases having taken place in the South. There was horror in the simple fact of it, but it was the festive atmosphere attending some of them that kept Negro writers in the grips of fascinated revulsion —and hatred.

The development of the Negro spokesmen's attitudes during the period from roughly 1890 to World War I followed the trend set by the ever-worsening relations between the races. It was a period of anguish and a growing sense of alienation from the white man and all his works. Negroes began to question, and then to reject, the white man's standards. The trend reached its consumation in a burst of bitter reproach and even hatred toward the white race. Nowhere is the trend better illustrated than in the thinking of the brothers, Francis and Archibald Grimké.

Francis J. Grimké and his brother were given birth by a slave, but, as the curious paradoxes of the slave system would have it, they were born into one of South Carolina's most prominent families. Moreover (while on the subject of paradox), they could count among their relatives the famous abolitionist sisters, Sara and Angelina Grimké. The brothers were born into slavery, but were set free in 1855 by their dying father. Francis was five years old at the time, and it would take some years and the Civil War to set him free in reality—years during which he was to be sold back into slavery by a half brother. After the war, arrangements were made (by whom we are not told) for him to study in the North, which he did. In 1878, Francis Grimké, now a rather fierce looking young man of dignified bearing, graduated from Princeton Theological Seminary and took a pulpit in Washington's Fifteenth Street Presbyterian Church at which he was to become a fixture (50 years), and at which he would win such distinction that Howard University would one day see fit to offer him its presidency (which he would refuse).

Francis J. Grimké is a wonderful example of how Protestantism throws man back upon himself—of how it makes the individual wholly responsible for his own actions. Week after week, year following upon year, with a regularity approaching monotony, this preacher whom men called the "Black Puritan" demanded of his people that they look to themselves—each man to the development of his own character. And each Sunday morning as Grimké rose to give his stern message a thousand other Negro preachers were climbing into a thousand other pulpits, preparing to deliver the same message to their congregations—the individual's responsibility for the self.[14] Preached as it was, at a time when the race's social and intellectual life was centered on and formed by the church, and when many of its most respected and famous men were ministers, this doctrine became the cornerstone of the Negro intellectual's consciousness. At a time when social scientists were starting to beguile the country with the comfortable doctrine that the individual is but the creature of his environment, when the most important liberal movement within the American church (the Social Gospel) adapted this doctrine to its needs, the Negro church went on unmindful of the clamor. Francis Grimké gave the environmentalist idea short shrift—it might say something about animals, he conceded, but nothing about man: "With man, however, it is different. He is a rational creature, a free moral agent, a responsible being, and therefore God's method of dealing with him is different."[15]

At about the turn of the century, when Francis Grimké was at the height of his powers, Booker T. Washington, from his school at Tuskegee, Alabama, was giving eloquent voice to a doctrine of

14 This is the impression gained from reading several hundred sermons—sermons meant, of course, for middle-class ears since they have found their way into print. The impression, no doubt, does not hold for the more primitive and evangelical sermons of the untrained rural and storefront preachers, who are famous for their vivid descriptions of the creation, heaven, hell, and the like.

15 Francis J. Grimké, *The Works of Francis J. Grimké: Vol. III, Stray Thoughts and Meditations*, ed. Carter J. Woodson (Washington, D.C.: The Associated Publishers, Inc., 1942), p. 42.

character development that had gained the attention of the nation. The Washington doctrine was a pragmatic thing: once the Negro develops character the white man will accept him as an equal. On the surface this position was not unlike Grimké's, but in its fundamental intent it was actually worlds apart. Being in essence pragmatic, Washington's definition of character meant that which will please the white man—that which will make the Negro just like the white man. During the early years of optimism, when white civilization was so often idolized by the Negro, Francis Grimké might have accepted this definition. Basically, though, the minister was concerned only with pleasing God, not the white man, and as time passed, and his respect for the white man neared the vanishing point, he came to see the Washington doctrine as conceived by the devil himself.[16] He was to become a bitter critic of the Tuskegee president and a member of the militant Niagara Movement. The seeds of the militant revolt against Booker T. Washington lay in the differing ideas of character.

The change in Francis Grimké's attitude toward the white man can be gauged rather accurately as we watch the never-ending, day-by-day grind of discrimination cast its shadow across his soul. In the early years of his ministry he was rather well disposed toward white America. On Thanksgiving Day, 1892, he thanked God for the evidences of Christian forces that he saw at work among the American people. He thanked God with equal fervor for the fact that this was a Christian nation filled with Christian homes. In another speech or sermon of that year he listed the signs of change for the better. Significantly, each sign that he mentioned was one which seemed to herald a change in the attitude of the white people toward the Negro. In 1892, he was still putting his faith in the benevolence and conscience of the whites.[17]

By 1900, Grimké had changed his mind about the white man's Christianity. He saw in the white church a blunted moral sensibility, a "mean, and cowardly, and despicable spirit." He could

---

[16] Francis J. Grimké, "Signs of a Brighter Future," *The Works of Francis J. Grimké: Vol. I, Addresses Mainly Personal and Racial*, ed. Carter J. Woodson (Washington, D.C.: The Associated Publishers, Inc., 1942), p. 263.

[17] Francis J. Grimké, manuscript of speech, 1892, Grimké papers, Howard University Library; Francis J. Grimké, manuscript of speech, June 26, 1892, *ibid*.

see little cause for optimism regarding the conscience of the white race. The South, he decided, was out to reinstitute slavery in everything but name, and the North could not care less. Largely because of the hypocrisy of the white clergy, the "Southern savages" had been sinking "lower and lower during these years of barbarism. . . ." Yet, as of 1900, Grimké had not lost his ability to distinguish between "good" and "bad" whites. In the same breath he proclaimed his lingering faith that there were still some white men and women above prejudice. "There are not a great many, I admit; but there are some."[18]

By 1918, the picture appeared grimmer to Grimké. Upon noticing a Pennsylvania Avenue sign which made obvious reference to the Germans, "SHALL HUMANITY RULE OR THE SAVAGE?" he turned with bitter sarcasm against white America. Germany hardly equaled the United States in savagery: "That shows, as clearly as anything can, that the whites are nothing but savages themselves; that they are still on a very low plane in point of moral development." American civilization, he wrote a few months later, "is about as low as it can be, measured by humane principles. . . ." The national greeting to the returning Negro veterans of World War I was widespread rioting and lynching. Grimké's mood began to verge on hatred: "If being a white man's country means a country where only white men may expect decent, humane treatment—where only white men may expect to have justice accorded them, then the sooner the white man is wiped from the face of the earth the better it will be for the world."[19]

Though he stood very near the center of prewar Negro radicalism, and though he came to stand on the brink of racism, Francis Grimké never stepped over the brink. His Christian faith remained too strong; his belief in the rationality of man never left him. Nevertheless, he walked far down the road to an invidious

---

[18] Francis J. Grimké, "Discouragements: Hostility of the Press, Silence and Cowardice of the Pulpit," Francis J. Grimké, *Works of Francis J. Grimké: Vol. I*, pp. 237–46; Francis J. Grimké, "Signs of a Brighter Future," *The Works of Francis J. Grimké*, ed. Carter J. Woodson (Washington, D.C.: The Associated Publishers, Inc., 1942), p. 270.

[19] Grimké, *Works op. cit., Vol. III*, pp. 44, 67, entry, August, 1819; *Ibid.*, p. 103. Entry, January, 1922.

comparison of the races. He succumbed to the temptation of categorizing all white men as money-mad moral freaks.[20] His opinion and his growing hatred was shared by others in his intellectual circle—men, who because they participated in the secularization of thought, sought a new faith to replace the old. The new faith they found was racism.

Constant and growing oppression rained hammerblows at the Negro intellectual's optimistic faith in a universe governed by moral law. But this was not all. Almost as devastating was the introduction into the post-Civil War American mind of new currents of thought—particularly the Darwinian-based idea that this is a universe of chance, of struggle, of chaos. To the Negro, struck by the absurdity of his plight, this had to be a compelling idea. It was the particular burden born by Archibald Grimké.

Like his brother, Archibald Grimké was a man of vast ability. A graduate of Harvard Law School, he went first into the field of newspaper editing, then into the field of history becoming an authority on the abolitionists and the biographer of William Lloyd Garrison and Charles Sumner. It was his admiration and respect for these men and the type of moral integrity they represented that he carried into the emergent radical movement of the early 20th century. He was a formative influence among the men who organized the Niagara Movement and the NAACP, and who elected him president of the Washington, D.C., branch of that organization. Measured by any standard his life was a success—yet he was a man plagued with dissolving certainties.

From 1883 to 1885, Archibald Grimké edited *The Hub,* a Boston weekly dedicated to advancing the cause of the Negro and the Republican party. The voice that spoke from the pages of the *Hub* was the voice of transcendentalism. It spoke of the "divine forces" that leap into the heart of the world in seasons of Pentecost, when "the eternal verities of the universe gravitate earthward and are incarnated in human thought and endeavor." The voice—and the voice was Grimké's—told its readers how society is governed by the moral force: "In its last analysis, civil society rests upon force— but this force is moral, not physical. . . . The visible is transient— individual and corporeal—and as a cause, must in the nature of

---

[20] Francis J. Grimké to Wendell Phillips Stafford, November 30, 1911, *Works, ibid., Vol. IV, Letters,* p. 125.

things be secondary. The invisible is eternal, impersonal, moral, and as cause, is beneath, in and above the merely visible, and, so far as it is concerned, ranks as primary. . . . The world is governed by mind."[21]

This transcendentalist orientation—a world governed by mind—pervades Grimké's biographies of Garrison and Sumner. The two abolitionists are shown to be agents of "Providence" working in history. History is shown to be the working out of the struggle between moral forces and the forces of materialism and greed. Garrison, especially, is depicted as being meek and forgiving in the spirit of Jesus ("Garrison was a full believer in the literal doctrine of non-resistance as enunciated by Jesus."), and it is this meek and forgiving spirit that Grimké equates with the moral forces that govern the world. Of the abolitionists he said: "Theirs was a moral warfare, the grappling of truth with error, of the power of love with the inhumanities of the nation." Actually, the spirit of love and nonresistance was a more accurate description of Grimké's ideal than that of the abolitionists. It was his favorite description of the Negro, for instance. But—going on with Grimké's analysis of history—we find him concluding that the forces of materialism have for the time being conquered the nation: ". . . the children of the nineteenth century worship but one god—the Almighty Dollar—and look with one accord upon Success as its supreme prophet."[22]

The period of Grimké's editorship of *The Hub* (1883–85), and of the biographies of Garrison and Sumner (1891, 1892), was his time of optimism. It was his time for the faith that moral forces are working themselves out in history. By 1898, Darwin had done his work on Grimké; tooth and claw, as he now saw, rule the world. On Thanksgiving Day of that year he announced to an audience of ministers his new belief in the doctrine of the survival of the fittest, and he held up to them a virtue quite unlike the meekness of Jesus—a "virile virtue" that makes for self-respect and is grounded upon a primitive consciousness of

---

[21] Archibald H. Grimké, "Our Apostolic Age," *The Hub*, Vol. 2, January 12, 1884, p. 1; Archibald H. Grimké, "Woman's Ballot," *The Hub*, Vol. 2, January 19, 1884, p. 1.

[22] Archibald H. Grimké, *William Lloyd Garrison: The Abolitionist* (New York: Funk & Wagnalls, 1891), pp. 118–122, 182; Archibald H. Grimké, *Charles Sumner: The Scholar in Politics* (New York: Funk & Wagnalls, 1892), p. 120.

power. As for meekness, he said, one day it might prevail. "But this I do not doubt, and you do not doubt, that the meek possess precious little of this earth today. . . . Might, not meekness, has covered the earth, and is covering it now at this moment, with its greedy, all-devouring rights and claims."[23]

By 1898, Archibald Grimké had lost faith in the efficacy of moral absolutes; the world had lost its guiding spirit for him; struggle and chaos had won. But though his vision had changed his heart remained divided. Sometimes he found it in himself to call upon the Negro to emulate the heavy-handedness of the white man. More often he praised the meekness of spirit and forgiving nature of his race. Repeatedly he extolled the behavior of the slaves during the Civil War for their devotion to their masters in time of crisis: "This behavior of the slaves," he wrote in 1915, "is the supreme example which American Christianity has yet given of the vital presence of the spirit of the divine founder in its midst."[24]

In his later years—years of dissolving certainties and deepening skepticism—one area of certainty remained for Archibald Grimké —his Christ-like image of the Negro. He had transferred from the abolitionists to his own race those virtues he held highest, and attributed to the white man a moral obtuseness and inhuman greed. In his last published paper (1924), Grimké sketched out his new faith in bold strokes. Using the examples of Washington, Jefferson, and Wilson he first made the point that the central fact of American history has been the great discrepancy between the white man's brave words and immoral deeds. Both the father of the country and the author of the Declaration of Independence were slaveholders; the Republican party brought emancipation, but abandoned the freedmen in return for economic gain—these and other examples Grimké used to point up the moral insensibility of white America. In sharp contrast is the picture presented by the Negro: "Yes, although black and despised, he, the slave . . . had risen above his centuries of wrongs, above their bitter

---

23 Archibald H. Grimké, "Lessons of the Hour," manuscript of speech, Washington, D.C., November 24, 1898, Grimké papers, Howard University Library, pp. 21, 22.

24 Archibald H. Grimké, "The Ultimate Criminal," *Occasional Papers*, Vol. 17 (Washington, D.C.: American Negro Academy, 1915), p. 5.

memories and bitterer sufferings to the love of enemies, to the forgiveness of those who had despitefully used him, aye, to those moral heights where heroes are throned and martyrs crowned."[25]

Out of the ruins of his former ideology Grimké had begun to build a new one based on this invidious comparison of the races. Essentially, he was a humanist. His early biographies of Garrison and Sumner were basically tracts calling American society away from crass materialism back to the humane values of those reformers. But his was a humanist response that, because (in his later years) its basic assumption was the invidious comparison of the races, could in less-mature or more volatile hands turn into racism and the complete rejection of American civilization.

The Grimké brothers belonged to a small circle of spokesmen and intellectuals who looked to 19th-century New England for their inspiration and their intellectual sustenance. This small circle of men took the abolitionists as their heroes, the Transcendentalists as their oracles. They read papers to each other at the meetings of the Washington, D.C., Bethel Literary and Historical Association, and its successor, the American Negro Academy. They formed the spearhead of early 20th-century Negro militant protest, providing a large share of the membership of the Niagara Movement (1905–09) and the early NAACP. Their closeness to Protestantism made them acutely aware of the self and of their personal responsibility for the self. Their closeness to Transcendentalism made them view the ongoing process of society as mere appearance—made them turn inward in their search for reality. Their situation as Negroes in white America deprived them of outward status and greatly reinforced the tendency to turn inward away from outward forms. The inner reality they found was character, and, more particularly, the Christ-like character. Their militant movement must be seen in this light. It stemmed in part from disgust at what seemed to be Booker T. Washington's submission to Jim Crow and to disfranchisement in the South. But, above and beyond that, they felt that Washington's doctrine of assimilation into materialistic American culture would lead

---

[25] Archibald H. Grimké, "The Shame of America, or the Negro's Case against the Republic," *Occasional Papers*, Vol. 21 (Washington, D.C.: American Negro Academy, 1924), pp. 1–17.

to the destruction of the Negro's unique humanity. In short, Negro protest, from the beginning of this century, has been basically opposed to assimilation.

The tendencies in thought thus far described are summed up well in the writings and doings of the shadowy figure, William H. Ferris--a man largely forgotten by historians. Though he stood near the center of the early militant protest (his claim was that he started the revolt against Washington), he was apparently too much the oddball, the misfit, to be taken seriously by his contemporaries. He was, nevertheless, a participating member of the Bethel Literary—where he first presented his case against Washington, in 1898—and later an active member of the American Negro Academy. He stayed on the sidelines while others organized the Niagara Movement and the NAACP. But he was active in cheering those groups on, and named their leader—W. E. B. Du Bois—the most formative influence on his thought.

Ferris' great effort, *The African Abroad* (1913), was a two-volume discourse on all subjects under the sun. In it he attempted to develop both a formal philosophy and a scheme of history. His ideas are the ideas of his Yale and Harvard professors as well as those of Du Bois. But if the work is second hand and imitative, it is a most valuable insight into the thinking of the more important men around him—the militants of his intellectual circle.

The African Abroad is a Transcendentalist work: "How can the mind of man impose its mental forms upon the world of sense, unless the world were the manifestations of mind, yea a mental being in its inner life?" Yet it incorporates into it the Darwinian struggle and the pseudo-Darwinian idea of the evolution of social life through conflict. The result is a scheme of history (borrowed from Du Bois) in which the world spirit (freedom and/or love) is working through the bloody struggles of peoples to the purpose of finally manifesting itself in the living reality of human intercourse. Ferris shows how each great nation and race has brought its gift to Western civilization. What must now be added to the theology of the Jews, the philosophical wisdom of the Greeks, the organizing genius of the Romans, and the spirit of freedom of the Anglo-Saxons, is the loving nature of the Negro: "We are a race possessing a lovable nature, a spiritual earnestness and a musical genius. The nineteenth century civilization, the nine-

teenth century Christianity, and especially the American civilization and American Christianity is absorbed in a gross materialism
which takes away the spirit of love and depreciates the spiritual
side of human nature. . . . The Negro possesses those spiritual
and emotional qualities which can soften human nature and
spiritualize religion and music." The Christ-like image of the
Negro coupled with this sort of evolutionary scheme of history
implies a mission ideology—the Negro's mission to spiritualize
Western civilization.[26]

The way Ferris understood it the great struggle of 20th-century
America would be that between American commercialism and
the humane spirit of the Negro. In this struggle Booker T. Washington was not exactly on the side of the angels: "Dr. Washington
has thus expressed the watchword of the modern world. 'The
world does not care so much what you or I know, as what we can
do.' And the masses of colored men and women have forsaken
soul-hunger for land-hunger and gold-hunger." As for himself
and the other militants, they were calling the race back from
Washington and the lust for gold: "It is a fact that this dissatisfac-
tion with the crass and sordid materialism of Mr. Washington's
teaching has voiced itself in Du Bois's 'Souls of Black Folk,' has
spoken in the trenchant and hysterical editorials of the Boston
Guardian, has uttered itself in the *Voice of the Negro*."[27]

Such, in broad outline, was the humanist line developed in
The African Abroad—the clearly expressed desire to recall
America from the lure of gold back to the humane values grouped
around love. It was in this mood that Ferris set Emerson up as
the ultimate in moral philosophy. But it is not a work of one
mood. It is a work that alternates back and forth between two
quite opposite moods—two world views. If love is to conquer, it
is to do so through the Darwinian struggle. If love is one guiding
force of history, the other is conflict. One world view portrayed a
universe governed by law; the other understood the historical
process in terms of struggle and chaos. In his Darwinian world
view the white man represented not the crass materialism of the

26 William H. Ferris, *The African Abroad: or, His Evolution in Western Civilization*, Vol. I (New Haven: The Tuttle, Morehouse and Taylor Press, 1913), pp. 15,
30, 35.

27 *Ibid.*, pp. 209, 396.

moral idiot but the fighter for freedom. From his Darwinian vantage point he could see that the greatest virtue is not love but courage and the fighting spirit. He wrote that, "The Anglo-Saxon race is the greatest fighting race that has yet appeared on the stage of history, combining aggressive force with dogged determination and a bulldog grit and tenacity of purpose, combining a daring, adventurous spirit with the ability to fight a hard, uphill battle." In this mood Ferris told the Negro to become a black white man, a "Negro-Saxon." The villain was still Booker T. Washington, but now because he was seen to be an "Uncle Tom" (Ferris was the first to use that particular epithet in reference to Washington) —he was a weak man calling for surrender.[28]

An explanation of the contradictions in *The African Abroad* begins to emerge when two other ingredients of the work are added to the picture. Ferris' fantasies of greatness constitute one of these ingredients. He informs us that in order to write this work he had to take time out from writing two important philosophical works and a volume of literary and historical essays. He tells us that he was the leader of the revolt against Washington. The other ingredient is self-doubt, a sense of inadequacy. He met attractive girls and informed them of his great talent ("I told her that I expected some day to startle and surprise, to astonish and electrify the world . . ."), but was unable to achieve normal relationships with them. These things suggest that his two world views correspond to a love-hate response to both the white man and to his own race, and that response, in turn, grew out of a love-hate response to himself. He countered his own sense of inadequacy with fantasies of greatness and of the greatness of his race (it is Christ-like). Yet, at one point he remarks that it is a shame that he is forced to associate with the "coarse and ignorant" lower class Negro. He counteracted his sense of inferiority to, and dependency upon, the oppressor by identifying with him and by glorifying his deeds. Both his world views were loaded with hostility—the one manifesting hatred through an invidious comparison of the races, the other by a tooth-and-claw view of a hostile world. His hostility was, as yet, undirected—or, rather, directed against everyone.[29]

---

28 *Ibid.*, pp. 287, 90.
29 *Ibid.*, pp. 124, 229.

Ferris broke out of the morass of conflicting loyalties and passions by turning racist—by joining the black nationalist Garvey movement of the 1920's. Garvey, a West Indian of magnetic appeal, brought to Harlem's masses a doctrine of emancipation through separatism—"back to Africa." He proclaimed the beauty of blackness, the greatness of the black man's past, and the promise of the future. His movement brought parades and uniforms and excitement to the streets of Harlem. To get his message across to a wider reading public he published the weekly *Negro World* (1918–33) and selected Ferris for his editor. As a child Ferris had often thrilled to the parades and speakers who celebrated Independence Day and the heroes who had made that day possible for America. His proudest moment had come when he had been asked to march in one of those parades. Now, years later, as a Garveyite, he could glory in other parades, other heroes—he could glory in his blackness. As a leading spokesman for the most virulent racist movement of the time among Negroes he now had a new absolute, a new set of certainties. The hostility that had been latent in his two opposing world views now came to the surface to become the core of a new world view. His earlier humanism had been a very real but a very frail plant. It was unable to survive the indignities suffered in 20th-century America.

II

Racial Christianity

The Negro intellectuals and spokesmen were faced with the problem of choosing between two world views as the new century approached. In the realm of religion it was a choice between an "other-worldly" and a "this-worldly" faith. Is the Christian message one which asks man to submit patiently to the evils of this world secure in the knowledge that paradise awaits the true Christian in the next, or is it a message of reform—calculated to bring to mankind a society based on brotherly love? A great many forces (which can be subsumed under the general heading, "the secularization of thought") were at work in the world of the intellectual to shift religious thought into "this-worldly" channels.

Rational religion in America, child of a clandestine marriage between Calvinism and the Enlightenment, had weaned the intellectual away from the fundamentalistic faith through a succession of theological vagaries ranging from William Ellery Channing's Unitarianism to Horace Bushnell's social Christianity to Walter Rauschenbusch's Social Gospel. Transcendentalism, socialism, Higher Criticism and Social Darwinism had done their work in convincing theologians like Washington Gladden and Walter Rauschenbusch that man is at least potentially good, and that God is working through history eventually to create a kingdom of heaven on earth.

These forces were generally absent from the Negro's religion, and for two very good reasons: first, the overwhelming majority of Negro clergymen were destitute of extensive education; second, the Negro's religious institutions were under the imperious domination of conservative-fundamentalist leaders whose power

26

rested less on book learning than on intrigue. As late as 1930 investigators found that a paltry 20 percent of urban Negro pastors (of all denominations) were college graduates. The corresponding figure for rural Negro churches was 3 percent. The majority of Negro churches had no educational standards for their ministries; anyone who felt "called" could usually be ordained. In the Baptist denomination (which accounted for two thirds of the churchgoing Negroes), freedom promoted the proliferation of untrained ministers—all that was needed to start a new church was the agreement of four laymen and three ordained ministers.[1]

But the Negro clergyman was not necessarily a man of small talent. On the contrary, the church was the one area in the Negro world where a man of talent might get ahead—it was the one institution not dominated by whites. The various denominations tended to become vast political arenas where power struggle and intrigue were as rife as was religious fervor. Somehow in the turmoil the more progressive minded got shoved aside. So, in Negro religion, the shift to "this-worldly" religion, when it occurred, was an isolated and sporadic thing. But it was important.[2]

Commitments to world views involve (beyond exposure to new ideas and calm deliberation on the alternatives) such factors as the cultural milieu, institutional pressures, and such attitudinal sets as are formed in the unconscious. With regard to the last-named factor, the handling and channeling of aggression must be taken into account as playing an important part in the process of choice. Admitting this, how is the historian to handle it? Probably only on the level of hypothesis.

The hypothesis of the present chapter is this: That the "Christlike" image (stereotype) of the Negro was born out of the formation of ego-defense mechanisms contrived in the slave's unconscious to maintain self-respect during a time when the choice in handling aggression was either to repress it or to be destroyed. The slave's patience, humility, and good nature were necessary

---

[1] See Benjamin E. Mays and Joseph W. Nicholson, *The Negro Church* (New York: Institute of Social and Religious Research, 1933), pp. 10, 238.

[2] See E. Franklin Frazier, *The Negro Church in America* (New York: Schocken Books, Inc., 1963), p. 43; and Carter G. Woodson, *The History of the Negro Church* (Washington, D.C.: The Associated Publishers, 1921), pp. 244 ff.

for his survival. Now, these were the very traits that the Christian religion set before the slave and the post-Emancipation generation as the ideal for which all men should strive—they were the traits of Christ, himself. It was not difficult, therefore, for the oppressed Negro to interpret his subservient behavior as being Christ-like. In fact, it was necessary for his self-esteem (ego-defenses) that he see himself as not servile; that he see himself, rather, as the realization of the Christian ideal. In time the Negro came to see himself as being Christ-like, and this self-image became (for him) a racial stereotype. As a stereotype it was an ideal self-image, and remained such even for many of those whose independence of the white world was sufficient to allow them alternate modes of behavior— alternatives to patience, humility, and good-natured forbearance.

As more Negroes gained relative independence, more were free to express their aggressions in ways other than sporadic outbursts of violence or in sullenness. For the independent Negro the Christ-like image was no longer needed as an ego-defense, but as a racial stereotype it continued its strong hold as an ideal and as a means of identifying with the race. The image was a source of self-esteem because it allowed the Negro to compare favorably the Christ-like Negro with the inhuman white man. The invidious comparison the image involved was also a first-rate way of channeling aggression. It was a particularly useful thing for the militant clergy: the invidious comparison allowed them to be racists and still be (as they thought) good Christians. Just as important, it was a way to rationalize a shift to a "this-worldly" religion. Though the vast majority of Negro clergymen stayed with their fundamentalism, an important few were pushed by their hatred of oppression into a "this-worldly" fight for civil rights. The Christ-like image of the Negro suggested a mission—a mission to make reforms in this world. So, the image that began its career as an ego-defense was turned into a weapon of militancy and became the core of a race ideology—a race-oriented religion. This chapter, then, is the story of a few religious leaders who could not tolerate the "other-worldliness" of the fundamentalist faith; who, because of their militancy, forged a "this-worldly" faith devoted to the Christian ideals of brotherhood, but based on racial antagonism.

It was this small band of religious militants that represented the Negro clergy in the Niagara Movement and the early NAACP just after the turn of the century. They were few in number (perhaps a dozen), but disproportionately influential in Negro intellectual and militant circles. Well-educated, articulate in the religious journals, they helped to formulate the ideology of the Negro mission and to bring it into the militant protest movements.

II

In the years following the Civil War and Reconstruction periods, the Negro clergy, like other race leaders of that period, accepted most of the pronouncements white men were making upon the state of their race. They idealized American civilization and contrasted it with African "savagery"; they proclaimed America's Christian virtues and hoped the Negro would one day live up to them, believing that the white man was waiting for the opportunity to welcome him into the full status of citizenship. This type of thinking was true even of those who considered themselves intrepid militants. Bishop Alexander Walters of the A.M.E. Zion Church, for example, esteemed himself as a staunch fighter for civil rights. Among a multitude of things, he attempted to organize the race leadership in the National Afro-American Council (1898), and tried in 1908 to lead the Negro voters out of the Republican party. In that same year, following Theodore Roosevelt's extremely biased handling of the race riots in Brownsville, Texas, Walters led a group of ministers in an indignant rejection of the President's offer to discuss the matter. But his was the voice of the conservative clergy, calling upon the Negro to get education and wealth in order to make himself fit to live in the white man's civilization; telling him that he must work for the possession of character if he was to command respect.[3]

The same rationale of Negro inferiority is seen in the words of another leading Negro clergyman, Bishop W. J. Gaines of the

---

[3] Alexander Walters, (*Boston*) *Guardian*, February 29, 1908; Alexander Walters, *My Life and Work* (New York: Fleming H. Revell Co., 1917), pp. 125–31, 208.

A.M.E. Church: "Oh! ye Southern whites! among whom we live, and with whom in the same soil we expect to lie at last, let your hand of love go out to your poor, struggling brother in black, who has toiled so long through the weary night of ignorance and servitude, and help to lift him to the same heights of knowledge and virtue upon which you so proudly stand." Gaines was just going along with the general content of thought of the conservative clergy (the overwhelming majority) when he called upon the "virtuous" white man to extend a helping hand to the suffering Negro and lift him to the heights of white civilization. No doubt he strongly believed in the superiority of the white man over the Negro. But deep down in his psyche, or wherever it is that stereotypes dwell, he held a strongly contradictory opinion—he was, in fact, a devotee of the Christ-like image of the Negro. "No race," he wrote in reference to slavery, "ever acted more like Jesus Christ, whose life was one long, patient non-resistance to wrong." Bishop Gaines was doing some sort of unconscious juggling act, at one moment holding aloft the superior virtue of the white man, at another comparing the Negro with Christ.[4]

One thing that helped the conservative clergy to avoid confronting the contradictions in their thought was their great faith that God is operating the world according to some great plan. They had the traditional argument of proslavery orators to confirm this idea—the argument that God had brought the Negro hither to Christianize him. Gaines sensed something of God's plan; he was beginning to perceive the "dawning light of the Divine purpose," as it even now "begins to reveal itself . . ." God intends, he said, to Christianize Africa through the agency of the Afro-American. For his part, Alexander Walters felt that God had brought the Negro to America that the *white man* be given the chance to learn true Christian leadership, which he would then go on to exercise over the world. In any case, both believed the Negro American had a mission—of sorts.[5]

The clergy was still full of optimism and faith in God's intentions as the 19th century began to run its course. L. J. Coppin, editor of the A.M.E. Church *Review* (1888–96), and later bishop,

---

4 W. J. Gaines, *The Negro and the White Man* (Philadelphia: A.M.E. Publishing House, 1897), pp. 70, 65.

5 *Ibid.*, p. 20; Walters, *My Life and Work, op. cit.*, pp. 244–45.

like many others would never forget the joyous moment of his emancipation. Was he not a personal witness to God's benevolent intent? He was convinced that one day the meek would inherit the earth—being Christ-like would pay off: "Now, if the Christian type of civilization is to be in the end the prevailing power, then the people who are the receptacles of the true Christianity will be the dominant people." In keeping with the conservative faith, Coppin instructed his people to wait and be good—it was at best a passive role.[6]

This was a concept of nonresistance, of submission and hope. It called for the repression of all hostile and aggressive tendencies. These clergymen were not ignorant of the daily depredations with which they were confronted, but the easiest way to handle hostility is not to have it, the easiest way not to have it is to have no enemies.

By the way of summing up this type of religious expression— the thought which appears to have been a near-consensus among the Negro clergy of the 19th century—it will be well to look at the ideas of perhaps the greatest Negro preacher of the time.

The Rev. Charles T. Walker was a Georgia Baptist who achieved fame in the 1880's. Neither of the famous white evangelists, Sam Jones nor Dwight L. Moody, claims Walker's biographer, was able to draw larger crowds to the revival meetings held in Atlanta's Exposition Park. Nor did anyone have more power in determining the selection of Negro ministers for the pastorates of the state. Walker (the "Black Spurgeon") first gained his reputation in a way reminiscent of Booker T. Washington. For several hours, during a National Baptist Convention in 1886, several of the brethren had been holding forth in derogatory terms against the whites. Walker arose, his face flushed with anger, and for some time held forth on the *goodness* of the whites. The same thing happened again in 1889. Walker was a devout believer in the goodwill of the whites, and argued that friendship should be returned for friendship.[7]

Again, in Walker, we see the peculiar blindness to oppression that characterized the clerical mind. God had freed the Negro

---

[6] L. J. Coppin, A.M.E. Church *Review*, Vol. 7 (July, 1890), pp. 102–103.

[7] Silas X. Floyd, *Life of Charles T. Walker* (no imprint, 1902), pp. 77–80.

from slavery. God was seeing to it that the Negro was getting a Christian education, wealth, and advancement in the professions. In all these things Walker was optimistic because God is in His heaven. His solution to the racial problem harked back to the individual redemption theme preached by Charles G. Finney in the 1820's: "The crying need of the age is men and women with pure, heartfelt, practical religion." There was nothing of militancy in Walker's message: "In this," he said, "we would do well to copy the life of our Savior. . . . He was sympathetic, tenderhearted, liberal, kind and generous. He was meek and, therefore, called a lamb; He was compassionate and charitable; He was content in poverty, patient in His deep afflictions. . . ." Walker's message was passively to endure fate—there was no room in his religion for the expression of hostility and aggression.[8]

In his optimism, Walker could not contain his admiration for the white man. "It seems to me," he said, "to be a logical conclusion, if honesty, truthfulness, chastity, industry and economy made the Anglo-Saxon great, the cultivation and practice of the same graces will make the negro great, prosperous and happy." Note that the Christ-like virtues were withheld from the Anglo-Saxon. These were reserved for the Negro. Like his contemporaries, Walker held dear the story of the slave's loyalty during the Civil War. He loved to relate Atlanta newspaperman Henry W. Grady's statement of it: "I want no truer soul," he quoted Grady as saying, "than that which moved the trusty slave, who for four years, while my father fought with the armies that barred his freedom slept every night at my mother's chamber door . . . ready to lay down his humble life on the threshold." The invidious comparison of the races was a potential in Walker, but never more than that. Optimism and faith in God's rule kept it on that level. He compared his race's situation with the great saga of the Hebrews in Egypt. His race, too, was being civilized for its great mission of bringing light to Africa. One need not question the ways of God, at least Charles Walker never did.[9]

---

8 Charles T. Walker, sermon, June 6, 1888, quoted in Silas X. Floyd, *Life of Charles T. Walker.*, pp. 125–29; Charles T. Walker, "The Negro Problem: Its Scriptural Solution," (Augusta, Ga.; Chronicle Job Printing Co., 1893), pp. 6, 8, sermon delivered at the Tabernacle Baptist Church, Augusta, Ga., June 4, 1893.

9 Walker "The Negro Problem," *ibid.,* p. 13; Charles T. Walker, *Forty Years of Freedom. The American Negro: His Hindrances and Progress* (Philadelphia: Christian Banner Printers, 1903), pp. 5, 3.

Such was the near-consensus reached by the older generation of clergy and held dear as generation followed generation. It was a consensus born out of slavery and reinforced by Emancipation—the supreme example of God's benevolent will.

But even as the conservative-minded fundamentalists held the reins of church government firmly in their hands, a younger generation was living through the systematic oppression being dealt out by the white man in post-Reconstruction America. In the late 1880's and the 1890's we begin to hear a few voices raised in opposition to the ruling consensus. The official organ of the A.M.E. Church, the *Christian Recorder*, stuck rigidly to orthodoxy, but editor Coppin of the A.M.E. Church *Review* now and then opened his pages to dissent. Examination shows two trends forming: rebellion against the white man, and a tendency to submit the tenets of fundamentalism to scrutiny.

One Rev. William Hannibal Thomas wrote in the October, 1888 issue of the *Review* that oppression was everywhere getting worse; that two centuries of submission and passivity had not worked. He called for "aggressive resistance" to replace compliancy, and implied that neither God nor the white man was going to help the Negro. He went further, asserting that this is not a moral universe at all, that "it is neither intellect nor religion that rules the world, but physical force—brute force, if you please. . . ." Thomas' ego-defenses were badly out of kilter—the mechanism for repressing aggression was not working at all well. "The Negro," he continued, "must lay aside humility . . . and manfully protect himself, his family and his fireside from the lecherous assaults of white invaders."[10]

Another contributor to the *Review*, R. R. Downs, dared to aim a blow at the time-honored tradition of the Negro's Christ-like role during the Civil War. "Now," he said, "Negro apologists, with their watery eyes, go sniffling over the country with a 'sorry-we-are-here-and-sorry-we-are-living' manner, basing their pusillanimous effort of speech-making on the Negro's 'faithfulness to old master's family during the war.' "[11]

Downs ended his article with an appeal for more manliness.

---

[10] William Hannibal Thomas, "Till Another King Arose, Which Knew Not Joseph," A.M.E. Church *Review*, Vol. 5 (October, 1888), p. 337.

[11] R. R. Downs, "The Negro Is Known," A.M.E. Church *Review*, Vol. 7 (April, 1891), p. 412.

This became a rising note. The Rev. S. Martin declared that true Christianity demands dignity for all. And the Rev. R. William Fickland warned that if the A.M.E. Church failed to lead the fight for civil rights, the progressive members of the church would leave it and carry on the fight from without.[12]

Meanwhile, the voices evincing a more liberal theology began to make themselves increasingly heard in the *Review*. The gradual shift was from an all-powerful God who had absolute control over history toward a benevolent but weak God who could do little of practical value for the Negro. In other words, some, at least, of the clergy were losing faith in God's ability to handle the situation. They needed a religion that was concerned with the here and now, that would not demand that they hold their hostilities in check on the theory that meekness would carry them into heaven. They were working toward a religion that demanded equality—civil rights.

In 1891 the Rev. A. W. Upshaw discussed biblical criticism and found that while the "higher" criticism was largely capricious, and therefore pernicious, much of the criticism had done a commendable work for religion in clearing up interpretations. At another time he had conceded that there was much in the Old Testament that seemed doubtful, and concluded that the "New Theology" of Lyman Abbott was right in believing that clear revelation progresses from Moses to John. The New Testament, he thought, is better on God than is the Old. Upshaw was expressing the tendency among some of the clergy to shift away from the concept of an awful, omnipotent God to the one of God as the loving Father of mankind. The Rev. S. B. Jones, a self-proclaimed evangelist, asked the question, "How Should We Present God?" Too often, he said, evangelists pictured God as a "demon ruling with an iron hand." Evangelists should put more emphasis on His loving, forbearing side: "Let us then, in our revivals, have more of the love, gentleness, forbearance and justice of God, for in no unmistakable language He says, 'Fury is not in me.' "[13]

---

12 S. Martin, "Education before the Christian Era," A.M.E. Church *Review*, Vol. 8 (October, 1891), p. 194; R. William Fickland, "The Church: Its Opportunities," *Christian Recorder*, Vol. 58 (August 4, 1910), p. 1.

13 A. W. Upshaw, "Biblical Criticism," A.M.E. Church *Review*, Vol. 8 (October, 1891), pp. 198–201; A. W. Upshaw, "Reason and Revelation," A.M.E. Church *Review*,

While some were probing the bastions of revelation and the omnipotent God idea, others had the temerity to suggest that the church pay some attention to the Negro's problems in this world —social problems. In 1894, one C. O. H. Thomas, in replying to a previous article in the *Review*, took an advanced position. The offending article had declared that the clergy should not discuss politics with their congregations. Not a bit of it, said Thomas, politics is based on moral law—the domain of the minister—and "it is the duty of the church and ministry to promote political and social reforms. . . ." If the church should omit this vital function, he continued, it will commit suicide. Should the church give "everything over to the control of the dreaded Socialist or fiendish Anarchist, give to them all the vital questions of the day, and confine the pulpit to 'Children's Day,' 'Missionary Day,' 'Education Day' and other meetings; together with belabored and prolixed discussions of either end of eternity . . . " the common people will quickly find other leaders. The Rev. Henry L. Phillips pushed further in this direction in his comments on General Booth's *Darkest England and the Way out of It*. Booth compared London's slums unfavorably with Dante's hell and with "darkest Africa." Phillips accepted this comparison and went on to say that it was foolish to preach the Gospel to those who are starving. "Man's first business," he wrote, "is with this life. Christ's first miracles were for the body." It is the minister's duty to attempt to lift people from slum conditions and "surround them with a new atmosphere, and give them an upward push."[14]

These were all timid steps away from what was basically a slave religion—a religion of acceptance and submission. If one were to criticize them, one would have to admit that their relevance is in showing how *little* the most daring of the clergy were disposed to question orthodoxy. Yet, the examples cited do indicate the direction that deviation from orthodoxy was taking in the 1880's and 1890's. Some of the clergy were beginning to question the

---

Vol. 5 (October, 1888), p. 328; S. B. Jones, "What Is the Best Way of Conducting Revivals in the A.M.E. Church?", A.M.E. Church *Review*, Vol. 8 (October, 1891), p. 221.

14 J. W. Smith, "Ministers and Politics," A.M.E. Church *Review*, Vol. 11 (July, 1894), pp. 181–84; C. O. H. Thomas, "Politics, Ministers and Religion," A.M.E. Church *Review*, Vol. 11 (October, 1894), pp. 277, 280; Henry L. Phillips, "General Booth's Darkest England and the Way out of It," A.M.E. Church *Review*, Vol. 7 (April, 1891), pp. 405, 407.

power of God to do what was needed for the Negro race; some were not so sure that a patient, submissive waiting for the favor of God and the white man was their cup of tea. The old slave religion was being questioned. It would take the combined efforts of a young intellectual and an old fire-eater to pick up these threads and weave them into open rebellion.

III

The two apostates from the slave religion were R. R. Wright, Jr., editor of the *Christian Recorder* (1909–36), and Reverdy C. Ransom, editor of the A.M.E. Church *Review* (1912–24). Together they succeeded in making God lovable but weak, and in taking the mission of making society better from His shoulders and giving it to the Negro. Together, they transformed Christianity from a God-centered religion to a race-centered one, and if few of the clergy cared to follow them there were others who did—W. E. B. Du Bois, for example.

Always Wright and Ransom were very close. Together, in 1900 they organized the Institutional Church and Social Settlement in the heart of Chicago's newly forming black belt on the South Side. This was the formative experience, for both of them—the struggle against poverty and crime among the low down. They had the help of Miss MacDowell of the Chicago University Settlements and of Jane Addams, whose Hull House was their model. They had the close friendship of Clarence Darrow; with him they negotiated a peace between striking stockyard workers and Negro strikebreakers—a peace which resulted in opening the stockyard unions to Negroes. They were close friends with Robert Ingersoll. Years later, Reverdy Ransom preached the eulogy at Ingersoll's funeral. That shocked and confounded the orthodoxy, but Ransom felt that Ingersoll, the atheist, was a better Christian than a good many of his clerical detractors. The experience at the Institutional Church in Chicago was basic for Wright and Ransom for another reason: for a period of four years they had to struggle against the orthodoxy simply to keep their church alive. The A.M.E. hierarchy opposed the operation from the beginning, and after a four-year fight Ransom and Wright had no alternative but to resign.[15]

That was just the beginning of Wright's career in the Chicago settlements. He went from the Institutional Church to the Frederick Douglass Center, and later founded the Trinity Mission in the heart of Chicago's slums. In December, 1905, we find him writing to Charles W. Chesnutt, the Negro author, concerning opportunities for opening a settlement house in Cleveland, Ohio. In the midst of all this Wright was in the process of getting an education. When he wrote the letter of 1905 to Chesnutt he was already a graduate of the University of Chicago, had studied in Berlin and Leipzig, and was working toward a Ph.D. in sociology at the University of Pennsylvania—a degree that he would get in 1912.[16]

Ostensibly, in 1905, Wright was working on a study of Negro migration from the rural South to Philadelphia—a study that was later published in 1912 as *The Negro in Pennsylvania*. Actually, he was rounding out a faith—a system of thought that flew directly in the face of A.M.E. orthodoxy. It was a totally "this-worldly" faith—the Kingdom of God must be made here on earth. "The teaching of Jesus on the Kingdom of God emphasizes," he later wrote, "the conversion of the social order: the making of the kingdoms of this world, the kingdom of our God." The Kingdom of God on earth would be based on the principle of brotherhood. Wright was calling for a moral revolution; more than that, he was calling for a social revolution: "It is revolutionary. It will change our industrial relations. It will change our politics. It will change our standards of morality." It was socialism—as he gladly admitted—but that, according to him, was the least of it. He called his program "Social Service"—but was far more interested in the moral aspects than in the industrial aspects of it. Socialism would come as a matter of course as man brought the reign of Christ to the world.[17]

---

15 Reverdy C. Ransom, "Ingersoll the Humanitarian," A.M.E. Church *Review*, Vol. 38 (April, 1922), pp. 173–175; Reverdy C. Ransom, *Pilgrimage of Harriet Ransom's Son* (Nashville: A.M.E. Sunday School Union, *ca.* 1948), pp. 93–136.

16 R. R. Wright, Jr. to Charles W. Chesnutt, December 5, 1905, Chesnutt papers, Fisk University Library.

17 R. R. Wright, Jr., *Social Service* (Philadelphia: A.M.E. Book Concern, 1922), pp. 21–22, 27–28; Editorial, *Christian Recorder*, Vol. 62 (March 19, 1914), p. 4.

Wright had to go through the painful process of throwing out his own boyhood beliefs before he could rebel against the orthodoxy prescribed by the A.M.E. Church establishment. His first beliefs came from a father who was a fundamentalist and the president of a Georgia industrial school. The story is told that once, when the senior Wright was yet a boy ("no bigger than a bar of soap"), the great General O. O. Howard asked him for a message to carry back to the boys of the North. "Tell 'em we're rising," replied Wright. Howard presumably carried out his end of the bargain, the boy carried out his. And President Wright, Sr., of the Georgia State Industrial College, was at least comfortably certain that his rise was due to his adherence to the fundamentals. Every morning in chapel he treated his students and professors to a large dose of those fundamentals. Every Sunday he taught the Bible. Once he found he had on his hands a professor who thought lightly of the Bible. Exit one highly trained Yale graduate from the premises.

If the experience of the Yale man is any guide, R. R. Wright, Jr., was not brought up innocent of the fundamentals. It seems equally unlikely that he escaped an early exposure to the Christ-like image. One of the extant speeches of the senior Wright is a talk on Lincoln—the Emancipator was attributed with "many of the traits for which colored people are noted . . . :" a sweetness of disposition, a great patience of the wrong, a forgiving nature, and a readiness "to wait for the slow process by which God accomplished great blessings for mankind." The fundamentals were the ideas of Booker T. Washington generously seasoned with "other-worldly" religion.[18]

Though the son was an apostate from the right, he always thought of his father's principles with a measure of affection. In April, 1914, for example, he related an instance when evangelist Billy Sunday was called upon by the University of Pennsylvania to quell an outbreak of suicides, and concluded: "Thus another valuable testimony from an unexpected source is given to 'the old time religion.' " On occasion, young Wright sounded very much like the famous Tuskegee president himself—calling for moral improvement by the race, economic self-help and education as the

---

18 R. R. Wright, Sr., "A Negro's Tribute to Lincoln," quoted in Elizabeth Ross Haynes, *The Black Boy of Atlanta* (Boston: The House of Edinboro Publishers, 1952), pp. 136–37.

way out of the race mire. In September of 1914 he defended
Washington's self-help ideas as one-half of the necessary program
of emancipation. On one occasion, Wright even went to the extreme of hoping for help from the white southerner. "We must,"
he then declared, "prove worthy of the service these noble men
and women render us." In Wright's defense it must be said that
he expected help from only a few whites at most. After the year
1915 Wright never again lost touch with reality.[19]

The year 1915 marked the crisis in Wright's intellectual life.
The last straw seems to have been a particularly brutal lynching
he had read about. On the day following the lynching he wrote:
"To-day is perhaps the darkest day in the life of the Negro race
during the past fifty years." The white man had, he said, entirely
deserted the Negro in both the North and the South. "We are
lynched," he wrote in intense anger, "we are hanged, riddled with
bullets and burned. Excursions are run to have the daughters and
sons of 'respectable leading citizens' witness the barbecuing of
a nigger. . . ." After the lynching his judgment of the white man
grew exceedingly bitter: "The white man is selfish and the American white man is the most grasping breed of humanity ever
made." Never again did Wright speak in the accents of his more
patient father. Never again did he make gestures in the direction
of the "other-worldly" religion of the church orthodoxy.[20]

The 1915 intellectual crisis served the purpose of severing
Wright's ties with the old faith, but it did more—it galvanized
him into becoming a militant. He continued to believe in and
develop his prayerful faith in the eventual advent of an earthly
kingdom of heaven based on human brotherhood—all of his experience as a settlement worker and student of sociology worked
in this direction. But his developing militancy sent him off in another direction. Building on his belief in the Christ-like Negro,
and on his disgust with the white man, he began to build a race-
centered religion.

Wright's "this-worldy" religion—his "Social Service"—was well

19 R. R. Wright, Jr., "A Testimony to Evangelism", *Christian Recorder*, Vol. 62
(April 9, 1914), p. 4; R. R. Wright, Jr., "Booker T. Washington and Segregation,"
Christian Recorder, Vol. 62 (September 24, 1914), p. 8; R. R. Wright, Jr., "The
Students' Conference at Atlanta," *Christian Recorder*, Vol. 62 (July 23, 1914), p. 4.

20 R. R. Wright, Jr., "Behind the Dark Clouds," *Christian Recorder*, Vol. 62
(January 21, 1915), p. 8; R. R. Wright, Jr., "Unlynchable Facts," *Christian Recorder*,
Vol. 64 (November 16, 1916), p. 4.

developed before his 1915 intellectual crisis: "And He only emphasized the Fatherhood of God as a basis for the teaching of the Brotherhood of Man," he wrote in 1914. It need only be said that he continued to develop this train of thought; continued to de-emphasize the importance of God and to increase emphasis on the spirit of brotherhood, until his religion ultimately pushed God into the obscure background. In 1935 (Wright was by then a bishop) we find him telling the World Fellowship Conference that any religion which preaches brotherhood and social service is valid. His rejection of A.M.E. orthodoxy was complete.[21]

The new note that appeared in Wright's post-1915 thought is one of militancy. He began to urge that the Negro race form an interest group and enter into the political arena. He gleefully urged the speedup of wartime migration of Negroes from the South as a boon to pressure politics. He called for the formation of a Negro political party to control the votes of its race and to elect Negroes to Congress. Then the idea suggested itself to him that the vast Negro wartime migration would force the northern states to arm men of his race and organize them into milita units. The South would have to follow suit. His imagination was working overtime.[22]

In his new militancy, Wright began calling for a new kind of Negro—one who would fight for the right. The meek Negro was not going to inherit the earth after all. More than anything else the colored man needed self-respect. Wright decided that Jesus had come carrying a sword—a spiritual sword to combat evil. "A man who shuns a fight with evil, with a lawbreaker, or a robber or a corruptionist," he said, "is not a peaceful Christian but a sinful coward." The race must always remember that before a Christian peace can come, right must triumph.[23]

Militancy, race consciousness, and a sense of God's impotence all conspired to redirect Wright's thinking into a new channel.

---

[21] R. R. Wright, Jr., "The Scriptural Basis of Social Service: What Jesus Christ Taught," *Christian Recorder*, Vol. 62 (August 27, 1914), p. 4; R. R. Wright, Jr., "Overcoming Racial and Religious Prejudices," Charles F. Weller (ed.), *World Fellowship: Addresses and Messages by Leading Spokesmen of all Faiths, Races, and Countries* (New York: Liveright Publishing Corp., 1935), p. 322.

[22] R. R. Wright, Jr., "Should Negroes Come North?", *Christian Recorder*, Vol. 64 (August 31, 1916), p. 4; R. R. Wright, Jr., "A Negro Party," *Christian Recorder*, Vol. 64 (September 28, 1916), p. 4.

[23] Wright, *Social Service, op. cit.*, pp. 23–24; R. R. Wright, Jr., "The Christian's Peace," *Christian Recorder*, Vol. 64 (December 21, 1916), p. 4.

He drew upon the Christ-like image of the Negro to fashion a race-centered religion. The ideas were introduced in a 1916 editorial entitled, "African Methodism in the Second Century." The world, he wrote, is in need of a rejuvenated Christianity. Who will give it new ideals? Not the white man, because "The Anglo-Saxon and the Teuton have failed." The white man does not have the religious temperament—a point that Wright felt was proven by the fact that he has never created a great religion. The European mind, materialistic and selfish, has never understood Christ. The Negro, on the other hand is of a poetic nature; he lives little on earth and much in heaven, and "he suffers too long, and is too kind to be a European." The Negro, he continued, is peaceful, loving and forgiving; it is up to him to instill new religious life in the world. "But what has this to do with the African Methodist Church's mission in the Second Century?", he asked. "This and only this: If European (and American) Christianty is to get back to Jesus, it will be because those people who understand the temperament of Jesus take it back." African Methodism will carry the Christian message of brotherhood to the white man, "she must be heard always proclaiming 'God our Father, Christ our Redeemer and Man our Brother.' This is her task for the second century." Wright had pushed God into the background and had given the mission of saving mankind to the colored race. It was a difficult role he had created for his race—the Negro was to be a patient, meek, Christ-like man and yet a militant fighter for the right. In fact, two incompatible elements were latent in Wright's formulation; one was aggression, the other was love; one was racism, the other was Christianity.[24]

When we turn to the ministry of Reverdy C. Ransom, Wright's older colleague at the Institutional Church, we find the tension between racism and Christianity becoming more overt, more pronounced. Ransom was torn between two concepts of Christianity: Christianity as an instrument of (possibly bloody) revolution, and Christianity as the means by which the Negro would save democracy and the white man's soul. At one time we find him speaking with the intensity of a Hebrew prophet, denouncing the ungodliness of the white man and proclaiming the necessity of

---

[24] R. R. Wright, Jr., "African Methodism and the Second Century," *Christian Recorder*, Vol. 64 (April 13, 1916), p. 4.

shedding a little blood in the cause of freedom. The next moment we find him extolling the Negro's inherent meekness and the need to conquer through love. Ransom could not decide whether John Brown or Christ should set the example for Negro religion.

We meet him in 1906 at Harpers Ferry telling the assembled militants of the Niagara Movement how John Brown was commissioned by God to strike down slavery by appeal to the higher law. Brown was a man who knew what few dare to admit, that freedom demands the shedding of blood: "A new birth of freedom within a nation," Ransom intoned, "is always accompanied with great suffering and pain. How much greater, then, the travail through which humanity must pass to bring forth its last and highest birth, for which all preceding ages have worked and waited until now." This note rang pleasantly in Ransom's ears. "Every good gift, even eternal salvation," he wrote in 1916, "has been bought with blood." It was a recurring theme.[25]

A deep and abiding lack of admiration and affection for the white man had possession of Ransom and nourished his militancy. He had red hair. It grated on his soul that he should have red hair. His boyhood companions derisively called him a "white man's nigger" because of it. He had a sneaking suspicion that somewhere back in the line of his progenitors there had been an Irishman. He stoutly denied that it could have been an Anglo-Saxon: "One thing I know, there is little of the Anglo-Saxon in me."[26]

When the post-Reconstruction movement was begun in the South to force the Negro race into a caste status, Ransom was a young man just entering the ministry (1885). He watched and agonized throughout the years that his race was jim-crowed and disfranchised. No romantic myth hid the actual conditions in the South from his eyes; he saw no paternalistic aristocracy there waiting hopefully for the day when the Negro would prove himself ready for citizenship. "Senator Tillman of South Carolina," Ransom knew, "fully represents the attitude of the Southern whites when he declares that they do not intend to accord Negroes,

---

25 Reverdy C. Ransom, "The Spirit of John Brown," *The Spirit of Freedom and Justice: Orations and Speeches* (Nashville: A.M.E. Sunday School Union, 1926), pp. 16, 25; Reverdy C. Ransom, editorial, A.M.E. Church *Review*, Vol. 33 (July, 1916), p. 38.

26 Ransom, *The Pilgrimage of Harriet Ransom's Son, op. cit.,* pp. 16–23.

under any conditions, political or any other kind of equality.
. . ." He had no illusions about white civilization being a high
plateau of achievement to be aspired to by the Negro. His critique
of that civilization was withering. When the Negro heavyweight,
Jack Johnson, won the championship (1903), Ransom noted caus-
tically that the real savagery occurred outside of the ring. The
betting, the feverish excitement, the garish advertising, and, when
Johnson won, the widespread spite shown against his race, all
convinced Ransom that in America civilization and Christianity
are only skin deep; that beneath them prowls the animal. He saw
the animal prowling whenever he read of another lynching—there
was evidence of the white man's brutal nature. It was time, he
said, for the Negro to treat the whites as the whites were treating
him—brutality should be "answered by a volley of bullets." "I
am unwillingly," he said, "but slowly, coming to the conclusion
that the only way for the Negro . . . to win and hold the respect
of the white people is to mete out to them a white man's measure
in all the relations of life."[27]

That was one side of the coin—the side in Ransom that opted
for John Brown and bloody retaliation. But Ransom had another
side that stood in opposition to bloodletting—a side that found
its satisfaction in benign contemplation of the Christ-like nature of his race: "The Negroes are a kind-hearted people. Their
nature is flooded with all the warmth of oriental sunshine which
for ages beat upon them." It gave him satisfaction to describe the
Negro's gift to America in terms that had none of the overtones
of revolt: "By [the Negroes'] influence the heart of America has
been softened with more kindness, a sweeter spirit has filled its life
and a stronger wave of emotion has swept the whole range of its
philanthropy and religion." And, as often as he counseled militancy to his people he counseled the emulation of Christ: ". . .
we need more and above all these, the spirit and power of the
Lord Jesus; purity, temperance, truth, justice, meekness, faith,
righteousness, love; against these prejudice, hatred, injustice, op-

---

27 Reverdy C. Ransom, "John Greenleaf Whittier," *The Spirit of Freedom and
Justice* (Nashville: A.M.E. Sunday School Union, 1926), p. 37; Reverdy C. Ransom,
"The Reno Prize Fight," *The Spirit of Freedom and Justice* (Nashville: A.M.E. Sun-
day School Union, 1926), pp. 124–25; Reverdy C. Ransom, "Lynching and American
Public Opinion," *The Spirit of Freedom and Justice* (Nashville: A.M.E. Sunday
School Union, 1926), p. 139.

pression, violence have no power." The two most important elements in Ransom's thought were, therefore, polar opposites, corresponding to the aggression that he felt, and to the Christian ideals that he believed in.[28]

Ransom's militancy ran deep and started early in life. He was expelled from Oberlin College for organizing a protest against segregated dining room seating arrangements. Then, at Wilberforce, he ran afoul of the Trinity, poked fun at Genesis, had the audacity to speak up for the science of geology; all this in spite of a stern resolve to keep his opinions to himself. For 15 years after graduation he worked quietly in the vineyards of the Lord. These particular vineyards happened to be the slums of Pittsburgh where, as he poked around the tenement flats and alleys, he learned something about squalor and human degradation. After that experience he lost interest in the wonders of heaven, there was too much wrong in this world.

In Chicago (1900–04) and again in New York City (1913–24) Ransom operated settlement houses in the heart of the black ghettos' worst slums, always with the church hierarchy in strong opposition. He got interested in city politics in 1907 when he went to the Republican mayor of New York and asked that Negroes be put on the police force. The mayor would not, but Tammany would—if its candidates were elected. Ransom helped Tammany win the election, and then watched the police force become integrated. After that he organized campaigns to switch the Negro vote in New York to the Democratic party, and in this again he had to fight the church hierarchy. It was perhaps inevitable that Ransom would get involved up to his ears in the militant protest movements.

In 1905 the A.M.E. hierarchy made the egregious error of sending the intractable minister to Boston, just when that city was becoming the storm center of agitation against Booker T. Washington's leadership of the American Negro. It would not have been like Ransom to remain aloof from the vilification of Washington; it would have been asking too much to expect the Wash-

---

28 Ransom, "John Greenleaf Whittier," *op. cit.*, p. 35; Reverdy C. Ransom, "Future Influence of Negro Scholarship in America," *The Spirit of Freedom and Justice* (Nashville: A.M.E. Sunday School Union, 1926), p. 165; Reverdy C. Ransom, editorial, A.M.E. Church *Review*, Vol. 33 (January, 1917), p. 158.

ington forces to refrain from dragging their clerical tormentor through the mud. It was a first-rate brawl. Ransom became a leader of the Niagara Movement (1905–09) in its revolt against Washington's policies, and then a leading speaker of the organizing campaign of the NAACP. In 1913 he captured control of the A.M.E. Church *Review* and turned its guns on Washington and religious orthodoxy. His war was mainly waged on two fronts, against "other-worldly" religion and against the caste system. The religion he fashioned as a result became "this-worldly" and race-centered.

Twelve years of editorials in the A.M.E. Church *Review* (1912–24) constitute a record of Ransom's religious formulations. One tendency was to make Christianity a doctrine of brotherhood on earth. In the January, 1917, editorial, he made Christianity stand on brotherhood and love, the upholding of justice, unselfish service to the poor and the weak, and opposition to oppression. Ransom decreed, in other words, that Christianity is a religion of civil rights and social reform. This was clearly phrased in his definition of African Methodism a year earlier: "This denomination," he wrote, "has prospered marvelously, its chief inspiration being not its religious doctrines, not its polity, but its spirit of manhood and equality for which it has stood these hundred years." But this was not a "love thine enemies" doctrine, for by this time hatred of the white man had become a dominant force in his thought. In 1918 he editorialized that if the whites continued with their white supremacy, the Negro had better abandon the dream of brotherhood and become "incarnate devils."[29]

As rebelliousness and the spirit of hostility grew in Ransom's breast, his religious ideas tended increasingly to become race-centered until it was a racial Christianity that he was preaching. In this racial Christianity brotherhood remained the ideal, but only the Negro was Christian. The teachings of Christ, the salvation of mankind, the kingdom of heaven on earth, all these became the mission of the more-Christ-like Negro:

As we face the present blight of the white man's civilization and the spiritual and social impotence of his Christianity, the spiritual leader-

---

[29] Ransom, editorial, January, 1917, *ibid.*, p. 158; Reverdy C. Ransom, editorial, A.M.E. Church *Review*, Vol. 33 (January, 1916), p. 206; Reverdy C. Ransom, editorial, A.M.E. Church *Review*, Vol. 34 (April, 1918), p. 265.

ship among men lies open and vacant for any people who will qualify to enter and ocupy it. . . .

If Americans of African descent can survive the social, economic, and political inferno through which they are passing, may now we hope with their growing intelligence and strength, they will arise in a great crusade for Justice and Righteousness and take the moral and spiritual leadership of the black race throughout the world to rescue the Cross of Christ from infidel Christianity.[30]

Ransom and Wright had taken the Christ-like image of the Negro, had added a mission ideology, and made it the core of their religion. Their religion had an important influence in the councils of the Niagara Movement and the early NAACP; it penetrated the classrooms of the Negro universities and colleges, became sociological dogma taught to thousands of students from the turn of the century through the 1920's. It represented the transformation of the old slave religion into a religion of militancy —the overthrow of the slave psychology. As such, it was a step in the emancipation of the Negro mind. But it had channeled aggression into the realm of mythology and so was itself an intellectual prison. It was a strange brew: part Social Gospel in its emphasis on the brotherhood of man, part racism. It set the Negro up as the moral arbiter of American civilization.

---

[30] Reverdy C. Ransom, *The Negro: The Hope or the Despair of Christianity* (Boston: Ruth Hill, 1935), pp. 3, 2 of Introduction.

III

W. E. B. Du Bois and the
crisis in intellectual leadership

The ideas and forces so far discussed were important in Negro thought because the men holding them and subject to their power represent an important element of the militant leadership of the Negro race between 1900 and World War I. In the Niagara Movement we find religious radicals such as Reverdy Ransom, J. Milton Waldron, and Sutton E. Griggs taking leading roles. In the National Association for the Advancement of Colored People during this period Archibald Grimké, R. R. Wright, Jr., James Weldon Johnson, and to a lesser degree, the author Charles W. Chesnutt, became important leaders. Most of these men also came together to exchange ideas in the American Negro Academy.

It would be a mistake to say that the mission ideology was anything like the official ideology of the Niagara Movement, and even more wrong to say that about the NAACP, for so long a time influenced by whites. But it would be right to say that all of the Negroes involved in these movements had to wrestle with the Christ-like image—to come to terms with it in one way or another. Of course, the towering personality in all three of these organizations was the mordant exhorter, W. E. B. Du Bois. In his thought, the more-Christ-like image and mission ideology were crucial.

Du Bois was torn by the same pressures that were at work on the Grimké brothers and the religious radicals. Like Archibald Grimké, he was vividly aware of the new world of ideas which seemed to strike down the old absolutes of the 19th century, yet he struggled mightily to hold on to those absolutes and to make them relevant to the 20th-century world. Like the religious radicals he revolted against the Christ-like Negro—no fit character for the new militancy—yet this same Christ-like Negro was the absolute to which he clung. The Christ-like image together with its mission ideology was his integrating myth—it gave meaning to a world which was beginning to be described as chaos.

Throughout his career Du Bois was to find his absolute being attacked on all sides by new ideas—ideas which he had either to fend off or to integrate into his system of thought. At the beginning of his intellectual career he embedded his absolute in racial theory. In that guise the Christ-likeness was a racial trait; it differentiated the Negro from the white man, made him better, gave him the mission of regenerating the world through a regeneration of its ethics. But during the 1920's Du Bois gradually discovered that racial theory does not hold water; that a new philosophical vehicle for his absolute had to be found. He found it in Marxism. In the guise of Marxist theory the Negro's Christ-likeness became the trait of the proletariat—of an oppressed people—of which the Negro was in the vanguard. In the new philosophical disguise the Negro's mission remained the same, but now it was in the context of class instead of race that the Negro would introduce the brotherhood of man. In the intellectual biography of Du Bois an understanding of the tenacity with which he held to his mythology is essential, because the crisis in intellectual leadership developed when there rose to prominence men to whom the mythology had no meaning.

Du Bois was a man intellectually divided against himself. He was the brilliant young sociologist open to the flood of ideas that were forging the modern temper and a new science; an empiricist whose skeptical eye doubted what it could not see. But he was also the mystic whose whole being sensed that the empirical world of the scientist is not enough. We must understand the Du Bois whose sociological inquiry into the black ghetto of Philadelphia is a landmark, as well as the Du Bois of the romantic (and melodramatic) novel. Early in his intellectual career the two sides of Du Bois closed in a struggle—a brief struggle. The mystic won and, in winning, made Du Bois a great protagonist for his race. In winning it also set the stage for the crisis in intellectual leadership.

In 1896 Du Bois was called by the University of Pennsylvania to make a study of the considerable Negro population in Philadelphia. The young sociologist was delighted. Two unrewarding years of teaching at Wilberforce University in Ohio were immediately behind him. Behind that were five productive years as a student at Harvard and Berlin. By training he was something of a philosopher-historian, but in terms of interest he was a sociologist. Those were years of birth pangs—sociology was issuing from the womb of moral philosophy. Harvard had no course in the new discipline so Du Bois could not have studied it there. His aim was to help pioneer the field. It meant much more to him than a mere profession, it meant a search for Truth (he always capitalized such words), and for ethical good. In a sense he was still a philosopher—a student of his Harvard professor, William James. He had learned from James that the age-old pursuit of truth and good had taken a wrong turn; that it had to begin anew, building its edifice out of experience. He had long and intimate talks with James on the subject.[1]

During his senior year at Harvard, Du Bois decided to set down such thoughts as he had on the subject of truth in his senior thesis, "The Renaissance in Ethics: A Critical Comparison of Scholastic and Modern Ethics" (1889). It was a good paper—at least James thought so, saying in the margin that it was highly original. But the famous philosopher voiced some reservations about its clarity. In fact, Du Bois was being pulled two ways and the paper showed it. On the one hand the young scholar called for ethics based on the scientific method. Ethical theory, he wrote, will forge ahead again when "it shall systematically study the facts accumulated and accumulating by (the mind's) wonderful manifestations for half a century . . . as the physicist studies heat not by its inner consciousness, but by what it does." Ethics, by this criterion, he made clear, was to seek not the absolute good but the relative good—the better. So far so good—this is proper thinking for a nascent sociologist. But at this point confusion and inconsistency entered his ar-

---

[1] For Du Bois's description of these years as well as his estimate of James's influence on his thought, see W. E. B. Du Bois, *Dusk of Dawn: An Essay toward an Autobiography of a Race Concept* (New York: Harcourt, Brace and Co., 1940), pp. 33ff.; and, W. E. B. Du Bois, "A Negro Student at Harvard at the End of the 19th Century," *The Massachusetts Review*, Vol. 1 (Spring, 1960), p. 449, in which he wrote, "I was repeatedly a guest in the home of William James; he was my friend and guide to clear thinking . . ."

gument. Ethics, he wrote, seeks the *why*, science the *what*, but we can never find the why—that must always remain shrouded in mystery. Here was an impasse. "Renaissance ethics" (the subject of the paper) will one day seek the why, but practical ethics will not —cannot—ask that question; it must rely on the study of day-to-day behavior. "Renaissance ethics" and practical ethics are clearly incompatibles. Though Du Bois's mind was with the latter, empirical ethics, his heart yearned to pierce through to a world of truths standing outside the thingness of phenomena. Scientists, he said, are wrong to think matter is the whole of the universe. Now, modern sociology decrees that there are no absolutes hiding behind phenomena, and Du Bois was a bright young man who, in 1889, stood on the brink of becoming a modern sociologist. His success in the newly opening discipline would depend upon how he resolved the dilemma embodied in his senior thesis—it would depend on his ability to content himself with the realm of the empirical. There was every reason to hope that the scientist would defeat the mystic in the struggle for Du Bois's mind.[2]

The study of the Philadelphia Negro community that Du Bois published in 1899 for the University of Pennsylvania is a first-rate work of sociology. It is well-balanced and calm in manner. It displays relevant factual data and its conclusions do the data no violence. The conclusions show large powers of understanding— an understanding that was about 20 years ahead of its time. Especially remarkable were his insights into the effects of the Negro's "social environment" (i.e., prejudice) on his self-esteem and achievement goals, the understanding that the Negro's main battle would perhaps be an inner one—the overcoming of low self-regard. In the realm of sociology Du Bois proved himself to be an advanced thinker. It looked as though the scientist in him was winning.[3]

All the returns were not in, however. From Philadelphia Du Bois went to Atlanta University to begin a 12-year interlude of teaching sociology. Once in Atlanta, he lost no time in inaugurat-

---

2 W. E. B. Du Bois, "The Renaissance in Ethics: A Critical Comparison of Scholastic and Modern Ethics," manuscript, 1899, pp. 22–23, 31–37, 24–25. James Weldon Johnson Memorial Collection, Yale.

3 W. E. B. Du Bois, *The Philadelphia Negro: A Social Study* (Philadelphia: University of Pennsylvania Press, 1899), p. 390.

ing a program aimed at producing a thoroughgoing sociological study of the Negro race in America. It was intended that, over a period of years, the study would look into all aspects of Negro life in the hope that knowledge would somehow puncture prejudice (an illusion of which Du Bois would later repent). There were problems: lack of funds, lack of trained researchers; but over a period of years he managed to get annual studies produced. The results, at best, were disappointing. Few of his deductions, for example, were made from sufficient samples. But beyond the mechanical difficulties another process was at work: each year the annual study was less objective and more impressionistic than the last. The 1914 study, *Morals and Manners among Negro Americans,* revealed a Du Bois in whom all scientific objectivity had stepped aside for mysticism. The mystic had ultimately won the day, and this time all the returns *were* in.

The 1914 Atlanta report was a paean to the "strength of purpose" and "purity of life" of Negro mothers. It was propaganda, not sociology. But it was more than that, it was an article of faith. Du Bois was not writing as a sociologist fresh from an exhaustive study of his subject; he was worshipping at the shrine of a myth: "It appears . . . as if the black race in passing down the steps of human culture gave the world not only the Iron Age, the cultivation of the soil and the domestication of animals but also in peculiar emphasis the Mother-idea." Du Bois needed no empirical evidence in this case, since one can assume that the race which produced the "Mother-idea" must have unusually pure and devoted mothers.[4]

The "Mother-idea" was but a small fragment in the pattern of an all-encompassing mosaic—a mosaic patterned around the Christlike myth and its mission ideology. By 1912 Du Bois had become what Eric Hofer has called "the true believer"; for by then he had committed himself to a mythology and to a set of supporting rationalizations. What had become of the scientific temper which made the 1899 *Philadelphia Negro* a notable success? The answer no doubt lies in his growing revulsion against the white man. It lies also in the development of his leadership of the radical wing of Negro thought—in finding himself conducting something of a

---

[4] W. E. B. Du Bois (ed.), *Morals and Manners among Negro Americans* (Atlanta: The Atlanta University Press, 1914), pp. 71–72, 67.

crusade against Booker T. Washington. The debate began in 1903 when Du Bois published his *The Souls of Black Folk* and continued with unabated fury until Washington's death in 1915. The very rhetoric of this impassioned debate had something to do with Du Bois's mental attitudes. Washington was calling upon the Negro to assimilate the commercial and competitive culture of America. Du Bois had to offer something more idealistic than the profit motive, something finer than the coarse materialism of American culture. This finer something had to come from within the race.

The intellectual seed which was to be fertilized by racial antagonism and the rhetoric of debate—the seed that would blossom, for Du Bois, into the invidious Black Christ image and the mission ideology—was present in Du Bois's mind even while he was making the Philadelphia study in 1897. He had, in fact, developed the Christ-like image as early as 1890 before a commencement day audience at Harvard University. The young Du Bois presented Jefferson Davis as a fine specimen of the white race, the "Teutonic" ideal of "stalwart manhood and heroic character, and at the same time [of] moral obtuseness and refined brutality." Against this he contrasted a new ideal to be given mankind by the Negro race: "It is the doctrine of Submissive man. . . ." Later in *The Souls of Black Folk* (1903), Du Bois had written ". . . all in all we black men seem to be the sole oasis of simple faith and reverence in a dusty desert of dollars and smartness," and had asked if America would be the poorer if she were to adopt the "light-hearted but determined Negro humility?" Ten years later, in the pages of *The Crisis*, organ of the NAACP, he thanked God for allowing him to be a member of the "kindliest race on earth."[5]

It was in his poetry and fiction that Du Bois carried out the implications of the Christ-like image to their fullest and rounded out the mosaic of rhetoric. "The Second Coming" of 1920 is a short story which depicts the birth of a Negro boy in a small Georgia town as the second coming of Christ. To complete the imagery implied by his central image a black madonna and a

5 W. E. B. Du Bois, "Jefferson Davis as a Representative of Civilization," microfilm, 1890, James Weldon Johnson Memorial Collection, Yale; W. E. B. Du Bois, *The Souls of Black Folk: Essays and Sketches* (London: Archibald Constable and Co., 1903), pp. 11–12; W. E. B. Du Bois, "Postscript," *The Crisis*, Vol. 6 (July, 1913), p. 130.

black God are needed; Du Bois supplied them. In his poem, "The Burden of Black Women," we find him supplicating:

> Down with their white men cheating of childhood,
> The drunken orgies of war—
>> down
>>> down
>>>> deep down,
> Till the Devil's strength be shorn,
> Till some dim darker David a hoeing of his corn,
> And married maiden, Mother of God,
> Bid the Black Christ be born!

In "The Call" (1920), a Negro maiden is called by God to go out and fight the heathen. The maiden demurs saying that she is but a girl, and black at that. God then reveals His face; it too is black.[6]

In the poem partially quoted above, Du Bois characterized the white man as the "Devil." This is some indication of his growing hostility toward the white race. The epidemic of gruesome lynchings, race riots such as the one at Atlanta in 1906, and the everyday meanness of whites toward Negroes were all having their effect on the Atlanta professor's already strained equanimity. The Atlanta riot of 1906, together with all the absurdities which led up to it, threw him into the mood of deep despondency and bitterness which informs his harsh "Litany of Atlanta." To fully reflect Du Bois's growing appreciation of the white man one need only quote the middle of the poem begun above:

> I hate them, Oh!
> I hate them well,
> I hate them, Christ!
> As I hate hell!
> If I were God,
> I'd sound their knell
> This day!

That was written in 1907.

---

6 W. E. B. Du Bois, "The Second Coming," *Darkwater: Voices from Within the Veil* (New York: Harcourt, Brace, & Howe, 1920), pp. 105–108; W. E. B. Du Bois, "The Burden of Black Women," *Horizon*, Vol. 2 (November, 1907), pp. 3–5; W. E. B. Du Bois, "The Call," *Darkwater* (New York: Harcourt, Brace & Howe, 1920), pp. 161–62.

So the white man was characterized as the "Devil," or more generally, as a barbarian. Such was his characterization of Jefferson Davis in 1890—a man of "moral obtuseness" and "refined brutality." Such was the characterization of the main white figure in his first novel, *The Quest of the Silver Fleece* (1911). John Taylor is a northern industrialist who despises Negroes for the sole reason that they are weak. Taylor is brutal, impersonal—a force involved in an economic enterprise that relentlessly ground its victims into the dust. Taylor is a man completely innocent of pity, tenderness, kindheartedness or love—a barbarian.

Such were the basic ingredients of Du Bois's mythology: the "Christ-like" Negro, and the white "barbarian." It was fully developed and firm by 1911, and pretty much accounts for the falling away from scientific objectivity of the 1912 Atlanta study. The world mosaic now had its pattern—the place of each piece was determined. Du Bois's critique of white civilization was in perfect accord with the mythology. Let one of his literary characters speak for him: "No, no. They don't really rule," exclaimed the swamp girl, "they just thinks they rule. They just got things,—heavy, dead things. We black folks is got the spirit." As the swamp girl inferred, American civilization is the logical realm of the money-grabbing white barbarian. The crisis of that civilization is, in the Du Bois critique, a crisis of the spirit.[7]

"A nation's religion," he wrote in 1920, "is its life, and as such white Christianity is a miserable failure." Du Bois struck the note often. America, he noted elsewhere, is in a state of "spiritual degradation," of "mammonism," putting a "premium on greed and impudence and cruelty. . . ." It was the lesson he sought to get across in his biography of John Brown. Brown and the abolitionist crusade represented for the Negro leader the high point in America's spiritual development. The decline from the pinnacle that was John Brown to the barren present was precipitous and, for Du Bois, not hard to understand. He reasoned thus: following the Civil War a moral revolution occurred owing to the influence of Social Darwinism. America had always been greedy and aggressive, but these traits had been sublimated into the conquest of the wilderness, not their fellowman. The Social Darwinist

<hr />

[7] W. E. B. Du Bois, *The Quest of the Silver Fleece* (Chicago: A. E. McClurg & Co., 1911), p. 46.

"survival of the fittest" idea directed the greed and aggression into racial chauvinism. The spirit of John Brown had been replaced by the spirit of conquest.[8]

Thus, the disparate pieces of the Du Bois mosaic began to find their pattern: the Negro, more Christ-like than the white barbarian; the critique of American civilization as a spiritual failure. Out of this pattern grew the Negro mission ideology—the mission of making that civilization better, of investing it with the Negro spirit. The logic of his position is analogous to that of the Puritans when they departed from England for the shores of America nearly three centuries before. Their mission had been to reform the world, but they had to withdraw from it if they were to maintain their spiritual integrity. Du Bois was confronted with the same twofold problem: to develop the Negro's spiritual gift so that it could perform its regenerative mission, and yet somehow to keep it free of the contaminating influences of American civilization. Speaking at the graduation of a Baltimore Colored High School class in June of 1910, he talked of going on "the Last Crusade, the crusade to deliver from the Heathen the sacred Truth of Human Equality and Brotherhood." He denounced the assumption that American civilization, "with its hypocrisy, lying and stealing, its prostitution and poverty, its ignorance and cruelty" is worthy of fealty, and ended with this exhortation: "To this high mark my brothers and sisters, let us lift our banners and march onward toward the ramparts of Jerusalem. It is the will of God."[9]

II

It does not seem likely that Du Bois believed in God. He operated, rather, in a twilight zone between his sociologist self and his true believer self. Going back, for a moment, to his senior thesis, we find the young Du Bois of 1889 proclaiming the central importance of duty; that duty must be based on Christian

---

8 Du Bois, *Darkwater, op. cit.*, pp. 35–36; W. E. B. Du Bois, "Sociology and Industry in Southern Education," *Voice of the Negro*, Vol. 4 (May, 1907), p. 175; Du Bois, *The Souls of Black Folk, op. cit.*, pp. 81, 164; W. E. B. Du Bois, *John Brown* (Philadelphia: George W. Jacobs & Co., 1909), pp. 359–80.

9 W. E. B. Du Bois, "Godfrey of Buillon," *Horizon*, Vol. 6 (June, 1910), pp. 4–5.

teleology; and that teleology lies outside the realm of science. The realm opened by science was never large enough for Du Bois. He operated beyond science in the realm of the seer, the truth giver. What it comes down to is that he was operating in the realm of myth and its rhetoric. The myth required the rhetoric of religion and that, in turn, required a God. The rhetoric went something like this: humanity has become alienated from God and is therefore in need of salvation—God has become lost, but the Negro Christ is on hand to save matters:[10]

> Prayest Thou, Lord, and to me?
> *Thou* needest me?
> Thou *needest* me?
> Thou needest *me?*
> Courage, *God*
> *I come!*

God existed for Du Bois not in the realm of belief but in the realm of need. God was a part of the mosaic; part of the pattern set by the Christ-like mythology and broadened by rhetoric. In a sense the God of Du Bois is a symbol of the fact that the universe does have meaning. The mission ideology makes sense only in a teleological universe and that, in turn, requires the presence of God. Yet, God need be only a three-letter metaphor for whatever it is that makes the universe tick in a meaningful way. This, it would seem, was Du Bois's (perhaps unconscious) usage. But the old tension between sociologist and seer was to remain until 1933. Du Bois could not be satisfied with a God that he needed but could not believe in. The mind had to come to the rescue of the heart; provide an understanding of the ticking of the universe, but do it in such a way that the Christ-like mythology and mission ideology would be preserved. For many years the Du Bois mind relied on the "germ" theory of history (in Du Bois's hands it was a racial theory). When the once widely held "germ" theory grew intellectually untenable in the 1920's, the Du Bois mind switched over to Marxism. During all this time the Du Bois heart was loyal to

---

10 For his most comprehensive statement of religious position, see W. E. B. Du Bois, "The Church and Religion," *The Crisis*, Vol. 30 (October, 1933), pp. 236–37; W. E. B. Du Bois, "Renaissance in Ethics," *op. cit.*, p. 39; Du Bois, *Darkwater*, *op. cit.*, p. 250.

its myth. In fact, that was the problem. In order to serve the heart, the mind had to winnow and sift as new ideas and concepts poured in from all directions.

The process began during the college years when Du Bois sat under the historian Albert Bushnell Hart, and continued during the period (1893–94) that he spent in Germany under Treitschke, Schmoller, Wagner and others. Hart and the Germans believed and taught Anglo-Saxon and or Teuton superiority. Hart's "germ" theory had it that the institutions from which free and constitutional government developed can be traced from their origins in the German forests to the New England town meeting. Reflecting this sort of thought, Du Bois recommended in 1899 that such a study of the Negro race be made, a study that would start with the development of the race in the African forests and then follow that development through the slave plantations to the present. At various times and places he told just what he thought such a history would reveal—the gradual unfolding of the Negro mission. In his 1897 "Conservation of Races" he fully expressed this idea. Each race, he told the assembled members of the American Negro Academy, carried in its racial idea or racial spirit its special and unique gift to mankind. The English, for example, gave us the ideal of constitutional liberty and commercial freedom; the Germans contributed science and philosophy, Romance nations literature and art. The Negro race, he said, had yet to make its full contribution. Just what that contribution was to be he did not fully reveal until six years later when he brought out *The Souls of Black Folk*, his opening shot against Booker T. Washington. The Negro, he would write then, carries within himself the pure spirit of the Declaration of Independence—the spirit of brotherhood—and more: "Will America be poorer if she replaced her brutal dyspeptic blundering with light-hearted but determined Negro humility? or her coarse and cruel wit with loving jovial good-humor? or her vulgar music with the soul of the Sorrow Songs?" [11]

Du Bois continued the development of a "germ" theory of

---

11 W. E. B. Du Bois, "A History of the Negro Race in America," *Southern Workman*, Vol. 28 (April, 1899), pp. 149–51; W. E. B. Du Bois, "The Conservation of Races," *Occasional Papers*, Vol. II (Washington: American Negro Academy, 1897), p. 7; Du Bois, *The Souls of Black Folk*, *op. cit.*, pp. 11–12.

Negro history with a thesis that he stated many times—the germinal institution in the Negro's development was his religious organization. It began, he believed, in the African forests with the medicine man (or voodoo priest), a leader and ideal-giver among his people. It crossed the ocean and adapted itself to Christianity in the form of the Negro slave preacher and his unlettered congregation. This preacher was the only contact the slaves had with the African past and with Western civilization. In this new guise the religious leader continued to cast his spell upon his people. After emancipation Negro community life became centered around its churches, and the Negro's peculiar and powerful spiritual force was thereby given a Christian texture—this was to be the Negro's gift to the world.[12]

The Gift of Black Folk was Du Bois's major work of 1924. It is a full exposition of the mission ideology expressed in terms of the Negro's gifts to America. The gifts he enumerated are these: the gift of labor, the gift of defense in time of war, the gift of the first real understanding of democracy, and finally, the gift of the spirit: "How the fine sweet spirit of the black folk, despite superstition and passion, has breathed the soul of humility and forgiveness into the formalism and cant of American religion." In that statement Du Bois was referring to the liberal religion of the religious modernists—the religious ideology that stressed first and foremost the brotherhood of man. In his opinion this liberal religion grew out of the union of English Puritanism and Negro emotionalism: ". . . the cold formalism of upper class England and New England needed the wilder spiritual emotionalism of the black man to weld out of both a rational human religion based on kindliness and social uplift. . . ." In a panoramic view, with which he ended the book, he saw the "sense of meekness and humility" spreading out from Negro religion to do battle with the white man's "contempt, lawlessness and lynching" to dominate the American spirit. Which would win in the end Du Bois's sense of the dramatic would not let him say.[13]

---

12 Statements of this evolutionary process are found in W. E. B. Du Bois, *The Philadelphia Negro, op. cit.*, p. 201; W. E. B. Du Bois, *The Negro* (New York: Henry Holt & Co., 1915), pp. 188–89; W. E. B. Du Bois, *The Gift of Black Folk: The Negroes in the Making of America* (Boston: The Stratford Co., 1924), pp. 320 ff.

13 Du Bois, *The Gift of Black Folk, op. cit.*, pp. 320, 331–32, 340.

Such was Du Bois's intellectual apparatus before World War I and well into the 1920's. The Black Christ, the mission ideology, the "germ" theory of history all fit the pattern of the mosaic. There was only one problem: the sociologist in Du Bois—the skeptic—was always on the alert for new trends of thought. The racial theory he had developed came under the attack of new ideas almost at its inception. At the turn of the century, for example, scientists were having a good deal of trouble discovering a method for distinguishing races by physical measurement. Apologists for racial theory found themselves under the increasing necessity of turning to the idea of inner (unmeasurable) differences. Du Bois, working out his own theory of race, closely followed this trend. Races, he claimed in 1897, are distinguished by "the race idea, the race spirit, the race ideal," which evolves in the course of their history.[14]

Another intellectual problem which soon confronted him was that of coming to grips with Social Darwinism. The "survival of the fittest" idea seemed to argue the white race's superiority as the most fit of the races. Du Bois had scoffed at this argument during his student days, but it had a certain cogency to a believer in race and could not be lightly dismissed. So he worked on the problem. We see his solution in *John Brown* (1909). The concluding chapter of that work contains a rather sustained philippic against the Social Darwinists as glorifiers of brute force. Du Bois turned the "survival of the fittest" idea around and aimed it at them. Not brute force, but spiritual strength is the key to racial survival, he wrote. The white man has an abundance of brute strength but little spiritual force.[15]

Meanwhile, more and potent intellectual forces were at work smiting the fortress Du Bois. Those who had built their theories of history and culture on race were beginning to find that they had built on shifting sands. By 1897, when Du Bois was building his "germ" theory of history with race as the central concept, historians were beginning to follow Frederick Jackson Turner in his

---

14 Thomas F. Gossett, *Race: The History of an Idea in America* (Dallas: Southern Methodist University Press, 1963), pp. 353 ff.; Du Bois, "Conservation of Races," *op. cit.,* p. 7.

15 Du Bois, *Dusk of Dawn, op. cit.,* pp. 147–49; Du Bois, *John Brown, op. cit.,* pp. 376 ff.

shift to an environmentalistic explanation of culture. August Weisman, meanwhile, was attacking the Lamarckian concept of acquired mental traits. William Z. Ripley and G. Finot challenged the idea that the various races represent successive evolutionary stages up the ladder from the beast. Du Bois was closely in touch with all the theories that dealt with race. In 1907 he recommended Ratzel's *History of Mankind,* Ripley's *Races of Europe,* and Denmiker's *Races of Man* as the latest word. Also during that year he promoted Finot's *Race Prejudice* as "must" reading. But in his own thoughts he trailed somewhat behind the most advanced of these writers. In *The Negro* (1915) he took advanced ground by admitting that no scientific definition of race is possible, but he pulled back a little when he wrote that, "Negroes differ from whites in their inherent genius and stages of development." [16]

Du Bois's ideas concerning race evolved under the pressure of the new ideas despite the reluctance on his part. By 1924 he was forced to conclude that, "Heredity is always stronger through the influence of acts and deeds and imitations than through actual blood descent. . . ." This was a clear admission that culture is more important than blood in molding a person's character. By 1927 he was forced to go the whole way with the environmentalists. In that year he proclaimed behaviorism to be the best explanation of personality growth. In the 1899 *Philadelphia Negro* the sociologist in him had held that social and cultural environment accounts for the high Negro crime and illegitimacy rates, but he had always been able to maintain that the Negro "genius" is innate. When he bowed to the vogue of behaviorism—the idea that man is a machine that merely reacts to environmental stimuli—in the late 1920's, the sociologist in him was reasserting itself. By then racial theory, per se, was hardly viable. [17]

The truly crippling blow to race theory came from another quarter—from Franz Boas and his anthropology. His work, *The Mind of Primitive Man* (1911), taught social scientists a new way

16 W. E. B. Du Bois to Forest Cozart, March 11, 1907, Francis L. Broderick notes for the Du Bois papers, Schomberg Collection, New York Public Library; Du Bois, *Horizon,* Vol. 3 (January, 1908); Du Bois, *The Negro, op. cit.,* pp. 13–14, 239.

17 Du Bois, *Gift of Black Folk, op. cit.,* p. 321; W. E. B. Du Bois, "Children," *The Crisis,* Vol. 34 (October, 1927), p. 275.

to study culture. No longer could race be considered in cultural development. No longer was it correct to say that one culture is, in any absolute sense, more advanced than another. Boas shelved racial theory by making it irrelevant to the study of culture and society.[18] And this is exactly how he affected Du Bois's intellectual development.

Over the years Du Bois had become quite familiar with the work of Franz Boas. In 1906 he had the anthropologist down to lecture his students at Atlanta University. In 1909 he reproduced a Boas article in the Niagara Movement's journal, *Horizon*, and in 1910 he heard Boas lecture before the National Negro Conference. *The Negro* (1915) is dotted with references to Boas' writings. And so it went. But, *The Negro* is anything but a wholehearted endorsement of the new anthropological doctrines, for Boas was cutting the ground from under the Negro leader's feet. Boas was busy maintaining that there had been absolutely no cultural carry-over from Africa to America; that the Negro-American's culture is American and nothing more; that it reflects the effects of slav-ery and oppression, but not of Africa. This was a devastating proposition for the Du Bois "germ" theory of Negro history and he ignored it . . . for a time.[19]

Du Bois's intellectual vehicle for his Christ-like mythology was being sorely taxed by 1920. Racial concepts were no longer ade-quate to account for the Negro-American's unique "soul life." The 1924 *Gift of Black Folk* marked the last time that Du Bois maintained in print his "germ" theory of history. Anthropology, history, and psychology had all conspired to make it obsolete. But his mystical faith in a Negro "soul life," or "racial ideal," re-mained firm. It was Du Bois the true believer who in 1928 an-swered the distress signal of a certain youth who wanted to know if the word "Negro" had any usefulness: "And then too," Du Bois wrote, "without the word that means Us, where are all those spiri-

---

[18] The opinion of Gossett.

[19] W. E. B. Du Bois, editorial, "The Achievements of Africans," *Southern Work-man*, Vol. 34 (December, 1906), pp. 649–50; Franz Boas, "Race Problem in America," *Horizon*, Vol. 4 (November, 1909), pp. 9–10; Franz Boas, *Horizon*, Vol. 4 (July, 1910), p. 12, address before the National Negro Conference by Franz Boas; Franz Boas, "Industries of the African Negroes," *Southern Workman*, Vol. 38 (April, 1909), pp. 217–19.

tual bonds, those group ideals and forward strivings of this mighty army of 12 millions? Shall we abolish them? Of course not. They are our most precious heritage." [20]

To ask Du Bois to give up the word "Negro" (the youth suggested replacing it with "American") was to ask him to relinquish his very identity. It was more; it was to ask him to give up his faith and begin casting about for something to believe in. It was to ask him to join the ranks of modern, 20th-century man. But, however much he might have tried to disguise the fact, his answer to the youth was partly a bluff. The old supporting rationalizations had dropped away from his mythology, leaving it naked and exposed to the scrutiny of a mind trained to doubt. After all, what is there in a name? The threat was that the word "Negro" would, without a supporting race theory, come to mean absolutely nothing more than having a black skin. In 1940 Du Bois stated the case succinctly: "Since then [1897] the concept of race has so changed and presented so much contradiction that as I face Africa I ask myself: what it is between us that constitutes a tie which I can feel better than I can explain? . . . The mark of their heritage is upon me in color and hair. These are obvious things, but of little meaning in themselves; only important as they stand for real and more subtle differences from other men. Whether they do or not I do not know nor does science." When he wrote that passage his belief in race as an entity in itself had all but disappeared. He could no longer talk about the Negro as a race with a racial essence brought to America and support it with an historical analysis of institutions developed out of the African forests. He could no longer talk about a racial soul innate in every black man. But he had not lost his faith in the Christ-like mythology. In 1940 the Negro was still a man who has the "courage to live and suffer in patience and humility, in forgiveness and in hope [with] eagerness to turn, not simply the other cheek, but the face and the bowed back [and] capacity to love." [21]

Du Bois had managed the job of retaining the Christ-like mythology by the simple expedient of transforming the Negro into a member of the proletariat. Marx had come to the rescue of the myth in its hour of danger. The Negro is more Christ-like than the

20 W. E. B. Du Bois, "The Name 'Negro'," *The Crisis*, Vol. 35 (March, 1928), p. 96.
21 Du Bois, *Dusk of Dawn, op. cit.*, pp. 116–17, 146–47.

white man because of his years of suffering under oppression. In 1933 Du Bois stated his new position this way: ". . . It is beside the point to ask whether we form a real race. Biologically we are mingled of all conceivable elements, but race is psychology, not biology; and psychologically we are a unified race with one history, one red memory and one revolt."[22]

Du Bois's on and off flirtation with socialism goes back to 1907. It was then, in the Niagara Movement, that he came into contact with the radical theologians and their religious modernism with its socialist overtones. Reverdy Ransom had come out for socialism back in 1897. J. Milton Waldron, modernist from Florida, recommended it in 1909 as the only possible solution for the race problem. The minutes of the Niagara Movement's August 27, 1907, meeting were given over to Waldron's description of his attempt to get the white Socialists of Florida to unite with the Negro in a common front. R. R. Wright, Jr., who had a Ph.D. in sociology and years of settlement house work behind him, was developing his theory of "social service," a close approximation to socialist theory. The atmosphere of the Niagara Movement meetings must have been dense with talk about the Christ-like Negro, the mission, and socialism. Du Bois was but reflecting the opinion of many of his fellow militants when he wrote in the Niagara Movement's journal that "In the socialistic trend thus indicated lies the one great hope of the Negro American." In his mind the Socialists and the later Communists were fighting the same fight, had the same mission, as the Negro—the fight for a society based on brotherhood, the mission of spiritual regeneration: First, he wrote in 1920, "must come the Spirit—the Will to Human Brotherhood of all Colors, Races, and Creeds; the Wanting of the Wants of All. Perhaps the finest contribution of current Socialism to the world is neither its light nor its dogma, but the idea back of its one mighty word—Comrade!"[23]

---

22 W. E. B. Du Bois, "The Negro College," *The Crisis*, Vol. 30 (August, 1933), p. 177.

23 Reverdy C. Ransom, "The Negro and Socialism," A.M.E. Church *Review*, Vol. 14 (October, 1897); J. Milton Waldron, "The Problem's Solution," *Proceedings of the National Negro Conference* (New York, 1909), pp. 159–66; Minutes, Third Meeting of the Niagara Movement, August 27, 1907, Francis L. Broderick notes from the Du Bois papers, Schomberg Collection, New York Public Library; W. E. B. Du Bois, "The Negro and Socialism," *Horizon*, Vol. 1 (February, 1907), p. 8; Du Bois, *Darkwater, op. cit.*, p. 159.

So, in the late 1920's Du Bois found his new intellectual home in Marxism. His courtship with Marx was a very tempestuous one for two reasons: he never attained more than a nodding acquaintance with the intricacies of Marxist theory, and he had always to confront the fact that the white American working class shut the doors of labor against the Negro. But despite this, beginning about 1928 when it shows up strongly in his novel, *Dark Princess*, Du Bois began to think of the social conflict in terms of class instead of race, with capitalism the enemy. He began to identify the millennium with the overthrow of capitalism by the proletariat. He began to identify the Negro as being in the vanguard of the proletariat: "In the hearts of black laborers alone, therefore, lie those ideals of democracy in politics and industry which may in time make the workers of the world effective dictators of civilization."[24]

III

Du Bois, proud, aristocratic, lonely, closeted in his editorial offices nursing his beloved *Crisis*, voice of the NAACP, to the press month after month, seeing his word overcome the word of Booker T. Washington, watching the circulation of his word swell till his name became a household symbol, until it drowned out the word of lesser men—this was the Du Bois of the 1920's. Defiant, hopeful, bitter, puzzled, he watched over the destinies of his race. Presidents came and presidents went, Du Bois eyed them, supported them, rejected them, heaped scorn on them—thundered it down from Olympian heights. His was the voice of Negro protest during the 1920's; he knew it, mastered the techniques of his trade—cool reason, molten sarcasm, the subtle turn of phrase, the shocking claim. Graciously he rendered judgments on the comings and goings of mortals—their literature, their religion, their social

---

24 Francis L. Broderick discusses Du Bois's courtship with Marxism in his *W. E. B. Du Bois: Negro Leader in a Time of Crisis* (Stanford, Calif.: Stanford University Press, 1959), pp. 144–49; W. E. B. Du Bois, "Marxism and the Negro Problem," *The Crisis*, Vol. 30 (May, 1933), pp. 103 ff.; W. E. B. Du Bois, "Postscript," *The Crisis*, Vol. 30. (June, 1933), pp. 141–42; W. E. B. Du Bois, "The Revelation of Saint Orgne the Damned" (privately printed, 1939), pp. 12–16, commencement address at Fisk, 1939. This shift of view is summed up in Du Bois's *Black Reconstruction* (New York: Harcourt, Brace & Co., 1935), in which the agrarian slaves and freedmen are represented as the vanguard of the proletariat.

events. He was listened to. Effortlessly, and with impeccable grace, he had shouldered the mantle of leadership handed down by the heroic Frederick Douglass and the faltering Washington. Then, in 1934, he was cast aside.

He was cast aside by the professionals, by men who had little time for grand visions, but much expertise in the pragmatic day-to-day business of lobbying before Congress and of arguing cases before the courts—expertise in the business of inching along. In 1933 and 1934 Du Bois stood accused by the professionals of forsaking his own fight for integration. He was allowed to withdraw gracefully from the NAACP (he was incapable of withdrawing gracefully). He was rebuked by the younger generation of intellectuals at a strategy session known as the second Amenia Conference. Old admirers sadly acknowledged him to be a backslider who after all those years of fighting for the right had capitulated to the Booker T. Washington philosophy.

It was not true—not in the deeper sense—that Du Bois was shifting his intellectual position when he formulated his new program for the 1930's—the program that cost him his leadership. His position remained the same; he was the seer following the myth of the Black Christ and the mission ideology in the directions they seemed to lead. It was, rather, the younger generation of intellectuals who had taken a new direction. For, the period from 1890 to roughly 1933 encompassed two intellectual revolts. The first one, of which Du Bois was a leader, was directed against the old slave psychology, which preached submission to things as they are. The second, and later revolt, was a part of a larger revolt in America and elsewhere—the revolt against the 19th-century absolutes. Bound up with the second intellectual revolt was a movement which lay at the heart of the "Negro Renaissance" of the 1920's, a movement which overcame the need to idealize the race—a movement which, in other words, rejected the Christ-like image of the Negro and its mission ideology. In this sense the second revolt was a psychological emancipation.

The first intellectual revolt involved turning the Christ-like image into a militant force for reform by loading the image with emotional antipathy toward the white man, and in giving the Black Christ a mission on earth to replace the hope of a blissful repose in heaven. We have seen how the myth developed in the minds of protest leaders. These men would no doubt have been militants without the myth, but the myth gave their militancy direction and based it in tradition. For Du Bois it served as an absolute—something which fixed his position in the universe, gave him a sense of participation in a great movement. What Negro militancy meant to Du Bois is summed up in a statement he made in 1914. "Evolution is evolving the millennium," he wrote, "but one of the unescapable factors in evolution [is] the men who hate wickedness and oppression with perfect hatred, who will not equivocate, will not excuse, and will be heard."[25] This is the spirit of the true believer, who will accept nothing less than perfection— the millennium.

In 1903 Booker T. Washington suddenly found himself confronted by a true believer; found that he had become a symbol of something that true believer despised. On the level of rhetoric the Washington-Du Bois controversy centered about what system of education was best for the race. Du Bois was attacking the theory of education which guided the Tuskegee enterprise, but, as many observers have pointed out, Du Bois, himself, favored such an education for all but a small minority. In any case, no controversy over education has ever been a sufficient cause to arouse the kind of wrath that this one did. On another level it was a struggle for power and influence. This was a very real struggle. Washington had the confidence of white politicians and philanthropists in the North, and this gave him control over the appointments of Negroes to political jobs and over the flow of funds into the coffers of Negro educational institutions. He had his hands on the purse strings. His power extended to the editorial offices of a great many Negro newspapers. The ideological battle could not be won by the militants while Washington retained these powers. But the essence of the battle waged by the militants was the struggle against the slave psychology, and on this level of the controversy Washington was little more than a symbol.[26]

For the militants Washington symbolized the slave psychology— the "Uncle Tom" (to use a more recent term). He represented

---

[25] W. E. B. Du Bois, editorial, *The Crisis*, Vol. 8 (May, 1914), p. 10.

[26] Washington's control of the Negro press is discussed in August Meier, *Negro Thought in America, 1880–1915: Racial Ideologies in the Age of Booker T. Washington* (Ann Arbor, Mich.: The University of Michigan Press, 1963), pp.. 227 ff.

compromise, the man resigned to things as they are. More than that, he represented submission to American materialism—the compromise of race ideals to the spirit of greed. Du Bois made it clear in his opening attack on Washington that the Tuskegee educator was being indicted on both of these grounds. He accused Washington not only of "the old attitude of adjustment and submission," but of developing a program that was based on the "gospel of Work and Money"; one that almost completely disregarded "the higher aims of life." [27]

Washington accepted—even praised—American society as he found it, asking only that the Negro be allowed to share in it. The militant revolt on the other hand had a strong puritanical element in it. Perfection was their aim. Were the Negro to assimilate American materialistic culture his spiritual endowment would be corrupted:

In the Black World, the Preacher and Teacher embodied once the ideals of this people . . . but today the danger is that these ideals, with their simple beauty and weird inspiration, will suddenly sink into a question of cash and lust for gold. . . . What if the Negro people be wooed from a strife for righteousness, from a love of knowing, to regard dollars as the be-all and end-all of life? What if to the Mammonism of America be added the rising Mammonism of the re-born South, and the budding Mammonism of its half-awakened black millions? Whither, then, is the new-world quest of Goodness and Beauty and Truth gone glimmering?

In this early struggle militancy was not on the side of integration, nor can Washington be accused of accepting segregation. The issue of integration versus segregation was not at stake. What was at issue was Washington's insistence that the Negro hurry up and assimilate the culture of capitalism, that he plunge in and start competing. It was essentially a controversy between the assimilationist and the puritan.[28]

The Washington-Du Bois controversy, begun about 1903, came to an end with Washington's death in 1915, by which time Du Bois's voice was clearly in the ascendancy. The way the story is usually told, Washington's approach went into an eclipse from

---

27 Du Bois, *The Souls of Black Folk, op. cit.*, p. 51.
28 *Ibid.*, p. 81.

that time on, never to be revived except among the pusillanimous. The usual account misses the fact (to be shown in a later chapter) that Washington's approach—assimilation of American culture— was picked up by both the sociologists in the schools and the professionals in the NAACP (who could not afford to admit the similarity between their program and that of the disgraced Washington). It was Washington's assimilationism, dressed up as integration, that undercut the Du Bois leadership in the early 1930's.

In 1933 and 1934, Du Bois called for a segregated Negro economy built on a cooperative basis. This call injected an ideological element into a power struggle already taking place within the NAACP leadership. The power struggle between Secretary Walter White and Du Bois need not detain us. White was the winner, partly because he was able to pin the tag of accommodationist on his antagonist. Du Bois argued vainly that the NAACP had never before made integration its cause. He was right, at least to the extent that it had not been pushed by *The Crisis* during all the years that magazine had been considered the voice of Negro militancy. The climax of the ideological battle was played out at the summer estate of NAACP president Joel E. Spingarn in 1934— the so-called second Amenia Conference. There, Du Bois heard the younger generation of intellectuals—lawyers, social workers, and college professors—ignore his advice to segregate and cooperate, and call instead for an even more concerted effort by the Negro to integrate into the American economy.[29]

To his contemporaries and to many later observers it looked as though Du Bois had returned to Washington's philosophy of compromise. The opposite was true. It was the new generation that was filled with the spirit of compromise. It was they who were willing to accept the imperfect American culture in return for equality. Du Bois's new position was simply a restatement of his old puritanical separatism in new garb—the garb of Marxism. The

---

[29] Du Bois introduced his new program in, "Our Economic Future," *The Crisis*, Vol. 35 (May, 1928), pp. 169–70, and reiterated it many times thereafter; W. E. B. Du Bois, "The N.A.A.C.P. and Race Segregation," *The Crisis*, Vol. 41 (February, 1934), pp. 52–53. His comments on segregation over the years were ambiguous. He recognized segregation as an evil because it was an affront to man's dignity and it was a denial of rights. His preference was always for a black society, see W. E. B. Du Bois, "Race Pride," *The Crisis*, Vol. 19 (January, 1920), p. 107, and "Atlanta," *The Crisis*, Vol. 20 (May, 1920), p. 5.

cooperative society was to be the society of the future. It was the kind of society, devoid of greed and plunder, toward which the Negro's racial soul pointed. It was to be the means by which the Negroes would introduce their spirit into the world as a regenerative force. It was not a new Du Bois but the same old seer, the same old puritan who at the 1938 Fisk University commencement exercises damned the "young intellectual exquisites," whose sole program is to "Do nothing, think nothing, become absorbed in the nation," and who developed the idea of the cooperative store, the credit union, the group insurance, and the building and loan association as the embodiments of the teachings of Jeremiah, Shakespeare, Jesus, Confucius, Buddha and John Brown. It was the same old vision which held that the Negro community, cooperating together, might be the "pipeline" through which a more human civilization would be extended throughout the world. And it was spoken with the same old millennial spirit: "This reformation of the world is beginning with agony of soul and strain of muscle. . . ." It could not be allowed to stop, he said. It had to go on, and the Negro had to decide what part he was going to play ". . . in this economic revolution for our own salvation and for the salvation of the world."[30]

In 1934, when he wrote his last editorial for *The Crisis*, Du Bois turned back in his mind to the beginning of his career, to the "Conservation of Races" speech he had made in 1897 before the American Negro Academy. Then he had developed his theory of the Negro mission. Looking back, Du Bois could see no reason to change his mind: "On the whole, I am rather pleased to find myself still so much in sympathy with myself." Marxism, being more intellectually acceptable, may have replaced the germ theory as an historical explanation of the Negro mission, but the essential vision was unchanged.[31]

With Du Bois pushed to the sidelines the grand vision of the Negro mission lost its last voice among the original militants. Archibald Grimké was dead. William Ferris had followed Marcus Garvey's black nationalism into obscurity. R. R. Wright, Jr. and Reverdy Ransom had both retired from the heat of earlier battles

---

30 Du Bois, "The Revelation of Saint Orgne the Damned," *op. cit.*, pp. 4–16.

31 W. E. B. Du Bois, "The Conservation of Races," *The Crisis*, Vol. 41 (June, 1934), p. 183.

to become sedate bishops of the church. The stilling of these voices meant a change that goes deeper than the rejection of a myth—it meant transition from the world of 19th-century absolutes into the 20th-century world of uncertainties. It meant, in fact, that the second revolution in Negro thought following Reconstruction had taken place. It meant that the Negro American intellectual was prepared to come to grips with the quandaries that so harass the 20th-century mind.

Du Bois took no part in this second intellectual revolution. His mind was too deeply attached to its New England roots. He still thought in terms of man transcending himself, the problem that gripped Ralph Waldo Emerson's mind. In 1928 he took time out from his labors for *The Crisis* to write a novel, *The Dark Princess* —a work that showed how a man thrust down by his environment, mired in his own hatred, bounded about by the temptations of mammon, was able to transcend these things into a higher realm of being. This was Du Bois the humanist at work, telling men to reach for an ideal that will lift them above their degrading culture. It was also Du Bois the racist writing. He would not have been true to form had he not made his hero a Negro, his hero's transcendental ideal the Negro's mission to save the world. The humanist and the racist—these were his two selves, forever in tension.[32]

Age did not mellow Du Bois. He continued his fight for unpopular causes after 1934, not without the old acrimony. When he was 84 (1951), the Department of Justice labored (after a seduction by McCarthyism) and brought forth an indictment against him. Du Bois was innocent and the case was thrown out of court, but not before the old radical perceived how isolated he really was from the leadership of his people—how few were those willing to defy public pressure to rally to his side. In his bitterness he turned his back on the civil rights movement and accused its leaders of the gravest of sins—apostasy from the grand vision. He saw about him a distressing tendency on the part of black intellectuals to bend their knees to "western acquisitive society." The slight relaxation of oppression of the previous few years had not, as he

---

[32] W. E. B. Du Bois, *Dark Princess: A Romance* (New York: Harcourt, Brace & Co., 1928).

had hoped, motivated black men to create ". . . a new cultural unity, capable of absorbing socialism, tolerance and democracy, and helping to lead America into a new heaven and new earth. But rather, partial emancipation is freeing some of them to ape the worst of American and Anglo-Saxon chauvinism, luxury, showing-off and 'social climbing.' "[33]

Oddly enough, that statement came a few short years before the grand vision was to find new spokesmen and attract (for the first time) something like a mass following. But before speaking of that it will be necessary to look at the plunge into modernity.

---

[33] W. E. B. Du Bois and Shirley Graham Du Bois, *In Battle for Peace: The Story of My 83rd Birthday* (New York: Masses and Mainstream, 1952), pp. 154, 155.

IV

Marginal men

W. E. B. DuBois's undeviating devotion to the Christ-like mythology suggests that to identify with the Negro race he needed to idealize it. If, for a moment, we look at the development of Negro thought as a process of emancipation—first from the slave psychology, then from the myths which grew from it—the second phase in the emancipation would appear to have come about when the Negro no longer needed myths to enable him to identify with his race. In short, the second phase would come when the Negro intellectual could identify with his race without needing to idealize it.

The three men who appear in this chapter were distinctly uncomfortable with their racial identity. They had two things in common: their inability to idealize the race, and their inability to identify with it in any meaningful way. They illustrate the plight of the intellectual freed from myths, but alienated from the masses. Indirectly, the three led to the second phase in the emancipation of Negro thought through their unsuccessful search for a new way of identifying with their race. They began the revolt against the Christ-like Negro, because they saw him as an "Uncle Tom." The revolt would reach its climax in the doctrine that Christianity is a slave religion.

A few words need to be said about the relationship between the Christ-like image and the "Uncle Tom" stereotype. The Christ-like image grew out of the Negro's helplessness. Being helpless, it was necessary to develop the traits of humility, patience, and the ability to forgive, in order to survive. The Christ-like image was the idealization of these traits. It was an ego-defense mechanism because it gave the Negro a modicum of self-esteem. But, if helplessness led to the Christ-like image when idealized, it led also to what was later to be known as "Uncle Tom," when that helplessness became the object of hatred. Although the term "Uncle Tom" did not come into general usage until the 1930's[1] the hatred of helplessness is evident in the religious modernists and Du Bois as well as the three subjects of this chapter. It led the religious modernists to modify the Christ-like image until it became a useful myth for militancy. Now, there is nothing in Du Bois's early or later life that suggests helplessness or humility. Nor is there anything that suggests them in the lives of the subjects of this chapter. For these people the Christ-like image was not a defense mechanism. For Du Bois it was a means of identification—a means of establishing his place and role in the grand scheme of things. It served the purpose of a social role for him. It could have done the same for the subjects of this chapter except that they were too busy attacking it. It was not an ingrained part of their personalities—not, for them, a defense mechanism—so they were able to attack it without loss of self-esteem. In doing so, they began a tradition which pictured the humble, patient, and forgiving Negro as a weak-kneed sycophant.

In 1931 sociologist Robert E. Park developed the concept of the "marginal man," the man caught between two cultures. The marginal man is in perpetual conflict between his two social roles—in the case of the Negro American, the conflict between being Negro and that of being American.[2] The three subjects of this chapter were marginal men. Each had to make a decision of identity.

One of these men, Sutton E. Griggs, never found the identity he sought. Griggs was a novelist of sorts who found in conscious escape the only alternative to the impossible situation of being locked out of the society to which he belonged. He was a minor figure at best. A lifelong resident of the South, he was one of the few southerners to join and actively participate in the militant Niagara Movement. He was something of a religious modernist. And, though not a scholar in any formal sense, he was in close

---

[1] In 1936 the conservative Charles S. Johnson used the phrase "Uncle Tom" without explanation in his *A Preface to Racial Understanding* (New York: The Friendship Press, 1936). He expected his readers to know what was meant.

[2] Robert E. Park, "Mentality of Racial Hybrids," *American Journal of Sociology*, Vol. 36 (January, 1931), pp. 534–51.

touch with the most advanced social thought. He toyed with the religiously acceptable ideas of Herbert Spencer and Benjamin Kidd until he decided that honesty demanded a more literally materialistic interpretation of Darwin. For a clergyman buried away deep in the Bible belt this kind of rugged intellectual honesty is astonishing. Life could not have been easy. As if religious radicalism were not enough, he kept abreast of, and propounded, the most modern American social thought, rejecting the work ethic of Booker T. Washington in favor of environmental determinism. He was well acquainted with the work in psychology done by Edward T. Thorndike, whose "law of effect" (latterly known as "reinforcement") was to be one of the building blocks of American behaviorism and its corollary that the human personality is a mirror of the culture around it. He quoted Rousseau, J. S. Huxley and William E. Locking in support of his own mature contention that social environment is all in the life of man. From this he drew the old socialist conclusion, that by controlling their social environment men can make themselves better.[3] A civil rights activist in the South; a Darwinist within the Negro clergy; a socialist swimming against the current of Washington's rugged individualism— all these things define Griggs as a man of large courage. But where the problem of identity intruded he fled in panic.

Griggs wrote four novels between 1899 and 1905, each a study in bafflement. For one thing, he was in a constant quandary about the discrepancy between his theory of social evolution and what he plainly saw going on around him. His theory, in those years adopted whole from Benjamin Kidd, was that the evolution of society from the lower to the higher forms is brought about by society's progressive embodiment of the Christian principles. It supposed that spiritual values, not technology, account for Western civilization's preeminent position. But, as he looked about him, Griggs saw nothing to support this conclusion. His novels agonize over the Negro's deteriorating situation in the South punctuated by the rise of the South's most vicious white elements. Onrushing social reality, as he understood it, thrust Griggs into the Darwinian universe of meaningless chaos. No feeling of community, no

---

[3] Sutton E. Griggs, *Kingdom Builder's Manual: Companion Book to Guide to Racial Greatness* (Memphis, Tenn.: National Public Welfare League, 1924), p. 8; Sutton E. Griggs, *Guide to Racial Greatness: or, the Science of Collective Efficiency* (Memphis, Tenn.: National Public Welfare League, 1923), p. 74 ff.

sense of belonging, was there to give him an anchor to windward in the Darwinian storm. Instead, he drifted in defeat.

Griggs opened his struggle with two novels, *Imperium in Imperio* (1899) and *Unfettered* (1902), both of which open with the symbolic passing of the benevolent old aristocratic class of the South. The first novels opens with the fine old teacher, Samuel Christian, dead. His successor's first words were: "Another black nigger brat for me to teach." From then on things went from bad to worse, giving Griggs occasion to comment on the white race: "Woe unto that race, whom the tears of the widows, the cries of the starving orphans, the groans of the innocent dying, and the gaping wounds of those unjustly slain, accuse before a righteous God!" That statement, uttered by the character Bernard Belgrave, was legitimate Griggs. Also legitimate Griggs was the statement made by another character, Belton Piedmont, that the white race is giving the untutored black savage "instruction in the arts of civilization, a knowledge of the English language, and a conception of the one true God and his Christ."[4] In each of his four novels the situation was repeated: two heroes appeared, one who was Christlike and nonviolent, one who was of hot warrior's blood. All of his heroes, violent and nonviolent alike, were studies in futility.

Griggs's heroes were based on the now familiar racial stereotypes; they were inevitably mulatto, and the Anglo-Saxon blood in each case did battle with the Negro blood. When the Anglo-Saxon blood got the upper hand, as in the case of Earl of *The Hindered Hand* (1905), a violent hero resulted. In Earl's case, "Ordinarily the well-known tractability of the Negro seemed uppermost in him, . . .", but as events progressed the Anglo-Saxon side of Earl took control. "Conditions have made me an outlaw among my kind," he said, "Rubbish aside, am I not as much of an Anglo-Saxon as any of them? Does not my soul respond to those things and those things only to which their souls respond? He that is without the law shall be judged without the law." In this mood Earl plotted rebellion and asked the Christ-like Ensal to join him. Ensal spoke of the Negro's "docility, his habit of cheerfulness when at work, his largely uncomplaining nature. . . ." Whereas Earl was mortified by the thought of the Negro's submissive behavior during the Civil

---

[4] Sutton E. Griggs, *Imperium in Imperio: A Study of the Negro Race Problem* (Cincinnati: The Editor Publishing Co., 1899), pp. 9, 231.

War, Ensal considered that to have been the race's finest hour. Earl's revolutionary plot was foiled—it was an exercise in futility. Ensal's task was different; he was to preach the Gospel to everyone. In the end this, too, was recognized as being futile.[5]

For a moment in the *Hindered Hand,* his last novel, it seemed as if Griggs would finally refuse to bow to the futility of it all. It seemed that he had made a new resolution—a union of the two natures into a stronger, more vital hero. He had Earl saying that "by the patience and optimism of the blood of my black forbears; by the energy and persistence of my grant of blood from Europe— by all these mighty tokens, I make oath that this nation shall rest neither day nor night until this shadow is lifted from my soul." But in the end this too was futile, and Earl departed for Africa. The answer was the inevitable escape.[6]

Griggs was caught up in a whirl of ambivalences. As Earl in *The Hindered Hand,* he eagerly assumed both identities—the black and the white—though neither without the other was enough. Both identities were, of course, pictured in terms of stereotypes, suggesting that neither the black nor the white *reality* would do. Revulsion toward both realities is the open secret of his books. The Negro's attempts to emulate the white man caused high indignation among his spokesmen for the Negro race: "We is lettin' dese white folks teach us too much," complained Aunt Mollie Marston, of *Overshadowed.* "Our church hes dun away wid dem good ole soul-stirrin' himes in which my soul jes' 'peared ter float right up ter God . . ." "Ef niggers stay heah in dis country wid dese cole hearted white folks we woan hab no 'legion 'tall." In part, *Overshadowed* was a sermon against assimilation; against the degrading effects of the white man's values. The book's climax was reached when the heroine discovered that her brother had stooped to revengeful murder: "Then the thought flashed over her mind that the Anglo-Saxon race, whose every advancing footstep had been planted in a pool of blood, was about to impart its mercilessness to the Negro, a being of another mold."[7]

---

[5] Sutton E. Griggs, *The Hindered Hand: or, The Reign of the Repressionist* (Nashville, Tenn.: The Orion Publishing Co., 1905), pp. 37, 52, 49–50, 140.

[6] *Ibid.,* p. 251.

[7] Sutton E. Griggs, *Overshadowed* (Nashville, Tenn.: The Orion Publishing Co., 1901), pp. 59, 75, 128.

If the whites were bad, the black masses were worse. Belton Piedmont, hero of *Imperium in Imperio*, voiced the author's antipathy:

Our grotesque dress, our broken language, our ignorant curiosity, and, on the part of many, our boorish manners, would have been nauseating in the extreme to men and women accustomed to refined association. Of course these failings are passing away: but the polished among you have often been made ashamed at the uncouth antics of some ignorant Negroes, courting the attention of the whites in their presence. Let us see to it, then, that we as a people, not a small minority of us, are prepared to use and not abuse the privileges that come to us.[8]

The speech is loaded with stereotyped phrases—phrases full of the revulsion of the cultured Negro, with his bourgeois values, toward the black masses. Griggs's heroes were always middle class and highly educated. They were mulattoes, half of one culture, half of the other. They, like Griggs himself, were marginal men.

So Griggs offered a confusion of alternatives—violent revolt, Christian patience, creation of a Negro community within American society, escape to Africa—none of which satisfied him. He could identify with no group of men. He was as much adrift as one of his heroes who became a citizen of the ocean—destined forever to drift between Africa and America, and avoiding both.

II

The forces working on Griggs in Nashville, Tennessee, were working on another novelist up North in Cleveland, Ohio. This was, of course, Charles W. Chesnutt, the best known and most successful of the pre-World War I Negro writers. Caught between the two worlds of color, Chesnutt's resolution of the conflict was unique and instructive. As in Griggs's case, we find in Chesnutt a strong sense of futility, a sense of inevitability—what will be, will be. But Chesnutt was quite content with life, and optimistic about the outcome of history.

Two identities fought for Chesnutt's soul. His ancestry, his childhood friends and haunts—these called him into the world of

---

[8] Griggs, *Imperium in Imperio, op. cit.*, p. 235.

the Negro; asked him to suffer its pains and fight its battles. But the call of the white world was strong as the passing years brought success and middle age. In appearance he was white. His adult friends were mostly white men: his stenographic business was conducted in the courts of Cleveland, his clubs were usually white clubs, and his home was flanked by white neighbors—friends. He liked the praise and friendship of famous white novelists. Two identities battled for his allegiance, but the white identity won. It gathered force after he left the South as a young man and settled in Cleveland. It won because thereafter he was a Negro only by an act of the imagination. For such a man the five-letter word "Negro" was an abstract mental category. Having no black skin, being subject to no daily-felt oppression, he lacked compelling reason to identify with the Negro race unless the category "Negro" itself could offer him some meaning. Had the Christ-like image satisfied his ego-needs, and had the mission ideology given him a sense of purpose, he might have remained a Negro. Chesnutt believed the stereotype to be true, but it repelled him. He equated the Christ-like Negro with the abject Uncle Tom. Rather than attracting him to the race, it caused him to flee it. He would always retain his sense of indignation over the Negro's plight; he was always to speak of himself as a Negro. But, in point of fact, some time in middle age he ceased to be one.

Chesnutt made gradual but steady progress toward his final identity. Born in Cleveland, he grew to maturity after the Civil War in Fayetteville, North Carolina, where his father ran a grocery store. The land was war-ravaged and life not easy, but there was little racial antagonism to cope with. His father, Andrew, became a county commissioner and justice of the peace for Cumberland County—something of a leading citizen. Chesnutt once watched a white man shoot a Negro down in cold blood, but the community tried and convicted the killer—an act inconceivable 10 years later. Charles's main antagonism in those years was directed against the country folk of both races. They were "good-sized liars, hypocrites, inquisitive little wenches, etc.," according to his diary. In short, one of them had refused him the loan of a mule. His problems were less racial than those of the typical country schoolteacher. Chesnutt, it seems, had little need to develop the defensive mechanisms of humility, patience, and the like, that made a man see himself as Christ-like.[9]

A good indication that Chesnutt built up no defensive, or oppression psychology is that as a young man he had great aspirations. Along with his duties as headmaster of the normal school in Fayetteville, he taught himself Greek, Latin, German, and French; he learned shorthand with the intention of using it in the North. He was a young man on the make and the South was beginning to get oppressive. In his diary he noted with what humor he could muster, words reportedly spoken of him by a white store clerk: "Well," said the clerk, "he is a nigger; and with me a nigger is a nigger, and nothing in the world can make him anything else but a nigger." With his boundless ambition he looked with longing to the freer atmosphere of the North.[10]

By 1884 Chesnutt was back in Cleveland working for the railroad as a stenographer, studying law, and writing short stories on the side. The stories, some of which were sold to S. S. McClure, dealt mainly with nonracial incidents typical of any northern business office. But the success of white writers like Thomas Nelson Page, George Washington Cable, Harry Stillwell Edwards, and others, who were using race as a subject, influenced Chesnutt to turn in that direction. His first racial efforts were conjure stories—tales of the Negro folk—that argued no cause. He was a success. The *Atlantic Monthly* published his first conjure story, "The Goophered Grapevine," in 1887, so neutral in tone a white man might have written it. Chesnutt was becoming an author; achieving that, he would do something about the color line. In 1881, while still in the South, he had written "Every time I read a good novel, I want to write one. It is the dream of my life—to be an author! It is not so much the *moustrari digito*,—though that has something to do with my aspirations. It is not altogether the money. It is a mixture of motives. I want fame; I want money; I

---

[9] Helen M. Chesnutt, *Charles Waddell Chesnutt: Pioneer of the Color Line* (Chapel Hill, N.C.: University of North Carolina Press, 1952), pp. 1–9; Charles W. Chesnutt, notebook and diary, July 1, 1874 to August 20, 1875, Chesnutt papers, Fisk University Library, entry August 20, 1875.

[10] Charles W. Chesnutt, journal and notebook, January 3, 1881 to September, 1885, Chesnutt papers, Fisk University Library, entry January 21, 1881.

want to raise my children in a different rank of life from that I sprang from."[11]

Chesnutt's first published book, *The Conjure Woman* (1899), was a collection of his conjure stories, the same neutral material. But, elsewhere, he had begun to work the racial vein, stories about mulattoes. Some of these, like "A Matter of Principle" (1899), featuring Cicero Clayton of the Blue Vein Society, were gentle satires of the mulattoes' pretensions of being white. Others, like "The Wife of His Youth" (1899), were melodramas concerned with the paradoxes which informed the lives of mulattoes. By now at home both in white and Negro society, he was keenly observant of the shades and nuances of the mulatto's life. He made no pretense (as some would do later) of identifying with the black masses. In mid-1890 he wrote a revealing letter to his publisher, George Washington Cable, commenting that the reading public seemed afraid of the mulatto, seeming to see him as "an insult to nature." Would that he were writing in England, he said, where such fears did not exist, for the mulatto was his chosen subject. Then he made clear his objection to his black-skinned brother:

. . . and I notice that all of the many Negroes (except your own) whose virtues have been given to the world in the magazine press recently, have been blacks, full-blooded, and their chief virtues have been their dog-like fidelity to their old master, for whom they have been willing to sacrifice almost life itself. Such characters exist; not six months ago a Negro in Raleigh, N.C., addressed a letter to the Governor of the State, offering to serve out a term of seven years' imprisonment in the penitentiary for his old master, and those who are familiar with the convict lease system know what that is better than the Negro did. But I can't write about these people, or rather I won't write about them.[12]

Chesnutt could not stomach the humble, devoted Negro—the Christ-like Negro of myth. But to him that humble, devoted Negro was no myth; he was a depressing reality.

That the Christ-like Negro was real for Chesnutt is evident in his novel, *The Marrow of Tradition* (1901), in which he described

---

11 *Ibid.*, entry March 26, 1881.

12 Charles W. Chesnutt to George Washington Cable, July 25, 1890, Chesnutt papers, Fisk University Library.

the Negro race as "docile by instinct, humble by training, patiently waiting upon its as yet uncertain destiny. . . ." He knew, too, the mission ideology. Adam Miller, the novel's hero, decided, after due reflection on the Negro's plight, that the patient, meek Negro must one day inherit the earth: " 'Blessed are the meek,' Miller mused one day on a train . . . , 'for they shall inherit the earth.' If this be true, the negro may yet come into his estate, for meekness seems to be set apart for his portion." But Chesnutt was not comfortable with Miller's solution. *The Marrow of Tradition* was written in a mood of anger and disgust. It was a fictional account of the 1898 Wilmington, North Carolina, race riot; an event, reports his daughter, that filled him with despair and deep disillusionment. The amiable William Dean Howells was shocked by the book's bitter intensity. It was the southern white man who bore the brunt of the attack, but the humble Negro of tradition in no sense escaped. "No doubt," one of the reactionary whites is made to say, "the Negro is capable of a certain doglike fidelity,—I make the comparison in a friendly sense,—a certain personal devotion which is admirable in itself, and fits him eminently for a servile career." Chesnutt went beyond such digs at the Christ-like Negro, and for the first time in Negro fiction created a character that was the epitome of the type which would later be stigmatized by the epithet, "Uncle Tom." This was the office boy Jerry, a cringing, cowardly, but shrewd servant of the despicable Captain McBane. Jerry scurries around doing favors for the whites; always obsequious, always fawning, and always keeping his eye on the main chance. Having implicated for murder an innocent Negro, he replied to congratulations: "Thank y', gin'l, thank y', suh! I alluz tries ter do my duty, suh, an' stan' by dem dat stan's by me. Dat low-down nigger oughter be lynch', suh, don't you think, er e'se bu'nt? Dere ain' nothing too bad ter happen ter 'im." [13] Chesnutt was tearing down a myth. In the process he destroyed what meaning the word "Negro" could possibly have for him.

---

[13] Charles W. Chesnutt, *The Marrow of Tradition* (New York: Houghton Mifflin and Co., 1901), pp. 80, 62; Helen M. Chesnutt, *Charles Waddell Chesnutt, op. cit.*, p. 104; William Dean Howells, "A Psychological Counter-Current in Recent Fiction," *North American Review*, December, 1901; Chesnutt, *Marrow of Tradition, op. cit.*, pp. 24, 184.

When a young man, Chesnutt wrote in his diary, "I hear colored men speak of their 'white friends.' I have no white friends. I could not degrade the sacred name of 'friendship' by associating it with any man who feels himself too good to sit at a table with me, or to sleep at the same hotel." But time and success changed that. By 1910 he was a member of Cleveland's exclusive, and exclusively white, Rowfant Club, and found it impossible to miss any of its weekly social gatherings.[14] During this period Chesnutt produced his last published novel, *The Colonel's Dream* (1905). Its main protagonist was a white man.

As Chesnutt's sense of identity with the Negro race grew weak he developed a certain detachment concerning its problems. His three novels, spanning the years 1900 to 1905, contain flashes of passion and anger, and little detachment. Commitment seems to have been greatest following the Wilmington riot of 1898 in which friends and acquaintances had been involved. But as time passed his involvement became that of an interested spectator. When the NAACP was formed in 1910, Chesnutt was invited to join. He did, but never found it convenient to attend a national convention. During a period when the Negro race was bitterly divided by the Washington-Du Bois debate, Chesnutt found it possible to oppose Washington in theory while keeping his close friendship.

In the fall of 1910 Washington traveled through England making optimistic statements concerning the Negro's progress in the United States. The outraged opposition, led by Du Bois, wrote a stinging protest entitled "Race Relations in the United States"— a vigorous condemnation of Washington—that Chesnutt was asked to sign. In refusing, Chesnutt wrote Du Bois a letter that was the ultimate in detachment:

But after all, it is largely a matter of the point of view. Mr. Washington says in that interview, "The Negro problem in the United States will right itself in time"; this I think we all hope to be the fact. He says further, "I believe that when America comes to a more accurate understanding of the difficulties which the masses of the working people in other parts of the world have to struggle against,

---

[14] Chesnutt, journal, entry March 7, 1882, *op. cit.;* Helen M. Chesnutt, *Charles Waddell Chesnutt, op. cit.*, pp. 288–89.

it will have gone far towards solving what is called the race problem."
I see nothing wrong in that; it is a philosophic reflection which
ought to have a great deal of validity.

Then, in the same letter, Chesnutt inadvertently revealed just how
slight was his personal sense of wrong:

Moreover, the protest is signed by a number of gentlemen, most of
whom hold or have held positions of honor and profit, political and
otherwise, which they certainly could not have attained without the
good will and sense of justice of the white people, however imperfect
that sense of justice may be in other respects.[15]

So, at a time when hatred was burning its impress into the souls
of men like him, Chesnutt was mellowing, losing his youthful hostility. The others were adopting stereotypes; Chesnutt was not.
Francis Grimké had begun to consider the white man a savage
beast. Archibald Grimké and Du Bois had developed a full-fledged
racism based on their Christ-like image. But Chesnutt's early life
in the South had given him no such illusions. Teaching in the
rural areas had brought him into close contact with the Negro
folk; he measured them against his own standards of culture and
found them sadly wanting. Idealize them, he could not. They were
Uncle Toms, full of mischievous servility.

Caught between two races, detached, yet content, Chesnutt was
not one to hack out a new path in the wilderness of racist America.
His perplexities were only deepened by the confluence upon his
time and place of two world views. He has been called modern by
some because of a tendency toward naturalism. His people were
caught in "the web of circumstance." Forces beyond human control had their fate in hand. "We make our customs lightly," said
one, "once made, like our sins, they grip us in bands of steel; we
become the creatures of our creations."[16]

In confronting this new specter Chesnutt could only fall back
upon the old 19th-century verities: his battle was still between
reason and unreason. "The very standards of right and wrong had

---

15 Charles W. Chesnutt to W. E. B. Du Bois, December 10, 1910, Chesnutt papers, Fisk University Library.

16 Charles W. Chesnutt, *The House behind the Cedars* (New York: Houghton
Mifflin Co., 1900), p. 35.

been confused by the race issue," thought the Colonel in his dream, "and must be set right by the patient appeal to reason and humanity. Primitive passion and private vengeance must be subordinated to law and order and the higher good." As it was with the socialists and their class war, so it was with Chesnutt and his race problem: solve the problem and the prophecy of the Enlightenment would come true, reason would reign on earth.[17]

But, if Chesnutt was the 19th century with its comforting certainties, he was that century distracted by the impending arrival of a new age. The Colonel's dream, after all, did not come true; the reign of reason did not come. Chesnutt had the Colonel's dream shattered by a particularly atrocious act on the part of some southern red-necks. He had the Colonel flee in horror and despair. The book ended as all of Chesnutt's novels ended, with reason in flight, with prejudice triumphant. In *The Colonel's Dream* Chesnutt stared straight into the modern abyss. The whole problem of his race in America needed to be redefined, but Chesnutt was not the man to do it. For one already detached it was easier to give up writing, to back away from the abyss, to contemplate the struggle from the safe niche his success had made for him.

Though 1905 ended Chesnutt's career as a creative writer, he was still a famous man called upon to speak and write on "the problem." From the heights of his eminence he propounded his solution. It was a simple solution, based on experience. The Negro race should simply disappear. "There are those," he said in 1908, possibly thinking of Du Bois, "who cherish the dream of a great Negro people in the United States, who shall make a mark upon the page of history. It is well to dismiss this dream—it is an idle dream. Under the condition of which I speak, the only condition under which you can secure your rights and your liberties and this free opportunity for upward movement of which I have spoken, there will no longer be a Negro race in the United States." When the Negro forgets he is a Negro and becomes everyman, then the Negro problem will cease to exist.[18]

---

17 Charles W. Chesnutt, *The Colonel's Dream* (New York: Doubleday, Page and Co., 1905), p. 247.

18 Charles W. Chesnutt, "Rights and Duties," manuscript of speech delivered before Bethel Literary Society, Washington, D.C., October, 1908, Chesnutt papers, Fisk University Library.

III

For Chesnutt the problem of self-redefinition solved itself. For James Weldon Johnson, a man of far tougher temperament, no such easy solution was within reach. He was not one to flee like Griggs and Chesnutt. It can perhaps be said that in his struggle—his search—he opened the Negro Renaissance in literature. In his *Autobiography of an Ex-coloured Man* (1912) he threw down the gauntlet to both white civilization and the Christ-like Negro. It was a declaration of independence from both—but independence from both, for this marginal man, was impossible.

Johnson went much further than Chesnutt in his revolt against the Christ-like Negro. For Chesnutt the Christ-like image lost meaning and faded away, leaving the category "Negro" without substance. It must have been an unconscious process. It was nothing of the sort for Johnson. He recognized his rejection for what it was, and systematically set about creating a new meaning for the category "Negro." This led him to become a propagandist of the Negro past—for the Negro's cultural achievements. It led him into making some doubtful claims for Negro culture; so doubtful, in fact, that it is hard to believe he himself was fully convinced. It also led him into some inconsistencies that make his life a paradox.

The *Autobiography* spreads wide its net of indictments against white civilization and culture. Is the Negro race accused of a high crime rate? Yes, the Negro has progressed in this respect, and yet "we are far from the point which has been reached by the more highly civilized white race. As we continue to progress, crime among us will gradually lose much of its brutal, vulgar, I must say healthy, aspect, and become more delicate, refined and subtle." Is London as much a city of vice as Paris? Yes, but unlike Paris, London is hypocritical about it—"the hypocrisy of the Anglo-Saxon." London stands for the "conservatism, the solidarity, the utilitarianism" of the Anglo-Saxon. "In the whole scene, not one ray of brightness, not one flash of gaiety, only maudlin joviality or grim despair." This sort of indictment was being made over and over in white *avant-garde* circles. Johnson merely changed the source of the trouble from "Puritanism" to "Anglo-Saxonism."[19]

If Johnson lacked enthusiasm for the white man, he was downright disgusted by the Christ-like Negro. To him the Christ-like Negro was a reality, a sad, disastrous reality. He had his fictional self of the *Autobiography* say that, "For my part, I was never an admirer of Uncle Tom, nor his type of goodness; but I believe that there were lots of old Negroes as foolishly good as he; the proof of which is that they knowingly stayed and worked the plantations that furnished the sinews for the army which was fighting to keep them enslaved." But that statement has a philosophical ring. A much more emotionally involved statement was made later, after he (his fictional self) had witnessed a lynching: "I walked a short distance away and sat down in order to clear my dazed mind. A great wave of humiliation and shame swept over me. Shame that I belonged to a race that could be so dealt with. . . ." In the story he could no longer bear to identify with the Negro race. Being of light complexion he decided to pass into the white race—the race he hated so: "I knew that it was shame, unbearable shame. Shame at being identified with a people that could with impunity be treated worse than animals." Here was the identity conflict starkly defined. His own race filled him with shame, the other with disgust. "I had made up my mind that since I was not going to be a Negro, I would avail myself of every possible opportunity to make a white man's success; and that, if it can be summed up in any one word, means 'money.' "[20]

For Johnson the subject of lynching was no abstraction. He had once witnessed a near-lynching and knew the terror in the heart of the victim; for the near-victim was himself. The incident occurred in 1900. Jacksonville had just been devastated by a fire. A lady reporter—white, but legally black in Florida—had come down from the North to report on conditions. Johnson, who had been in the thick of it, agreed to meet her for a talk in a nearby park. Shortly after taking a seat in the park the baying of hounds and the shouts of men reached their ears. Someone had reported

---

[19] James Weldon Johnson, *The Autobiography of An Ex-coloured Man* (Garden City, N.Y.: Garden City Publishing Co., 1912), pp. 151, 138–39.

[20] *Ibid.*, pp. 41, 187, 191, 193.

them, a black man and a white woman alone together in the park. Understanding and horror struck Johnson simultaneously. Maddened men were approaching and he was to be the victim. What emotions struggled in him as the mob tore as his clothes and at his person—terror, humiliation, outrage, helplessness—one can only guess. The outcome was, of course, anticlimactic, but his soul bore the scar. "For weeks and months," he wrote later, "the episode with all of its implications preyed on my mind and disturbed me in my sleep. I would wake often in the night-time, after living through again those few frightful seconds. . . . It was not until twenty years after, through work I was then engaged in, that I was able to liberate myself completely from this horror-complex." Johnson was a proud man; the humiliation of it must have been nearly unbearable. The humiliation ascribed to his fictional self in the *Autobiography* was his own. In revolting against the Christlike Negro, Johnson could never take the path of Chesnutt, become detached and philosophical. He was too much involved; too emotionally committed to the struggle. So he deliberately set out to create a new "Negro."[21]

A significant theme in the *Autobiography* is Johnson's attempt to promote and popularize the idea that the Negro has a unique racial genius. Where white culture tends to be drab, materialistic and emotionless, culture created by the Negro is full of humor and rich emotion. Before his final disillusionment, the novel's hero had been filled with the desire to transform his race's folk music into great art—into classical masterpieces somewhat in the vein of what Dvořák did with the spirituals in his "New World Symphony." Here again, the hero of the *Autobiography* was not entirely fictional. The real-life Johnson devoted a good deal of his time and talent to creating such an art, not in music but in poetry. Johnson relates in his autobiography how he began to grope in this direction while collaborating with his brother and Bib Cole in writing songs. The year was 1900. Up to that time the professional stage and the public knew of Negro artistry only through the grotesque distortion provided by minstrel shows and "coon songs." The three men passed beyond "coon songs" with their simple ballads, and gained something of a reputation on Broadway; but Johnson

---

[21] James Weldon Johnson, *Along This Way: The Autobiography of James Weldon Johnson* (New York: The Viking Press, 1933), p. 170.

was not satisfied. He saw the limitations of the dialect poetry he had been writing. When he read *Leaves of Grass* all he had done suddenly seemed puerile. Dialect poetry could express something of humor and something of pathos, but great art it could never be. He started out to blaze a new trail.

Johnson was still groping when he published the *Autobiography* in 1912. His poetry had become inspirational in nature, but was less than inspiring:

> Oh Southland! Oh Southland!
>   Have you not heard the call,
> The trumpet blown, the world made known
>   To the Nations one and all?
> The watchword, the hope-word,
>   Salvation's present plan?
> A gospel new, for all—for you:
>   Man shall be saved by man.[22]

Apparently unable to capture the thing he was seeking in poetry, he turned to expounding his faith in the public forum. In 1917 Johnson told a Socialist conference that the only true art of America had been created by Negroes. He was speaking of the spirituals, of jazz, of the Uncle Remus folklore. Thereafter, from time to time, he elaborated on this theme. In the preface to an anthology of Negro poetry, he wrote that the measure of a civilization's true greatness lies in its literature and art, and that "the Negro has already proved the possession of these [artistic] powers by being the creator of the only things artistic that have yet sprung from American soil and have been universally acknowledged as distinctive American products." In other words, what greatness American culture can claim, it owes the Negro.[23]

My suspicion is that in trying to reestablish his identity with his race Johnson was creating a new image of the Negro—the image of the Negro as a creator of culture, a fresher and better culture than America had known. This kind of thinking had a great many possibilities. One could visualize the Negro's culture as that of a folk and set it over against the outworn, even decadent,

---

22 James Weldon Johnson, "Oh Southland!" *Horizon*, III (June, 1908), 8.

23 Johnson, *Along This Way, op. cit.*, p. 327; J. W. Johnson (ed.), *The Book of American Negro Poetry* (New York: Harcourt, Brace & Co., 1922), pp. 9–10.

civilization of America. The more youthful, vigorous folk culture, it might be thought, could be used to revive American culture, to bring it back to the cleaner and more human passions of primitive man. This is a sort of cultural pluralism, but it gives the Negro a mission, and it gives meaning to his life.

Johnson never gave his thinking the full or systematic statement that I just have, but it is clear that he had something like it in mind. At times he wrote without embarrassment about the Negro's primitive nature: "Being shut up in the backwoods of Georgia forced a comparison upon me, and a realization that there, at least, the Negro woman, with her rich coloring, her gayety, her laughter and song, her alluring, undulating movements—a heritage from the African jungle—was a more beautiful creature than her sallow, songless, lipless, hipless, tired-looking, tired-moving white sister." In a speech to the Washington, D.C., branch of the NAACP Johnson talked of "us who are warmed by the poetic blood of Africa— old, mysterious Africa, mother of races, rhythmic-beating heart of the world. . . ." He often spoke to audiences of the rhythm and emotion that the black man had brought over with him from Africa. It was the message of cultural pluralism. In his mind the Negro's contribution lies in the realm of art: "I believe," he told a Howard University audience, "the richest contribution the Aframerican poet can make to American literature will be the fusion into it of his own racial genius. Extreme rhythm, color, warmth, abandon, and movement."[24]

Added to this kind of proselytizing was Johnson's efforts to popularize the Negro past. In his pamphlet, "Native African Races," he extolled Africa's culture and contributions to civilization. In *Black Manhattan* (1930), he attempted a revision of Negro history. Much more important, however, were his labors in the field of creative art. It is in this area that the true paradox of Johnson's life becomes evident.

Johnson was seeking a new social ideal to replace the Christ-like image he so violently rejected. The new social ideal was to be that

---

24 Johnson, *Along This Way, op. cit.*, p. 121; J. W. Johnson, manuscript of speech delivered to Washington, D.C. branch of the N.A.A.C.P., *c.* 1924, Johnson papers, James Weldon Johnson Collection, Yale University Library; James W. Johnson, "American Negro Poets and Poetry," manuscript of speech delivered at Howard University, April 10, 1924, Johnson papers, James Weldon Johnson Collection, Yale University Library.

of a creator of culture; but, what was to be the content of this uniquely Negro culture? Johnson found it in (of all things) the Negro's primitive Christianity—his childlike religious faith. The sense of discovery is found in both his fictional and his real autobiographies where he tells of coming upon a Negro preacher of the primitive type speaking to his people of creation, of heaven and hell. Johnson was overcome with the poetry of it, with the pure emotion and strength: "He intoned, he moaned, he pleaded— he blared, he crashed, he thundered. . . ." Johnson was captivated by the beauty of the black man's religious faith; by what he thought its finest expression—the spirituals. "I never heard these songs," he said, "but that I am struck by the wonder, the miracle of their production." They are the expression of the Negro's innermost experience; they unite his primitive African heritage with the Christianity of America: "The result was a body of songs voicing all the cardinal virtues of Christianity—patience—forbearance—love—faith—and hope—through a necessarily modified form of primitive African music. The Negro took complete refuge in Christianity, and the Spirituals were literally forged of sorrow in the heat of religious fervor. They exhibited, moreover, a reversion to the simple principles of primitive communal Christianity."[25]

Johnson wrote a poem apotheosizing the creators of the Spirituals, a poem of some beauty which is a clear statement of his reverence for the Black and Unknown Bards: ". . . You—you alone, of all the long, long line/ Of those who've sung untaught, unknown, unnamed,/ Have stretched out upward, seeking the divine." It is indeed a curious thing that Johnson should lavish such praise upon the very thing that he despised in the Negro.[26]

It is even more curious that in his pursuit of creativity Johnson should have written religious poetry: "Courage! look out, beyond, and see/ The far horizon's beckoning span!/ Faith in your God-

---

25 Johnson, *Along This Way*, *op cit.*, p. 336; James W. Johnson, "What America Owes to the Negro," manuscript of speech, *c.* 1924, Johnson papers, James Weldon Johnson Collection, Yale University Library; Johnson (ed.), *The Book of American Negro Spirituals* (New York: The Viking Press, 1925), p. 20.

26 James Weldon Johnson, "O Black and Unknown Bards," from *Saint Peter Relates an Incident* by James Weldon Johnson. Copyright 1917 by James Weldon Johnson. All rights reserved. Reprinted by permission of The Viking Press, Inc.

known destiny!/ We are a part of some great plan."[27] This fits in well with the mission ideology of myth, but it is curious because Johnson was an agnostic. As he made clear in his autobiography, he gave up religion at an early age and did not give it much thought thereafter. Furthermore, far from believing in "some great plan," he actually believed the forces at work on man to be so "arbitrary . . . as to make fatalism a plausible philosophy."[28]

Johnson's poetry reached maturity with his *God's Trombones* (1927), seven poems inspired by the sermons of primitive Negro "exhorters." The seven poems, ranging from "The Creation," to "The Judgment Day," are attempts in free verse to render into poetry the traditional or folk sermons that have no one author but were the common possession of most of the successful preachers of the Negro's old-time religion. They are successful poems. They do capture the spirit of the old-time preacher, and something of his power. But, in a sense, they are fakes. The poems were not expressions of Johnson's religious sentiments. *God's Trombones* was anthropology, not creativity. As much as he might empathize with the Negro folk, as much as he might believe in the genius of the race, he was not himself a part of it—not in terms of self-identity.

The paradox of Johnson's life was this: even while he labored to create a tradition for the American Negro he was in the process of isolating himself from that tradition. He was himself a stranger to what he thought best in the race. The primitive, emotional Christianity of the spirituals was what he had found at the end of his search. He had been cut off from that tradition both by his revolt against the Christ-like Negro and by the modern world. There is, he said, little "evidence to refute those scientists and philosophers who hold that the universe is purposeless; that man, instead of being the special care of a Divine Providence, is a dependent upon fortuity and his own wits for survival in the midst of blind and insensate forces." He was rootless. Among Negroes, he was the first modern.[29]

---

27 James Weldon Johnson, "Fifty Years," from *Saint Peter Relates an Incident* by James Weldon Johnson. Copyright 1917 by James Weldon Johnson. All rights reserved. Reprinted by permission of The Viking Press, Inc.

28 Johnson, *Along This Way, op. cit.*, p. 95.

29 *Ibid.*, p. 413.

V

The sociological imagination

Before the 1930's the social science taught at those Negro colleges and universities staffed by Negroes (a small, but important, group) began with the "more Christ-like" image and built up its theories from there. Its main—its only—concern was the race question, and its answers were provided by the image and the mythology surrounding it. As it was at other colleges and universities throughout the land, social science in Negro colleges was in its infancy. Basically, the Negro schools of higher learning were not oriented toward either scientific research or the social sciences (e.g., economics or psychology). The great names in Negro education belonged to men whose chief concern was either religion or the humanities. John Hope, first Negro president of Morehouse College, specialized in Greek and philosophy. Benjamin Brawley, one of the ruling triumvirate for many years at Morehouse, was a scholar in English and American literature. William Henry Crogman, for decades a revered professor at Clark University, taught the classics. William Scarborough of Wilberforce was famed (among Negroes) for his Greek textbook. And so it went.

The reasons for the concentration on religion and the humanities were not hard to find. As late as 1926, only 4 of the 62 Negro colleges and universities were nonsectarian. That is the first striking fact. The second is that until World War I the Negro colleges were largely manned and administered by dedicated white educators whose main concern was to bring culture and enlightenment to a benighted race. The white educators tended to steer clear of the controversial race question, and so were not much concerned with scientific probing into social causes. Many of the sources of funds for operating these schools were controlled by people who were under the influence of Booker T. Washington's educational theories. Atlanta University found it difficult to obtain funds for Du Bois's Atlanta studies during the first decade of the century. His budget for the year 1901 was a minuscule $250. In 1908 only a last-minute grant of $1,000 from the Slater Fund made continuation of the work possible.[1]

The agencies that founded the Negro colleges were various, but all had strong religious affiliations. The American Missionary Association had a hand in the creation of Howard University, Atlanta University, Berea College, Talladega College, Fisk University, Tougaloo College, and still others. The influence of white religious organizations was strong or dominant in all of these. The Association originated as an organ of the abolitionists in 1846, but was adopted by the National Council of Congregational Churches in 1865. In association with the Freedmen's Bureau it founded and nursed Fisk from high school to college status, giving the presidency to Reverend Erastus Milo Cravath, an A.M.A. field secretary. Howard University's early history shows the same influence of white religion. It existed first as the dream of a Washington, D.C., Congregationalist minister. Its first president (1866) had been pastor of the First Congregationalist Church of Washington, and the list of subsequent presidents up until the mid-1920's reads like a Who's Who of Congregationalism.[2] It was not until 1926 that Howard got its first Negro president, Dr. Mordecai W. Johnson, a Baptist minister.

Often the Negroes had to wage a fierce struggle to capture their colleges from white control, and they were not always successful in the early decades of this century. In 1899 a wing of the Negro Baptists felt it was time to remove the dominance of northern whites from Atlanta Baptist College (now Morehouse). They demanded that the administration and presidency of that institution be given to William E. Holmes, a rather fierce Negro radical. The northern Baptist leaders concerned—E. L. Morehouse and Gen-

---

[1] J. A. Gregg, "Christian Education and the American Negro," A.M.E. Church *Review*, Vol. 43 (October, 1926), p. 79; Francis L. Broderick, *W. E. B. Du Bois: Negro Leader in a Time of Crisis* (Stanford, Calif.: Stanford University Press, 1959), pp. 56–57.

[2] Nine of the first 13 presidents of Howard were Congregationalists.

eral T. J. Morgan—threatened withdrawal of financial support. The scheme fell through. Morehouse remained under a white president until John Hope became its first Negro president in 1906.

Even the advent of the Negro college president and Negro teaching staffs did not soon alter the situation; these men were more often than not the products of Negro colleges, and in many cases merely carried on the old traditions. Mordecai Johnson (Howard), Benjamin Brawley (Morehouse), John W. Davis (West Virginia State College), were all products of Morehouse. It was not until 1928 that Atlanta University, during the process of reorganization, got its first Negro president in the person of John Hope. Even so, the president was still either appointed by whites or represented the choice of the white community. Under the white missionaries the colleges tended to be paternalistic toward the students. Often, after the Negro administrations assumed control, the colleges became feudal in nature. The presidents wielded dictatorial control over the instructors and their subject matter. Educational values lost out to status seeking within the faculties as status meant power. There was little or no tradition of scholarship and learning. Negro college heads followed their white predecessors in placing "moral" character above intellectual development.[3]

In the best of the Negro universities Negro control gradually brought change. The Chicago-trained sociologist, E. Franklin Frazier, took a post at Howard University. Ira DeA. Reid, trained in sociology at the University of Pittsburgh and Columbia University, was brought to Atlanta University by John Hope. Charles S. Johnson went to Fisk as head of the division of social studies in 1928 and took with him the ideas of the "Chicago school" of sociology—a system of ideas which were an important part of the Negro Renaissance.

The importance of the new sociology to the Negro university, and to Negro thought in general, can be understood only when juxtaposed to the patterns of thought that dominated before it

---

[3] These are the observations of Howard University sociologist, E. Franklin Frazier, who had to contend with the problem throughout his professional career. E. Franklin Frazier, *The Negro in the United States* (New York: The Macmillan Co., 1957), pp. 478–97.

came. The old social science, as taught in Negro institutions, was shot through with myth, wish fulfillment, and sometimes, as in the case of Du Bois, hatred. The important figure at Fisk in sociology was George Edmund Haynes; at Howard it was Kelly Miller. A glance at their ideas will give some indication of the magnitude of change brought about by the new sociology.

George Edmund Haynes, a product of Fisk University (1903), Yale (1904), and Columbia (Ph.D., 1912) was Fisk's professor of economics and sociology from 1910 to 1920. He was important enough in his field to be made director of the Division of Negro Economics, U.S. Department of Labor (1918), one of the very few Negroes to get a government job under Woodrow Wilson. His speciality was the Negro migration north and the conditions of Negro labor in northern urban centers. In 1912 he published a study of the Negro in New York City that shows a good grasp of the importance of quantification (it abounds with statistics). If it added nothing (except statistics) to what was already well known (crime and disease are a reflection of the urban environment), it at least shows a sound grasp of research techniques and avoids flights of fancy. It was his interest in the social conditions of the urban Negro that led Haynes to join with others in organizing in 1911 the National Urban League. The new organization was to open opportunities for Negroes in industry and, in general, aid migrants to adapt to city life. This sort of prosaic work seems a welcome contrast to the general preoccupation with the Negro "soul"; the Haynes of these years appears to modern eyes to have been a very down-to-earth sort. But these years of his life are deceptive. Actually, Haynes was gravitating toward a spiritual solution to the racial problem. In 1921 he terminated his relationship with Fisk to join the Commission on the Church and Race Relations of the Federal Council of Churches. He had come to see the solution as resting on the spread of the Christian faith among both races.[4]

In 1922 Haynes published a book that he hoped would give the problem of race relations its proper scientific framework; instead of that it put the problem in the framework of the Christ-like

---

4 George Edmund Haynes, *The Negro at Work in New York City* (New York: Columbia University Press, 1912); George Edmund Haynes (ed.), *Toward Interracial Cooperation: What Was Said and Done at the First National Interracial Conference* (New York: The Federal Council of Churches, 1926), p. 97.

myth and its mission ideology. *The Trend of the Races* opens with a bow to the theory of social folkways and *mores* developed by A. G. Keller's *Societal Evolution* and to some recent ideas about social milieu. But all that turns out to be window dressing—the modernity that rings through his opening statement does not go far beneath the words. His real thesis turns out to be that it is the Christ-like nature of the Negro that will ultimately solve the race problem.[5]

The Trend of the Races is shot through with the expression of the Christ-like image, the following passage being in no way exceptional: "Another characteristic expression of the Negro mind in race relations may be called its attitude of patience, tolerance and sustained optimism. These are illustrated in Negro forbearance under opposition, restriction, and oppression, in his method of meeting difficult problems and situations, and in the hopefulness and loving kindliness of his folk songs and in his enthusiasm." In their lucid moments present-day sociologists would give that statement the Bronx cheer. But imagine the effect of such a statement on the "talented tenth" in the Fisk classrooms. Its relation to reality is nil, but it is the kind of thing the future leaders of the race were listening to in their sociology classes. With Haynes it was a simple statement of fact. He went on to reduce human nature to two opposing forces, greed and charity, leaving no doubt as to which race had been entrusted with the preponderant share of the latter.[6]

Haynes' optimism was the faith of the pre-World War I progressives—he saw the world as tending toward a society based on the principles of Christ. He felt that it is the job of religious bodies such as the Federal Council of Churches to bring about the new society. He looked to that body in particular because it seemed to be trying to bring the races together. "The great hope of the future," he wrote, "is that the ideals of Jesus may determine the conditions of these experiences and the conditions of these contacts." Haynes worked all his life to bring about that mutual understanding; there is none of the antiassimilationist tendency in his thinking that was found in Du Bois. Nevertheless, he did have

---

5 George Edmund Haynes, *The Trend of the Races* (New York: Missionary Education Movement of the United States and Canada, 1922), p. 19.

6 *Ibid.*, pp. 82, 136.

a strong sense of the Negro's mission to save America from the commercialism he saw overwhelming her. "A type of Negro," he wrote, "has developed with an interracial mind and soul passionately responsive to ideals beyond the bartering commercialism of the hour. . . . There is still such spontaneous altruism in the souls of black folk, in spite of the centuries of exploitation, that America may have a demonstration of the democratic cooperation the future holds for peoples and races which can share the purposes and aspirations each of the other."[7]

Haynes's twin in thought and inclination was the sociologist at Howard University, Kelly Miller. The Howard sociologist was himself thoroughly religious and guardedly optimistic. At times he allowed his optimism to carry him away, as when he happily declared that the Bolshevik revolution was another long step away from slavery and toward the millennium. But that kind of radicalism was not characteristic of the staid institution that was and is the capital of the Negro bourgeoisie. Miller was soon back in line and became an ardent anti-Communist.[8]

Most of Miller's life and thought were the very essence of moderation and respectability. He was a product of Howard, and soon after graduating in 1886 he was back there teaching mathematics. It was at the insistence of Miller that Howard instituted a course in sociology, gave the job of teaching it to Miller, and kept him teaching it for 39 years. Most of that time he was either head or dean of the department, so it might be said that sociology at Howard and Kelly Miller were, until 1934, just about identical.

But, was it sociology? After his retirement in 1934, Miller bitterly complained of the drift by Negro colleges away from the religious milieu that is, he said, so suitable to the Negro's uniqueness "In spiritual talent, hedonistic capacity, and certain forms of artistic expression. . . ." If Miller's classroom proceedings resembled his books and pamphlets they were more like revival meetings than dispassionate discourses on social structure. His writings were didactic, turgid, and uncompromising. They were deeply rooted in the Christ-like image and mythology. The following is an example:

---

7 *Ibid.*, pp. 192, 21, 98.

8 Kelly Miller, "The Negro in the New World Order," *The Everlasting Stain* (Washington, D.C.: The Associated Publishers, 1924), pp. 44–49.

The Negro embodies the assemblage of Christian virtues and graces to a degree unequalled by any other member of the human family. Meekness, humility and forgiveness of spirit are undetachable coefficients of his blood. He is incapable of deep-seated hatred and revenge. . . . When he is reviled he reviles not again. The Negro nature strangely fulfills the apostolic definition, "Charity suffereth long, and is kind; charity envieth not; charity vaunteth not itself, is not puffed up, doeth not behave itself unseemly, seeketh not her own, is not easily provoked, thinketh no evil; rejoiceth not in iniquity. . . ."[9]

For Kelly Miller as well as for Haynes and Du Bois the basic problem to be solved by sociology was, of course, the race problem. But given the conceptual framework within which these men operated the race problem in America was unsoluble. The problem as they saw it revolved around this set of alternatives: Is the Negro to demand full integration and risk losing his racial attributes through assimilation, or, is he to accept segregation as the means to develop his peculiar genius, safely protected from the contaminating *mores* of American civilization? One could not logically follow both courses (though most tried), but to follow either one to the exclusion of the other was to give up a cherished dream. If the policy of developing the racial genius in Negro colleges were followed, the Negro would be forever a minority group with minority group status. If the policy of assimilating America's materialistic culture were pursued the Christ-like Negro would be lost and the Negro mission would have to be abandoned. This was the quandry of the pre-Renaissance Negro mind; it was the rock on which Du Bois foundered.

Until World War I, the Washington-Du Bois controversy obscured this basic dilemma. Washington wanted the Negro to adopt the ethos of the competitive society (with its materialistic bias) and simply to begin competing, albeit by beginning at the bottom. He had no illusions about a racial-soul, no Christ-like images to protect. The Du Bois faction attacked Washington for supinely accepting segregation (and therefore inequality), but the real segregationists were those, like Du Bois, who believed in the Christ-like Negro and his mission. For Washington, segregation was a tactic—

---

9 Kelly Miller, "The Reorganization of the Higher Education of the Negro in Light of Changing Conditions," *Journal of Negro Education*, July, 1936, pp. 484–94; Miller, *Everlasting Stain, op. cit.*, pp. 255–56.

a means of placating the whites until such time as the Negro got
a toehold on the economic ladder. For Du Bois segregation meant
inequality and was not to be tolerated. And yet—and yet, he rejected the very society into which the Negro was to be assimilated
by integration.

This overriding controversy of the prewar era, fought at a
white-hot pitch, settled nothing and confused everything. The first
man to take up the cudgels against Washington was Monroe Trotter, editor of the Boston *Guardian*. Nowhere in Trotter's writings
does one find the slightest hint of the Christ-like image. For the
editor the issue was integration versus segregation, pure and simple. But then Du Bois entered the controversy bringing with him
the Niagara Movement loaded down with ministers who were developing a militant religion based on the Christ-like image. All
became confusion.

Not the least confused among the disputants was Kelly Miller.
The Howard sociologist considered himself a moderate—a medi-
ator between the extremes. In 1913, in an obvious effort to bring
together both sides of the controversy, he pointed out that each
was one-half right with its educational premises, that both industrial education and liberal education were needed by the race.
Later, in 1923, he called for a Negro "Sanhedrin"—a conference of
all factions. The Sanhedrin met and satisfied no one. His moderate
counsels availed nothing; it is difficult to see how they could have
in the light of his confusion. Like Du Bois he felt that greed and
materialism are the standards of American civilization: "To all
outward appearances," he wrote, "our civilization is intensely materialistic in its tendency, the dollar is its highest denominator."
Like Du Bois he believed it to be the Negro's mission to change
these values: "Those that suffer and are overborne have always
moral and spiritual advantage over their haughty oppressors. . . .
Who knows but that you have been placed here to bring an arro-
gant world back to the simple teachings of the Son of God?" But,
what was his counsel?—what was his position on integration? "The
Negro," he said, "is more apt to win in the race that is set before
him by following the precepts of Jesus than by joining the great
white throng that bows down and worships at the shrine of the
Almighty Dollar." That statement, it appears, represents the heart
of his thought on the subject. It was as precise a formulation of

reform as he was capable of. It can be interpreted as either segregation or integration, depending on one's inclination.[10]

With his inability to prescribe a program for racial betterment Miller fell back on exhorting the Negro to become better—a strange thing for one who believed in the Christ-like goodness of the Negro. In pamphlet after pamphlet Miller labored his readers with demands that they become more industrious, more intelligent, and more manly—each pamphlet being an exercise in futility. He simply did not deal with the real world, with the psychological and sociological problems confronted by the race. In talks and speeches to Negro educators, he admonished his listeners to stress the education of the will and the spiritual faculties of their students. He maintained that somehow this was the solution to the race's problems. All this was so much wasted breath, but Miller cannot be blamed for it—he was simply saying what Du Bois and what other spokesmen for the Niagara Movement said.[11]

The emancipation from mythology could not readily come from within the Negro schools; they were too much dominated by men like Miller and Haynes—too much dominated by the Christ-like image. When it did come it was largely through the effects of the new sociology—sociology that came from the great northern university. Most responsible for bringing new thought were the two giants among Negro sociologists, Charles S. Johnson and E. Franklin Frazier. When these two men had done with it, the sociology represented by Miller and Haynes was a thing of the past, and gone with it (at least in the social science departments) was the Christ-like image and its mythology. By 1933 the revolution in sociology was complete, for by then Frazier and Johnson were completing their formulations and were about to take over at Fisk and Howard.

If the new orientation toward race relations by sociology can be said to have a father he was Robert E. Park. Both Johnson and Frazier studied at the knee of Park at the University of Chicago.

---

10 Kelly Miller, "Education for Manhood," *Kelly Miller's Magazine*, I (April, 1913), p. 8; Kelly Miller, *The Negro Sanhedrin: A Call to Conference* (Washington, 1923); Kelly Miller, *The Primary Needs of the Negro Race* (Washington, D.C.: Howard University Press, 1899), p. 7. Kelly Miller, address to the Alumni Association of the Hampton Normal and Industrial Institute, June 14, 1899; Kelly Miller, "A Word to the Twentieth Century Negro," *Voice of the Negro*, January, 1905, p. 678.

11 See, for instance, Kelly Miller, "Moral Pedagogy," 1913, Miller addresses and speeches, Moorland Collection, Howard University Library.

Johnson began his four-year study under Park in 1917, and Frazier worked under him, on and off, for a decade before receiving his Ph.D. in 1931. It was the "Chicago school" of sociology and particularly Park's formulations on race relations and the city that became the foundation of the Negro sociology.

Park shifted the whole question of race relations away from "race" and "racial differences" and fitted it into the conceptual framework of class and status conflict. Until the "Chicago school" began its formulations American sociologists[12] worked on two basic assumptions regarding race relations. First was the belief that the Negro is "an inferior race because of either biological or social heredity or both;" and second was the idea that because of his physical character the Negro cannot be assimilated by the dominant race in America.[13] Charles Horton Cooley, one of the early greats of American social psychology, said in his *Social Process* (1919) that it is a reasonable conclusion that "during the process of biological differentiation of races, mental differences had developed." But, as Cooley himself admitted, these mental differences had to be assumed. How, for instance, does one measure "racial temperament?" Or, how does one compare the mental capacity of races when the individuals in each race range from genius to imbecile?, and when the social environments of the two races have differed significantly?

Park's reorientation of the study of race relations went hand in hand with the broad movement in the sciences to redefine problems in terms of operational definitions. In Park's redefinition of basic conceptual tools that would make for objective study, data collecting, and measurement were introduced. He made use of such concepts as *attitudes, social distance,* and *mores,* concepts which enable researchers to begin systematic investigation of social problems. But more important, this approach enabled social scientists to begin to think in concrete terms about improving race relations. If it was found that racial antagonism in a certain area was being compounded by exaggerated social distance between races steps could be taken to reduce the social distance. The older thinkers, the Kelly Millers and Du Bois's thought in terms of a "moral

12 This world, of course, excluded Kelly Miller, George Edmund Haynes, W. E. B. Du Bois, and other Negro sociologists. I have never seen a statement by a Negro that admitted of anything but equality or superiority to the white man.

13 See E. Franklin Frazier's discussion in "Sociological Theory and Race Relations," *American Sociological Review,* Vol. 13 (June, 1947), pp. 265–71.

revolution" as the answer to the race problem. They could wait and hope for a more Christ-like Negro race to bring about such a revolution in the ill-defined future, but they could offer few concrete programs beyond pleading (or demanding) that the whites break down the racial barriers. But once the problem could be defined in terms of social distance one could demand school integration and be quite sure that he meant it. Before this, when one demanded school integration, he was demanding it as a democratic right to equality. Henceforth, he would be demanding it as a sociological necessity.

E. Franklin Frazier was born in Baltimore (1894) and graduated *cum laude* from Howard University in 1916. He became perhaps the most widely known of Park's Negro students, partly through his devastating portrayal of the Negro upper classes, *The Black Bourgeoisie*, written near the end of his life. However, he had long held an eminent position among Negro scholars. It was Frazier who replaced the ailing Kelly Miller as head of the sociology department at Howard in 1934, a position he was to hold for 25 years—years during which he influenced countless students and, probably, most of the present Negro leadership class.

The sociology that Howard students began to learn in 1934 bore hardly a family resemblance to that of the Miller regime. Frazier had nothing but contempt for the type of moralizing that had been passing as science. "Negro education in the past," Frazier had written in 1924, "to characterize it briefly, has been too much inspiration and too little information." Certainly 1934 brought a new atmosphere to the Howard sociology classroom. Gone was the emotion of the seer; it had given way to dry objectivity. Absent was another old friend—no longer did the familiar Christ-like Negro hover near, lurking behind each assumption and coloring every observation. Frazier, of course, was no stranger to the mythology. In a sense he even accepted it as a fact. He accepted it as an anthropologist accepts a tribal rite, to be studied and analyzed. He believed that the Negro in America does have a surfeit of religious emotionalism; that it can be explained by countless evangelical sermons; that it has nothing to do with "racial temperament."[14]

---

[14] E. Franklin Frazier, "A Note on Negro Education," *Opportunity*, Vol. 2 (March, 1924), p. 76; E. Franklin Frazier, "The Mind of the American Negro," *Opportunity*, Vol. 6 (September, 1928), p. 266.

Frazier's basic formulation of the race problem was one he made early and held onto for life. It was that enunciated by Park. He gave his first published exposition of it in an article entitled, "Social Equality and the Negro" (1925). The formulation was as follows: The Negro is caught in a vicious circle, he has been categorized as an inferior, and, because so categorized by the dominant culture, he is enmeshed in a caste system which maintains his economic and cultural inferiority in fact. So far as Frazier was concerned, the only thing that could break down this deadly categorization was increased social intercourse between the races. With this in view, he denounced the tendency of Negroes to voluntarily isolate themselves from the dominant society; he deplored the idea of developing a self-sufficient Negro culture. This was no plea based on democratic or humanitarian grounds—it was a demand grounded in social theory. Moreover, here is none of the backing and filling of a Kelly Miller, caught between two opposing tendencies. It is a straightforward call for integration and assimilation. It is a matter of caste, not of race, and "Caste breaks down when social intercourse becomes general." [15]

Frazier was still a research assistant at the University of Chicago in 1927 when he began using the tools forged by the "Chicago school" to probe the mysteries of "the problem." At that time certain sociologists at Chicago were carrying out a program of research based on an article Park had written back in 1916. In that article Park had suggested the overwhelming importance of the city in modern life. He thought that in the light of the fact that the city seemed to be creating an entirely new culture it was time that sociologists go into the city as anthropologists go into a primitive culture. So Park's students and associates did just that, beginning a whole new style of investigation of which Frederick Thrasher's *The Gang* (1926) became the classic. Thrasher lived with the subjects of his study—became one of them. [16]

In another paper Park suggested what was to be the guiding theory of these studies, the theory of "social disorganization." The basic premise of this theory is that the rapid social mobility found

15 E. Franklin Frazier, "Social Equality and the Negro," *Opportunity*, Vol. 3 (June, 1925), pp. 165–168.

16 Robert E. Park, "The City: Suggestions for the Investigation of Human Behavior in the Urban Environment," *American Journal of Sociology*, Vol. 20 (March, 1916), pp. 577–612.

in the city (including the movement from rural communities to the urban slums) together with the impersonalization of life that occurs in the city, breaks down the *mores* and community sanctions which govern group behavior in the stable community. This disorganization hits the family unit with devastating force, destroying this last and most important citadel of well-structured interpersonal relationships. The result is disorganized and, many times, antisocial behavior on the part of the individual—vice, crime, alcoholism, juvenile delinquency, and all the rest of it.[17]

The young Frazier, himself engaged in Park's program, was sufficiently impressed by this line of reasoning to use it as the basis of his explanation of Negro behavior in Chicago. He used it to sweep away some of the foundations of the Negro's older social thought. His attack on three of the traditional positions needs comment— three positions that were cornerstones of the older thought. First, there was the idea that many of the American Negro's cultural traditions have originated in Africa before enslavement. Frazier followed Franz Boas in stoutly denying the possibility of this. Secondly, he attacked the very notion that an oppressed minority such as the Negro can maintain or build a separate and viable cultural tradition. And finally, by strong implication, he repudiated the theory that the Negro is somehow Christ-like. This last he did by contending that, if anything, the Negro's tendency is toward antisocial behavior.

We saw how Du Bois in his "germ" theory of history, used the idea of African cultural survivals to support the contention that the Negro has a peculiar racial soul or genius. The scholar who did most to bolster Du Bois's ideas here was not a Negro but a white student of Franz Boas named Melville Herskovits. In a long series of articles and books, anthropologist Herskovits attempted to trace back to Africa what he considered to be the Negro American's religious emotionalism and "matriarchal" family organization. From start to finish Herskovits had an uncompromising adversary in Frazier (who had much the better of it). Frazier's massive refutation of the anthropologist was his *The Negro Family in*

---

17 Robert E. Park, "Community Organization and Juvenile Delinquency," Robert E. Park, *et al.*, *The City* (Chicago: University of Chicago Press, 1925), pp. 99–112.

the United States—a work that, incidentally, put him in the front rank of scholars.[18]

Frazier began laying the foundations for his argument in 1927 when he began his study of the Negro family in Chicago. The argument, based squarely on the "social disorganization" theory, was simple: the history of the Negro American is a history of social shocks, each resulting in disorganization of the family and other institutions. First there was the original act of enslavement, accompanied by bloodshed and the uprooting of the individual from his African family and community. The trans-Atlantic voyage, where the individual was packed for months like a sardine, unable to move, and subject to every kind of sickness without medical attention, was a thoroughly destructive thing for the victim's personality. Then came slavery in which only the most rudimentary family organization was permitted to exist: the husband was given no authority to enforce discipline, indeed was treated as a child, and the mother was away all day at work. The next shock was that of emancipation. What family organization slavery had built up was in most cases destroyed in the transition to freedom. The final social shock (for many) is the rupture of rural community life when the individual migrates to the city.[19]

Frazier would concede to those who dreamed of an American Negro culture that folk communities had developed in isolated plantation areas following emancipation, and that a folk culture of sorts had developed there. But, at best, he thought, it was (and is) a low order of culture, mired in superstition and ignorance. It was a culture, moreover, that grew out of personal defeat and despair. It was not something Frazier wanted to see retained.[20]

As far as Frazier was concerned, the cataclysmic events that repeatedly disrupted the Negro's social life had an effect opposite to the creation of such an ideal type as the Christ-like Negro. The

---

18 Melville J. Herskovits, *The Myth of the Negro Past* (New York: Harper & Bros., 1941), p. 170; and Melville J. Herskovits, "Social History of the Negro," Carl Murchison, *A Handbook of Social Psychology* (Worchester, Mass.: Clark University Press, 1935), pp. 256–57.

19 E. Franklin Frazier, *The Negro Family in Chicago* (Chicago: The University of Chicago Press, 1932), pp. 22, 32–33.

20 E. Franklin Frazier, *The Negro Family in the United States* (Chicago: The University of Chicago Press, 1939), pp. 110–11.

destructive effects of these events freed the Negro from social organization and control leaving his impulses unrestrained. The result was widespread antisocial behavior in the form of illegitimacy, crime, and vice in the more disorganized of the urban ghetto areas.[21]

After saying all this, Frazier went on to commit an even greater heresy. In his mind the move from the folk community of the South to the city and the attendant breaking up and falling away of the folk culture was a good thing. It brought the race that much closer to the necessary assimilation of American culture and integration into modern civilization. Frazier did not particularly like the commercialism and status seeking of American civilization, but he had no myth about a racial "soul" to defend—he was cutting through the fog surrounding the segregationist-integrationist controversy.[22]

All this got Frazier into some trouble with the Negro fiction writers of the 1920's and led to a spirited debate over whether the Negro writer should concern himself with Negro culture. A rather light-hearted exchange was being made between writers George Schuyler and Langston Hughes in the pages of the *Nation* in June, 1926. Seeing an opening for the academic mind, Frazier trod in. "If the Negro," he wrote, "had undertaken to shut himself off from the white culture about him and had sought light from within his experience, he would have remained on the level of barbarism."[23]

Frazier thus marks a significant and abrupt rupture with the traditional Negro thought and must be considered an important factor in the break the 1920's made with the Christ-like image and its mythology. The Christ-like image was not by any means dead, as will be shown. Nor was the sociological imagination introduced by Frazier enough to stop the emergence of another strain of mythology that became important in the late 1950's. But the issues were sharpened; the sociological approach was something that every Negro intellectual, whether he preferred assimilation or separatism, would be obliged to come to grips with.

---

21 Frazier, *The Negro Family in Chicago, op. cit.,* pp. 161, 166, 193–94.

22 *Ibid.,* p. 252.

23 E. Franklin Frazier, "Racial Self-Expression," Charles S. Johnson (ed.), *Ebody and Topaz, a Collectionana* (New York: National Urban League, 1927), p. 120.

It cannot be said of Frazier that in making assimilation the goal he gave up the idea of a Negro mission. On the contrary, such an idea was one of his major messages—brought out time and again. But the mission idea had to be drastically altered. Frazier put the Negro not morally above American civilization but outside it. Because, he thought, the Negro has never been fully assimilated he stands outside in the position of observer. "Negro leaders," he wrote, "have enjoyed a cosmopolitan experience that enables them to view objectively their racial experience, as well as American culture and cultural traits in general. This appears to be increasingly one of the chief functions of the Negro intellectual." Frazier's version of the mission idea shifted the Negro's role from moral leader to social scientist.[24]

Frazier's idea of mission (attenuated as it was) appears to have been an outgrowth of another of Park's ideas, that of the "marginal man." The marginal man's strategic position between two cultures supposedly enables him to stand apart from and objectively view each. Such, at least, is the optimistic aspect of the marginal man's situation. But it is not impossible to interpret his situation in an entirely different way—in a way that stresses his cultural dilemma. He is a man, in the latter view, whose personality is rent by the conflict of values—a conflict between two cultures.

It was the second, and pessimistic, approach to the Negro's situation as marginal man that Charles S. Johnson chose to develop. As far as Johnson was concerned the marginal situation is neither a happy nor an advantageous one. It is a situation that calls forth disorganized and even antisocial behavior. To Johnson (who did not for a minute accept the idea of a separate culture for the Negro in America), the movement from the folk culture of the rural South to the industrial culture of the city is an inevitable, if painful, process. As such it would be acceptable. But the problems involved in making the adjustment to new cultural surroundings are vastly complicated by the problems of race. So long as discrimination and segregation are realities the Negro can never hope to complete the transition from one level of culture to the next—he is more or less permanently suspended in the marginal situation. His folk culture can no longer serve him in his new urban surround-

---

24 *Ibid.*, p. 121.

ings; but neither does the white man's culture have much relevance to the Negro's racially segregated situation. It cannot teach him to cope with a situation for which it was not developed. Caught in this anomalous position, the Negro youth's personality suffers deterioration. He makes use of all the defense mechanisms— avoidance, displaced aggression, and the like—but his basic problem is underlying frustration and hostility from which there is no escape.[25]

Johnson's developing thesis opened a new area for consideration: the effects of oppression in creating personality conflicts in the oppressed. The question had long since been opened and treated, of course, but on a most superficial level. A great many words had been expended in exhorting the race to take more pride in itself, to overcome the sense of inferiority that comes from being treated as an inferior. But it was Johnson who began to realize how futile such exhortation is.[26]

It was not long after he took up sociology that Johnson began to feel that a sense of inferiority lies near the root of the Negro's problems, and that a systematic attack on this infirmity was the first order of business. He called this feeling of inferiority an "oppression psychosis," a term that implies that the sufferer is a patient in need of treatment.[27] Johnson, however much he may have wanted to do so, never led a crusade for the removal of the oppression; instead, he called for treatment of the patient. He called for the patient's adjustment to the real world—the world as it exists for the black man now. His basic proposition was that men must treat with reality and not build impossible castles in the sky. This, of course, was the Booker T. Washington approach.

All this made men call Johnson impossibly conservative, and, in a sense, they were right. He was most certainly not a militant.

---

25 Charles S. Johnson, "The Problems and Needs of the Negro Adolescent in View of His Minority Racial Status: A Critical Summary," *Journal of Negro Education*, Vol. 9 (July, 1940), pp. 344–53.

26 In his 1925 paper, "Community Organization and Juvenile Delinquency," Robert E. Park, citing the work of Alfred Adler, discussed the problem of feelings of inferiority as they relate to pathological behavior growing out of the disorganized community. As of that time the problems stemming from low self-esteem had not yet been widely explored.

27 Charles S. Johnson, *A Preface to Racial Understanding* (New York: Friendship Press, 1936), p. 12.

There was little in his background to produce a fire-eater. His father was a highly literate Baptist minister in Bristol, of western Virginia, and apparently something of a leader of the community in which he had preached for 43 years. So his son had something so many Negro youths lack—a respected father. The younger Johnson went on from what was perhaps a passably happy childhood to complete his courses at Wayland Academy, Richmond, as president of his class and editor of the college newspaper. In the fall of 1917, legend has it, he arrived at the University of Chicago with $1.19 in his pocket and a yearning to learn the secrets of sociology. He did not have to wait long. The year 1919 brought Red Summer and race riots to Chicago. Johnson was given the job of directing the investigations that led to the production of *The Negro in Chicago* (1922), a landmark in the study of race relations. The work established him as a scholar.[28]

Park's influence was not only all-important in molding Johnson's approach to sociology; it apparently also gave direction to his attitude toward the problem of race. Before assuming his teaching position at Chicago in 1914, Park had spent seven years in association with Tuskegee Institute learning about human relations from a master on that subject, Booker T. Washington. In fact, a direct line of influence can be traced back from Frazier and Charles S. Johnson through Park to Washington. Back in 1904 when he began working with Washington as a ghost writer and general propagandist for Tuskegee and all its works, Park was a man at loose ends with no sense of direction. He decided that, having nothing original to contribute to the world himself, he would attach himself to the Negro leader in the hope of being useful to a man performing a great work. Many years later, when he was at the height of his influence, Park looked back on his association with Washington as the formative period of his life: ". . . the man who has influenced me most and brought me into a practical,

<hr>

28 For a sketch of Johnson's life, see Edwin R. Embree, *13 against the Tide* (New York: The Viking Press, Inc., 1944), pp. 47–70; Chicago Commission on Race Relations, *The Negro in Chicago: A Study of Race Relations and a Race Riot* (Chicago: The University of Chicago Press, 1922). The work of the Chicago Commission and the contribution of its various members is discussed by Arthur I. Waskow in his *From Race Riot to Sit-In, 1919 and the 1960s* (Garden City, N.Y.: Doubleday & Co., Inc., 1966).

healthy normal attitude toward the world has been Booker T. Washington." Something needs to be said concerning Washington's thought.[29]

It is well known that Washington preached a pragmatic doctrine of adjustment. It is well known that in emphasizing the accumulation of property as the fastest way to power he tended to minimize the importance of political and civil rights; in saying that the Negro race should concentrate its efforts in agriculture and in producing such basic goods as brick Washington was, in effect, saying that the Negro should begin at the bottom and build an economic base for his later rise. These were the things people heard Washington say day in and day out, but they had little lasting influence on Negro thought. For the things he said of lasting import we must turn to those that influenced the sociologist. First in this category was his rejection of the Negro's other-worldly religion and his reasons for doing so. Du Bois and the religious modernists, R. R. Wright, Jr. and Reverdy Ransom, had poured out their contempt on the old-time religion because they had seen it as a slave religion. They had created a this-worldly mythology as a vehicle for their anger. Washington's position was altogether different. He understood the old-time religion to be an escape mechanism for a people whose prospects in this world were dim. He wanted the Negro to start thinking about accumulating property. The black man was to make his way in this world, not escape from his responsibilities. If we realize that religion was in Washington's day the Negro's dominant ideology, we realize that he was calling for an end to ideology and an adjustment to the real world. He was calling for an end to escape and his call was heard by the sociologists, was made their major theme.[30]

Both revolts against the old-time religion—that of the religious modernists and that of Washington—had the effect of liberating the Negro mind from the slave psychology of old, but each revolt led in a different direction—one to militancy and separation, the other to compromise and assimilation. While they liberated they

29 Robert E. Park to Emmett J. Scott, April 18, 1904, Booker T. Washington papers, Library of Congress; Robert E. Park to Charles W. Chesnutt, Chesnutt papers, Fisk University Library.

30 Booker T. Washington, manuscript of speech to the National Unitarian Association, Saratoga, N. Y., September 26, 1894, Washington papers, Library of Congress.

introduced new problems. Washington's assimilation without militancy led to a policy of accepting Jim Crow and lower class status. Du Bois's pure militancy led him into the realm of mythology. He struggled against reality by escaping into myth. Washington came to terms with reality by submitting to it—by submitting to the status quo. At bottom the question they left unresolved was this: How can the black man conquer the forces of circumstance without resorting to myth (racism)?

Du Bois's approach to freedom through self-transcendence implied withdrawal from the constant pull and tug of the real world. Washington, to the contrary, saw freedom in terms of self-mastery, in terms of a plunge into the real world and in terms of competing with it on its own terms. He called for "a freedom that is forced, and one that is the result of struggle, forbearance and self-sacrifice." Du Bois was led to emphasize the spiritual values of race, Washington was let to emphasize the moral value of economic competition. Du Bois was in constant danger of betraying his humanism to racism, Washington was equally in danger of perverting liberalism into crude materialism. In rejecting escape into myth as a viable approach to freedom, Washington emphasized the need to deal with the real world, but he often fell into the trap of identifying the real world with things. Yet, in spite of his tendency toward materialism, he did leave a most valuable clue to Park and through him to Johnson—that in the struggle for freedom the first round is with oneself, and that this first round must take place in the ongoing social world.[31]

For Johnson, whose great concern was the Negro youth's "oppression psychosis," the problem of identity and meaning was central. Given his lack of alternatives he was forced to create another option, a new possibility—the possibility of dragging freedom and identity and meaning out of the brute facts of reality which of themselves negate these things. Such was the problem faced by Johnson. Such is the problem faced by 20th-century man. Such was the legacy of Washington.

In 1919 Johnson began doing studies on the urban situation of the Negro for the National League on Urban Conditions (National Urban League), an organization that reflected Washington's

---

31 Booker T. Washington, manuscript of speech to the Brooklyn Institute of Arts and Sciences, February 22, 1903, Washington papers, Library of Congress.

philosophy in that it confined itself to improving the race's situation within the existing framework of race relations. Johnson later became one of the League's guiding spirits as editor of its magazine, *Opportunity*. He conceived as his function the task of setting facts grounded in objective research across to his readers under the assumption that the race problem could not be solved until it was understood. In the April, 1928, issue of *Opportunity* Johnson set forth a strong plea for the Washington approach. How, he asked, would a disinterested philosopher advise the Negro?:

This philosopher would reasonably argue that since men hold passionately to opinions which are founded upon intangible emotions, the wiser strategy would shift proof from a subjective to an objective plane, from immaterial belief to visible reality. Such a diplomacy would select from the "emotional clusters," the most favorable features and extend their implications, and it would spare itself the energy of combatting unfavorable features futilely by the expedient of pointing out, to the strong group, the self-destructive qualities inherent in them. It would as frequently as possible, divert unpleasant attention from itself, by directing attention to greater "menaces." It would deprive the stronger group of the satisfaction it might get through insults, by developing the defensive coating of a sense of humor; it would rid the inferior position of that debasement which engenders scorn, by deliberately rationalizing this position into one which gave its enemy no satisfaction. It would constantly divert attention from abstract and undefinable theories while it laid an unmovable foundation at the base of this scorn.[32]

What Johnson was saying is that you can't make a slave of a free man—that emancipation must come from within. The Negro's first step is to resolve his inner conflicts and conquer himself. Black youth, he wrote, are in the chains of the historical implications of the black man's status within American culture. "These implications, both direct and insidious, have tended to warp perspective, to consume energies futilely in conflict, in disconsolate brooding, bitterness and sensitiveness; they have imposed dangerous dual standards, constricted life aims and expectations, and contributed mightily to the defeat of the very spirit of youth." The first need,

---

32 Charles S. Johnson, "The Philosophy of Booker T. Washington," *Opportunity*, Vol. 6 (April, 1928), pp. 102–03. Reprinted with permission of the National Urban League, Inc., from *Opportunity:* Journal of Negro life.

he continued, is a "freedom from within." And, if the first step toward emancipation is to free oneself from inner conflicts and self-hatred, the second step is to gain self-knowledge by coming to grips with reality. The latter is the job of Negro education.[33]

During the late 1920's and the early 1930's, a heated discussion arose among Negro educators over whether or not Negro youth should be educated with the view to developing a group culture, as Du Bois and Kelly Miller argued, or whether they should rather be educated with the view to assimilation into the dominant culture. This was, of course, the transfer into the realm of education of the current debate in literature. Johnson felt that the debate was just plain silly—"an amusingly specious one." The Negro's hope, he felt, does lie in education—in the school—but the type of education he envisioned was encompassed by neither side of the debate in progress. In order to explain his theory of education he went back to the "marginal man" theory. To educate the Negro youth exclusively in the ways of the white world is to overlook the fact that he is denied access to that world. Such an education would bear little relation to his future experience—it would not be functional. But on the other hand, to seek out a racial culture one would be forced to go to the primitive folk culture of the rural South—a culture that bears no relevance to the urban-industrial world the child must live in. The Negro must be educated to function as a marginal man—educated on two levels of culture: the one he is in, and the broader, dominant culture toward which he, as a member of the race, is headed. But, more than that, he should be educated to value the experiences he has in the marginal world and to value himself because of his experiences. Johnson wanted the Negro American to understand and love the very human record established by his race in America.[34]

As the editor of *Opportunity*, Johnson had the chance to do something about bringing that record to the awareness of his people. He became, in fact, one of the leading promoters of the literary "Renaissance" of the 1920's, opening his pages to all comers.

---

33 Charles S. Johnson, "To Negro Youth," *Opportunity*, Vol. 6 (September, 1928), p. 258.

34 Johnson, *Preface to Racial Understanding, op. cit.*, p. 85; Charles S. Johnson, "Education of the Negro Child," *Opportunity* (February, 1936), pp. 38–41; Charles S. Johnson, "The Problems and Need of the Negro Adolescent in View of His Minority Racial Status: A Critical Summary," *op. cit.*, 244–353.

As editor, and therefore something of a critic, Johnson became more than a sociologist—he became something of a philosopher. That age—the age of the 1920's—was a time when writers, artists, and critics everywhere (especially in Chicago and New York) were looking to art to step in and fill the function of discarded myths— the function of giving value to life.

Johnson developed his philosophy in this spirit. No longer, so he thought, can we look to such abstractions as "group mind, race, social equality, superiority" for our values. The same goes for religion: "In an organized religion life itself has been treated as being without meaning and value, except it was taken to testify to a reality beyond itself." Johnson made his appeal to experience; nothing beyond experience can be given credence. It is out of experience, he said, that we must forge our values and bring meaning into life. Johnson had worked his way to a kind of humanistic naturalism and his authority was, not surprisingly, John Dewey, who spent his life trying to draw a humanistic position out of the naturalistic view of the world. He was citing Dewey when he said that men must develop "faith in the possibilities of human experience. . . ." "I am convinced," Johnson continued, "that the road to new freedom for us lies in the discovery of the surrounding beauty of our lives, and in recognition that beauty itself is a mark of the highest expression of the human spirit." It was Johnson rather than Du Bois who reflected the spirit of the artistic impulse of the 1920's. Du Bois was searching for meaning and inner freedom in his racial absolutes, Johnson sought them in experience— the human condition: "There is a thrilling magnificence and grandeur," he said, "in the fact of survival itself, in the tread of unconquerable life through two centuries of pain." [35]

The message of the sociologists was that freedom comes only to those who come to terms with reality—for them that reality was the hard one of life in white America. This, as a minimum requirement, meant adjustment and therefore integration. Their first concern was not with external oppression but with freedom through self-mastery over personality disorganization; gain that,

---

[35] Charles S. Johnson, "Some Notes from a Personal Philosophy of Life," manuscript of speech, February 13, 14, 1937, Johnson papers, Fisk University Library.

and oppression would die of its own impotence. The two sociologists pointed the way for the emancipation of the Negro mind from myth by demanding that the Negro come to terms with the real world. Frazier taught that the mythical world of Negro cultural uniqueness did not, and could not, exist in America. Johnson taught that the real world—the world of experience—is the source not only of truth but of beauty; that it is not only in the truth of the real world but also in its beauty that freedom lies.

Partly because the sociological imagination made its attack on the Negro mythology, future writers and intellectuals of the race would turn their attention to the problem of finding beauty and meaning in the Negro's American experience. But myths have a way of flowering in unsuspected gardens. The *experience* of the Negro in America proved a most fruitful garden. And, because the sociological imagination had done its job well in its attack on myth, and because the writers and intellectuals began to look to experience, the new mythology would lack the rational humanistic structure of the old. The new myth would be the fruit of the search for beauty in experience. The search for authentic experience would cause a turn inward to emotion. The new myth would raise an irrational emotionalism unhampered by the rational framework that Du Bois' humanism had required of the old. But, this was all far in the future.

II

It was not a sociologist but a student of philosophy who picked up the various strands of thought and interpreted them in terms of art and literature. Alain Locke became the spokesman (and salesman) for the Negro Renaissance of the 1920's. Much derision was directed at Locke by Renaissance poets and writers—as often as not he was set up as a symbol of what the writers were in revolt against. It was easy to caricature Locke because he was small and fastidious, perhaps even dapper. He did not try to hide the polish usually associated with a Rhodes Scholar and Harvard Ph.D. In short, he was easily stigmatized as "dicty"—he stood apart from the masses—by those writers who were in a great lather to escape from that category themselves. But in spite of these things, Locke got grudging admiration from the Harlem literati as a man who could hold his own in verbal give-and-take with their best.

Locke, in some ways, epitomized the strengths and weaknesses of the literary Renaissance of the 1920's. On the positive side, he recognized the need for inner freedom and was a force in the movement which turned toward a probing of the psyche and away from the fatal attraction to the grotesqueries of white oppression. On the negative side, he reflected the inability of the middle class (and all the Renaissance writers but one were middle class) truly to empathize with the city masses. These bourgeoisie writers were beginning to understand—trying to understand. They were learning something of the complex psychological problems of the masses. They sought to write about the masses. But they were not, after all, of the masses. They had their own moments of bitterness and despair, but it was not the bitterness or the despair of a wasted, ugly existence. They tried to capture the reality of such an existence, and often succeeded only in grasping the picturesque. They opened the way to an understanding of the masses but rarely succeeded in going deeper than an intellectual understanding. Locke's strengths and weaknesses, then, were those of the Negro intellectual in the 1920's. His main strength lay in the intellectual preparation for a later communion with the reality that is the masses. He had, like the new sociologists, sloughed off the myths, and, without quite realizing it, he was searching for a substitute.

Locke was unique in that he was able to turn his critical faculties to things other than the race question—it was not his all-consuming passion. In fact he tended to see the solution of the Negro's problems in the broader terms of curing the ills which trouble Western civilization. Du Bois had plenty to say about the ills of Western civilization but it was always with the Negro as the referent—to solve the Negro's problems would solve the problems of civilization. For Locke it was rather the other way around: the problems of his race were part of the larger problems of modern civilization. "I know," he once told his Howard students, "how difficult this advice will be to carry out. America's chief social crime, in spite of her boasted freedom, is the psychology of the herd, the tyranny of the average and mediocre; in other words, the limitations upon cultural personality." Here was the cry of the modern intellectual—the critique that became so popular in the recent past. It is David Riesman's lament about "other-directedness." But long before the sociologists and popularizers heard it, it was echoed and reechoed through the pages of the "little reviews" of the pre-World War I "Little Renaissance."[36]

A new mood was beginning to make itself felt among artistic and literary circles in the decade preceding World War I. It was a feeling of emptiness. Despite a jubilant feeling of freedom and discovery, the deeper feeling was one of lack. Van Wyck Brooks, thought by some best to represent the prevailing mood,[37] expressed it as a deficiency in, or lack of, American culture. America, as he put it, had always been a pioneering people given over to conquest. This had once been enough, in a sense it had been heroic; but with industrialism came a deep change. Conquest had gone hand-in-hand with greed, and now with all frontiers gone, with the empires of industry built, only greed remains. With no traditions other than that of exploitation, Brooks said, American culture is little more than the profit motive. The result is the wasteland. "One looks out today," he wrote, "over the immense vista of our society, stretching westward in a succession of dreary steppes, a universe of talent and thwarted personality evaporating in a stale culture, and one sees the inevitable result of possessing no tradition." This search for culture was deeply associated with a personal emptiness—in Brooks' phrase, he felt "externalized."[38]

It is this sense of being "externalized" that appears to have informed the "Little Renaissance" as it did the later "lost generation." It was this sense that sent the artists off on their search and its persistence that later made them feel "lost." In a most revealing prewar article, Waldo Frank called this sense of externalization being "objectified." "To an astonishing degree," he wrote, "we have objectified our lives." Frank used a term that was to become popular among the followers of the existentialist Sartre when they wanted to describe the modern condition. What Frank seems to have meant by it is the feeling of being nothing other

---

36 Alain Locke, "The Ethics of Culture," *Howard University Record*, Vol. 17 (February, 1923), p. 183.

37 See Alfred Kazin, *On Native Grounds: An Interpretation of Modern American Prose Literature* (Garden City, N.Y.: Doubleday & Co., 1956).

38 Van Wyck Brooks, "Young America," *Seven Arts*, Vol. 1 (December, 1916), p. 147.

than what others see us as (a feeling of "other-directedness")—the sum of our social roles. We are an unknit welter of unrelated facts, he wrote, "So, as the chaos cools and the specific groups congeal, we find ourselves inexorably set within them. Each of our little clusters of activity has become a world." Frank felt fragmented— broken up into his social roles. There was a lack of the sense of wholeness, of the sense of having a humanity that belongs uniquely to the self, that is not bound up with the roles we play, that is not the product of what others think of us—that is not objectified.[39]

What he and the "Little Renaissance" writers and the later Negro Renaissance writers lacked was an integrating myth: a myth that pulls all the fragments of oneself together into a whole; a myth that tells one who he is above and beyond the various social roles he is required to play. For them no church or sect could provide it, no sense of nation or of community bestowed it. The myths that had been were dead. James Oppenheim, editor of the *Seven Arts* made that clear. He could not crusade for God or Christ, he wrote, there were no kings to overthrow in the name of liberty, he could believe in no imperial destiny. F. Scott Fitzgerald's famous remark was that his generation had awakened "to find all gods dead, all wars fought, all faiths in man shaken."[40]

These men thought for a while they had found the answer in art. With myths gone, there remained to man his inner humanity, his experience of the world—this to be expressed in art. Van Wyck Brooks looked enviously toward Germany whose soul-life, he thought, had been given expression by Goethe. No American "Goethe" could be seen on the horizon, but Goethe had set the direction toward which American writers must work. To Frank also art held the answer: "By art [man] lifts up the hidden bases of existence and makes them his experience; he achieves that sense of unity and *at-homeness* with an external world which saves him from becoming a mere pathetic feature of it."[41]

Although it is not necessarily true that everyone accepted Brooks's analysis of causes, most people within the literary circles

---

39 Waldo Frank, "Vicarious Fiction," *Seven Arts*, Vol. 1 (January, 1917), pp. 294–95.

40 James Oppenheim, editorial, *Seven Arts*, Vol. 1 (March, 1917), p. 505.

41 Van Wyck Brooks, "Our Awakeners," *Seven Arts*, Vol. 2 (June, 1917), p. 238; Frank, "Vicarious Fiction," *op. cit.*, pp. 295–96.

of the time were in complete agreement with his conclusion that American art had always lacked vitality, that to fulfill its function it must become something new and different. Brooks posited two extremes within American culture—the purely intellectual and the purely practical—and tried to show that the extremes had captured the culture, that there was no middle ground. Americans, he wrote, are at times driven by the practical motives of self-gain, at times by theory, but American practice and American theory are so at odds that they have never effected a union—they remain incompatibles. American art has never come down from the plane of unreality to dirty its face in the hard facts of life. Because of this, American life has never been touched by the artist—he has always been the impractical theorist cavorting around on the level of the abstract. The ideals American artists have established are divorced from the realities of American existence, and so are given mere lip service as the unrelieved pursuit of gain goes drearily on. For art to become meaningful, Brooks said, it must stop trying to moralize, it should come down out of the clouds and be concerned with the facts of existence. The artist must stop trying to escape from the crudities of American life and start trying to make them meaningful. He should put his life, his passion into his art. Passion informed by intelligence will be creative. Beauty will be drawn out of reality passionately experienced, and this, not some abstraction, will become the new ideal.[42]

Here is, in essence, the dream of Charles S. Johnson—to create beauty out of experience. Johnson saw this ideal fulfilled in the Negro spirituals. Into those songs went the pain and longings of the slaves. Here, in essence, was the hope of James Weldon Johnson who tried to capture in *God's Trombones* the feelings of the primitive sermons. And, as we shall see, it was also the hope of those of the Negro Renaissance who looked to the "blues" as the embodiment of their race's true experience. The Negro writers were caught up the spirit of the artistic yearnings of the time—which is to say that their experience was part of the common experience.

---

[42] Van Wyck Brooks, *America's Coming of Age* (New York: B. W. Huebsch, 1915), pp. 9–27, 60–64, 129.

Alain Locke was, by analogy, the Van Wyck Brooks of the black Americans. In announcing the "new Negro" he was, in effect, proclaiming "the Negro's coming of age." He was the self-appointed spokesman for what he thought was a new birth of Negro art. But he went further than advertisement. Like Brooks, he attempted to give direction to the literary movement—a direction that he took from the new sociology. In his 1925 announcement, "The New Negro," Locke talked of the Negro American's objective. Those of the Negro's "outer life," he said, are already sufficiently formulated, "for they are none other than the ideals of American institutions and democracy." But beyond this are the race's inner objectives, and these are largely a matter of self-esteem, ". . . an attempt to repair damaged group psychology and reshape a warped social perspective."[43]

The white writers, with Brooks as their spokesman, were trying to lift Americans out of a cultural wasteland. Sociologically speaking, they were searching for something that would replace the unifying myths that their time had rejected. The dilemma and perhaps the tragedy of their (and our) time was that the unifying myth for which they searched was something in which they could never believe. They hoped to find a spiritual essence, but to talk in terms of essences is to pass over into the realm of mysticism. Man, as the feeling went (and goes), has no such thing as a spiritual essence (soul). But man acutely feels the need of one. To fill the vacuum and to avoid mysticism, to embrace a new myth while knowing that it is a myth—that was the problem. So the artists turned to art for the solution.

To avoid mysticism art must come out of experience. Embodied in art, experience would shape man's ideals. Art would somehow bridge the gap between the world of reality and the ideal; it would enable man to cross over from the all-too-human to the divine. The Puritans of the 17th century relied on science and reason to carry man to the outskirts of the divine. But times had changed; man, by the time of World War I, would have to find a more circuitous route; he would need to blind himself to the implications of what he was doing or it would not work. So, in the "Little Renaissance," he tried to disguise what he was doing in

---

43 Alain Locke, "The New Negro," Alain Locke (ed.), *The New Negro: An Interpretation* (New York: Albert and Charles Boni, 1925), pp. 10–11.

art. The sadness of it was that the closer one approached the divine the closer he approached mysticism—myth. The danger was that in creating beauty one was merely creating myth. Brooks asked American artists to emulate Carlyle, Ruskin, and Nietzsche, who, through their art, created "social ideals"—the "hero" idea, the "idea of interaction of harmonious art and Harmonious life," and the "superman." Each of these men gave us an ideal growing out of their ages, or, as Brooks put it, a "focal centre." This focal centre, or social ideal that unites a people and gives them direction—makes life worth living—is not an absolute, is not to be taken as a universal truth (that would be mysticism). Rather, said Brooks, it must grow out of experience, it must suit the age. It would be more on the order of a working hypothesis than on the order of a truth. What Brooks was saying, while trying not to say it, was that he desperately needed a cause: ". . . the happiest excitement in life is to be convinced that one is fighting for all one is worth on behalf of some clearly seen and deeply felt good and against some greatly scorned evil."[44]

It was all very well to say that, until the very unmystical Walter Lippmann happened by and roundly scolded the *Seven Arts* writers. They were, said Lippmann, asking for another myth at a time when "The youth of Europe is being devastated because the people of Europe are fed on large symbols and great myths." Parenthetically, the day was not far off when Lippmann, himself, would be captivated by the idea of saving the world for democracy.[45]

Here was the modern existential dilemma: to create meaning for one's life one must deal in myths, in self-deception. This was the dilemma of Alain Locke. He felt the need of a unifying myth for the same reasons that were acting on Brooks. But he had the added problem of race: a unifying myth, or "social ideal," created by art out of racial experience was needed to bind the psychic wounds caused by oppression. A new myth to replace the Christ-like mythology was needed by the Negro if he was to believe in himself. It was needed to do what the Christ-like mythology did for Du Bois, but it could not be Du Bois's "racial soul," it must

44 Brooks, *America's Coming of Age, op. cit.*, pp. 105–20, 171–72.
45 Walter Lippmann, "A Reply," *Seven Arts*, Vol. 1 (January, 1917), p. 305.

grow out of reality. It was the sociologist Charles S. Johnson, not the romantic Du Bois, whom Locke echoed when he called for a renaissance in Negro art: "Race for the younger generation is but an idiom of experience, a sort of added enriching adventure and discipline, giving subtler overtones to life, making it more beautiful and interesting, even if more poignantly so. . . . Our poets . . . have carried the folk-gift to the altitude of art."[46]

The similarity between the thought of Locke and Brooks in this matter is striking—each was reacting in the same way to the modern age. An understanding of Locke gives insight into the essential unity between the two movements, one white, one Negro. An understanding of Locke's plight gives insight into the essential division between the two artistic movements. The Negro Renaissance writers' reaction to Locke tended to be a muffled snicker. The Renaissance was in revolt against myths, it had had enough of "racial souls" and "racial geniuses." To it, the Christ-like Negro was an Uncle Tom. Locke's plight was that in trying to formulate the requirements for Negro art—in trying to say what Van Wyck Brooks was saying, but to say it to the Negro—it was necessary to cross the boundary into mysticism. He did not believe in a racial soul, but it sounded as though he did when he spoke in terms of the Negro's "great folk-epic," "folk-spirit," and "folk-gifts." Locke echoed Brooks when he talked about Negro life finding "a new spiritual dynamic in artistic self-expression," but the Renaissance did not understand him. The Renaissance writers went their way until they ultimately found what Locke hoped they would find. He had, however, believed they would find it in the singer of the spirituals, in "Patience, adaptability, loyalty, and smiling humility." That was the road James Weldon Johnson had taken—it was unconvincing. The Renaissance writers ultimately found their "social ideal" (for that is what it would be, and in Brooks's sense) in the "blues," in what they believed was their race's real experience.[47]

---

[46] Alain Locke, "Negro Youth Speaks," *The New Negro, op. cit.*, p. 48.

[47] See Alain Locke, "The Concept of Race as Applied to Social Culture," *Howard Review*, Vol. 1 (June, 1924), pp. 290–99; Alain Locke, *The Negro in America* (Chicago: American Library Association, 1933), pp. 10, 43, 45, 11.

VI

The Renaissance in literature

As World War I ground to a close in 1918, Negro thought entered a new period—one of disintegration, reexamination and reformulation. What had been a near consensus among intellectuals suddenly split apart. The mainstream of thought turned away from Du Bois and left him isolated by the end of the 1920's. The Renaissance writers of the postwar decade scoffed at, and made merry of, the idea of a racial soul. They had no room in their thinking for the mission idea. But their merrymaking was tinged with anxiety. The Christ-like myth had given comfort; without it one felt exposed. The racial soul had been an absolute; now all absolutes were gone, and Negroes began to feel themselves in an incomprehensible situation—a situation devoid of meaning. The Christ-like image and mission ideology had given meaning to a situation which otherwise would have bordered on the intolerable.

The Negro Renaissance in literature was a search for new meaning. The search led in various directions: to the social sciences, toward introspection, toward self-revelation. It led at times to self-hatred and despair, at times to doubtful hope, and, when at its best, to a tough and prideful affirmation of the human spirit.

As the decade of the 1920's opened, various and disparate forces were at work in the Negro world. Young people whose abilities unfitted them for the inconspicuous drudgery of lives in the remote corners of the Negro world flocked to black bohemia—to the brutal, ugly, joyous Harlem, there to find what their individual temperaments were bound to find—fulfillment, or despair, hope, or nothingness. The young writers turned out not-so-good books

123

ranging from the frivolous to the exploration of naked reality. But always the tendency was to turn inward, to expose the inner hurt, to probe the ragged wound of self-hatred, or to peer into the inner emptiness. These writers, who had come together to join in the search for inward beauty, turned finally to striking at the roots of myth in an orgy of despair. Those who had come to take part in the gaiety of New York's wider artistic colony, found themselves, not participants but objects of wonder and amusement— lionized for the novelty they represented. They found that even the world of art was segregated, not on the surface, but deep down. And so they mocked themselves. And they played the necessary role because a man needs to make a living. But alienation came with the role—and that could not be laughed away.

The writers were foam on the surface of a mightier wave of dark humanity—the Great Migration. In 1910 it was a mere whisper of a promise. Within the decade it had become a roar. But not really a roar, perhaps, it was so weary, its feet so sore. The war had come. Men were needed to tend the machines that built the machines of destruction. The call went out to the South-land. Soon thousands of faces etched themselves in black against the soot-gray slums of the cities. It was not really the war, though. It was really something else. Something very elusive and very intangible had swept the South and triggered the response. Whole communities disappeared in the night. The Baptist minister awoke to find his flock gone and he hurried North to find it. The barber, the doctor, the storekeeper—these had soon followed. But in the lead was the field hand, the lowest of the low. His gifts to the North were few. He brought his share of crime, disease, and ignorance. Yet, he brought other things, too, things of the human spirit. Whatever else, this black man, this field hand, had looked despair in the face, and then had looked beyond it. He knew the hardness of the road from Memphis to Chicago, and yet he had looked beyond. He knew the desperation of the jobless, the fear of the hunted, and the isolation of the uprooted—and had looked beyond. And he sang about it. He sang the blues.

The 1920's were, for the Negro, years of self-discovery. Self-discovery had to come from outside the Negro colleges where the myths prevailed undiminished, where the spirituals were held to be the supreme gift of Negro culture even while the blues poured forth from every cabaret and every home. The new thought had to come from outside the tight little communities kept by the Negro upper classes—the communities that supplied teachers and pupils for the colleges. The books of the Renaissance writers that seemed so blatantly to broadcast the word "nigger" horrified the upper class sensibilities. This, indeed, was the crux of their rejection of the new thought. The young writers dared to look that devil in the face until it dissolved into limbo. The upper classes with their cloistered minds exorcised the word from their vocabularies, but it remained their most potent psychological reality. They glorified in the lightness of their skin or shamed in the darkness of it because of that word. They denied its validity a thousand times but consciously copied white society in minute detail in order to escape from it. Above all, they repressed the anger and aggressiveness that they associated with "niggerness" and convinced themselves through the psychological mechanisms of ego-defense that they were truly Christ-like.

With the migrating Negroes it was different. They broke away from the enforced etiquette of their home communities and merged into the impersonal ghettos of cities North and South. Aggression became an everyday fact of life—"niggerness" held no terrors. The blues singer shrugged his shoulders at the word, but used it—used it as a shorthand symbol of the persecution which was one more of life's hard realities. His psychological problems were, no doubt, legion, but they did not include the secreting away into the unconscious the imagined horrors of "niggerness," and the consequent elaborate pretensions that he was anything but human with normal human passions.

The literary Renaissance was a release of Negro literature from the mode of reform and special pleading. The subject ceased to be "the Negro's plight" and became "the Negro." Characters began to emerge as individuals. They gradually ceased to represent the Uncle Tom type, the militant-young-Negro-in-revolt type, or the ravished-but-virtuous-maiden type and achieved some uniqueness of personality. The Renaissance, in short, broke away from the restrictions imposed by the needs of reform and found the freedom to seek a literary gender. Just what direction this search should take was a question that caused much heated discussion. Should it attempt to achieve a racial expression, or should it merge in the broader stream of American literature? The pros and cons of this debate are not nearly as important as the fact that the Negro writer was gaining freedom to determine his own course. Du Bois might fret over the new direction and call for art that is propaganda, but the writers paid no attention. They were looking for something Du Bois had not consciously sought—self-definition.

To Du Bois there was no question concerning self-definition or purpose. One was a Negro and one's purpose was to fight for the Negro's rights. To the young Negro writer of the 1920's the answers were not all that certain. He was a Negro (who would let him forget it?), but a feeling of uniqueness had begun to take precedence. He was, first of all, a unique individual, and as such was not all certain just what his purpose in life was supposed to be. He had ripped away the identity-giving myths, and by doing so had cast himself into the mainstream of American thought. He now faced a hostile world alone, in his black skin.

The Renaissance was a liberating experience, but in the modern world liberation can be terrifying. He was like the college freshman who exuberantly casts off his childhood beliefs and looks around for a rationale that will give his life meaning—and finds none. The new Negro had to find a rationale that would sustain him in the everyday plight of being a Negro in white America. In his poetry he bitterly reiterated the absurdity of a destiny which made him black and set him down in America. Where was the meaning in that? The danger was that the seemingly futile quest would turn into resignation, or worse, self-pity.

II

The postwar world broke in upon the consciousness of the Negro American in a way that the white man could never experience. For most Americans it was a time of weariness and reaction against noble sentiments, a time of artificially induced superpatriotism, a time of disillusionment, a time of fear—fear of dimly perceived forces that heralded change. For the Negro American it was a time of shock, a time of high hopes smashed to rubble. He had marched to war in the belief that new forces were working for democracy. He marched back knowing he had been wrong. He returned to race riot and lynching.

The riots spread through the South and into the North like the winds of plague—Knoxville, Tennessee; Elaine, Arkansas; Charleston, South Carolina; Atlanta, Georgia; Norfolk, Virginia. Then Washington, D.C., in mid-July, a newspaper alleged that white women had been raped. A city crowded with soldiers went beserk. For two days the soldiers ran amuck. Up on Seventh Street and on Georgia Avenue, up around Howard University and the homes of the "black bourgeoisie," the fighting swirled. It left the Negro population stunned and angry, and vaguely proud, . . . the Negroes had fought back. Ten days later it was Chicago. A Negro had the audacity to be swimming in an area reserved for whites. He was stoned and killed. Negroes retaliated, killing several white men that afternoon. Gangsters became active, stabbing and beating dozens of black men that evening. Trolley cars were stopped by organized mobs of whites. The Negroes were pulled from the cars and killed. An aged Italian peddler, one Lazzeroni, was stabbed to death by Negro boys. Gangs of white boys terrorized the homes of those Negroes unfortunate enough to be living in white residential districts. Negroes opened fire upon automobiles in the black belt. And so it went for seven days. Thirty-eight people were killed, 537 injured. Again there was anger and despair among the Negro population. And again a touch of pride. They again had fought back.

It is hard to measure the feelings of a people after a year like 1919. Robert T. Kerlin tried to do it in *The Voice of the Negro, 1919*—a survey of editorials from the Negro press that year. The press, of course, did not speak with one voice, all shades of opinion were expressed. But dominating it all seems to have been a hard, steady beat of bitterness, anger, and pride. Most militant were the New York periodicals, *The Messenger, The Crusader, Challenge Magazine*, and, of course Du Bois's *The Crisis*. Let *Challenge Magazine* speak for the New York press:

America hates, lynches, enslaves us not because we are black, but because we are weak. A strong, united Negro race will not be mistreated any more than a strong united Japanese race. It is always strength over weakness, might over right.

But with education comes thought, with thought comes action; with action comes freedom.

Read, Read! Read! Then when the mob comes, whether with torch or with gun, let us stand at Armageddon and battle for the Lord.[1]

The editor of the *(Oklahoma City) Black Dispatch* expressed a widespread hope that a "new Negro" had emerged from the war:

The corner stone upon which rests all of our difficulties is YOUR white man's UNWILLINGNESS TO RECOGNIZE THE NEGRO AS A MAN. Now the Negro is a man, and a free man. I might say to make clearer my point that you have now with you a NEW NEGRO.[2]

The Kansas City colored paper, *The Call*, also expressed the new hope and the new pride:

Hell seems to have broken loose in Washington, D.C. within the past few weeks. These outbreaks of the mob in Washington and Chicago have taught it one thing which it will not soon forget, viz.: That the Negro means to be as merciless in repelling attacks upon him as the attackers. The NEW NEGRO, unlike the old time Negro, "does not fear the face of clay." . . .[3]

The Negro of postwar America was restless, and, as the riots proved, in certain areas he was becoming aggressive, even belligerent. The late Booker T. Washington (died 1915) could not set the ideal for the city Negro. Accommodation no longer rang true. New figures arose to dominate the horizon. There was nothing of the "Uncle Tom" in the squat and heavy, scowling, figure of Marcus Garvey. The West Indian was out to set the Negro American free. He called on the masses to turn their backs on white civilization—to follow him back to Africa where he would build an empire that would outshine anything the white man had done. He told the Negro to reject whiteness, to see the beauty of his own dark skin. He demanded racial purity, not in the name of whiteness, but in honor of blackness. His "African Orthodox Church" painted God black. His Universal Negro Improvement Association gave culturally deprived men and women a chance to gain

---

1 Editorial, *Challenge Magazine*, October, 1919, quoted in Robert T. Kerlin (ed.), *The Voice of the Negro 1919* (New York: E. P. Dutton & Co., Inc., 1920), p. 19.

2 Editorial, *(Oklahoma City) Black Dispatch*, October 10, 1919, quoted in Kerlin, *op. cit.*, 1920, p. 63.

3 Editorial, *(Kansas City) The Call* (n.d.), quoted in Kerlin, *op. cit.*, p. 77.

a little status and self-respect by creating for them a nobility with titles, honorary orders such as the Knights of the Nile, and such uniformed groups as the African Legion and the Black Cross Nurses.[4]

Garvey's voice was the voice of militancy. It was the voice of Du Bois, but directed to a different audience—to the multitudes, not the "talented tenth":

We are face to face with environments in a civilization that is highly developed; a civilization that is competing with itself for its own destruction; a civilization that cannot last, because it has no spiritual foundation; a civilization that is vicious, crafty, dishonest, immoral, irreligious, and corrupt.[5]

Garvey's star fell with his imprisonment in 1925, but for a short time he had awakened the masses of the cities. And, more important for this study, he helped awaken the intellectuals to the existence of the city masses and their unrest—to the "new Negro."

The outrage felt by the masses was being given literary expression by a new group of young writers just beginning to arrive in Harlem:

> If we must die—let it not be like hogs
> Hunted and penned in an inglorious spot,
> While around us bark the mad and hungry dogs,
> Making their mock at our accursed lot.
>
> Oh, Kinsmen! we must meet the common foe!
> Though far outnumbered let us show us brave
> And for their thousand blows deal one death-blow!
> What though before us lies the open grave?
> Like men we'll face the murderous, cowardly pack,
> Pressed to the wall, dying, but fighting back![6]

---

4 Amy Jacques-Garvey (ed.), *Philosophy and Opinion of Marcus Garvey* (New York: The Universal Publishing House, 1923), pp. 5, 14, 37; see Edmund David Cronon, *Black Moses: The Story of Marcus Garvey and the Universal Negro Improvement Association* (Madison, Wis.: University of Wisconsin Press, 1955).

5 Jacques-Garvey (ed.), *Philosophy and Opinion of Marcus Garvey, op. cit.*, p. 31.

6 Claude McKay, "If We Must Die," *Selected Poems of Claude McKay* (New York: Bookman Associated, 1953), p. 36.

Such was the cry of a young man up from the West Indies named Claude McKay. It was the cry of one unused to slavery, and unready for it. Already an alien in spirit, McKay perfectly expressed the new alienation of the 1920's: "My spirit is a pestilential city." Outside of the tradition of the American Negro, he had no particular compulsion to renounce the old myths—they had no meaning for him. But his boyhood experiences as an agnostic—and avid reader of Huxley and Haeckel—his short career as a Pullman porter careening through the industrial wilderness, hating the people he served—these helped cut him loose from certainties and drove him to give expression to a growing sense of lostness: "In this vast world of hate and greed Upon my knees, Oh Lord, for Truth I plead." The Renaissance poets were discovering America.[7]

In the early 1920's Claude McKay appeared to be a pole star guiding the feet of the other young writers. But he was really just a passing comet lighting the sky for a moment. In the fiction of the Renaissance one finds small echo of Jake, or Banjo or Bita —the primitive types who people McKay's novels. The search was the same—and the sense of lostness—but the note his characters sounded was false to the ears of the American writers. It was to the whites that McKay appealed—white apologists for the "new Negro." It was the whites who seriously listened for the sound of the jungle beat in every Negro breast—it was for them that McKay set the tone of the Negro Renaissance. Langston Hughes reports his reaction when his white patron grew impatient to hear him express his supposed exotic nature: "But, unfortunately, I did not feel the rhythms of the primitive surging through me, and so I could not live and write as though I did. I was Chicago and Kansas City and Broadway and Harlem. And I was not what she wanted me to be."[8]

McKay's search for certainties, moreover, led him down paths which the Renaissance writers could not follow. It led him first to Russia and Marxism, then to a vagabond life on the French

---

[7] Claude McKay, "Desolate," *Opportunity*, Vol. 4 (November, 1926), p. 338; Claude McKay, "Truth," *Selected Poems of Claude McKay* (New York: Bookman Associated, 1953), p. 46.

[8] Langston Hughes, *The Big Sea* (New York: Alfred A. Knopf, Inc., 1940), p. 325.

waterfront, and finally into the haven of Catholicism. McKay had been all the while merely searching for the right absolutes; the Americans had lost the ability to believe in absolutes.

The course taken by American Negro literature in the 1920's was roughly that taken by the larger literary movement of white America. The latter has been described by Henry May as a revolt against the 19th-century beliefs in the certainty of moral values, the inevitability of progress, and the efficacy of culture. Such men as W. E. B. Du Bois, Benjamin Brawley, Kelly Miller, and Charles W. Chesnutt, despite their strong reservations about American culture, sincerely held these 19th-century faiths. These were the men who staffed the Negro colleges and the early NAACP. The conflict between these "custodians of culture" and the young Negro writers would, in part, revolve around the latter's revolt against these basic faiths. The Negroes participated in this debate because they were Americans. But because their more basic identity was a racial one, their deeper conflict revolved around the myths that had given an older generation of Negroes a feeling of identity and purpose. The Renaissance writer, in short, though he joined in on the onslaught against the 19th-century American certainties, reserved his ferocity for the beliefs that peculiarly characterized Negro thought. It was not just the idea of progress that crumbled, but the idea that the Negro is destined to lead the march of progress. It was not only the belief in moral good that fell, but the faith that the Negro uniquely embodies this good.

The job of destruction was not done in a day, nor was it accomplished without inner conflict and confusion. The men and women who took up the self-appointed task were not of a nature to coolly weigh and assess it; the kind who could approach it without emotion, self-doubt, and cynicism. Nor could the atmosphere in which many of them lived be called conducive to the dispassionate search for truth. Their ideas cannot be disassociated from the lives they lived—the ritualized but disorganized world of Harlem's bohemia.

This was the Harlem of the cabaret, the black bottom, the house-rent party. It was a black man's world suddenly gone self-conscious and self-consciously vulgar with the onslaught of waves of white sensation seekers. It was a quiet middle-class neighborhood that one day awoke to find itself discovered—not discovered as it really was, but as an exotic spot. The bombs that awakened the world to what Harlem was supposed to be were the play *Lulu Belle,* produced in in 1925, and Carl Van Vechten's novel, *Nigger Heaven* (1926). A dozen imitations sprang into being The world was put on notice that Harlem was a place of high night life, of jazz bands, of mixed parties of Negroes and whites. Harlem's clubs sprang to meet the challenge. Clubs like the Cotton Club, Small's Paradise on Seventh Avenue, and Barron's Exclusive Club at 104th Street and Seventh—these and a dozen others became famous downtown. Jazz bands were called in—Cliff Jackson's Krazy Kats at the Lenox Club, Charlie Johnson and his Small's Paradise Orchestra, Duke Ellington and his Cotton Club Orchestra came in and brought with them the high point of jazz in the 1920's. There were dozens of others, each as good as the next. They held epic contests. A crowd of 5,000 gathered at the Savoy Ballroom in May, 1929, to hear five of the best jazz bands in the world in the "Battle of Jazz." The sensation of the night was an acrobatic Missourian, Cab Calloway, whose "Tiger Rag" stopped the show. It was all very sensational; it was all very artificial. It had little relation to the lives being led behind Harlem's brownstone fronts. And the tables were reserved for whites.[9]

For the Renaissance writers black bohemia's focal point was the dwelling of Wallace Thurman—brilliant, consumptive, desperate. There one would find Langston Hughes, a young man of huge ambition, whose method was that of understatement—simulated nonchalance—which rarely did credit to his intensity of feeling. There one found Rudolph Fisher, combining the writing of stories with medicine, whose brilliance of wit left mortal minds (like Hughes's) spinning. His too was a flame that would quickly spend itself. To complete the inner circle, Zora Neale Hurston would have to be present. Hers was the sprightly but strong mind, full of earthy humor and tough of fiber—springy but finely tempered.

These four constituted the inner circle—the hard core of the literary Renaissance. When together they were black bohemia. They danced and sang and laughed and drank and joked . . . and

---

[9] I have followed the description of Samuel B. Charters and Leonard Kunstadt, *Jazz: A History of the New York Scene* (New York: Doubleday & Co., Inc., 1962).

wondered at themselves. They attended the gatherings of the great—the Du Boises, the James Weldon Johnsons, the Van Vechtens—and had fun at the gatherings of the lowly. When with the great they met and discussed weighty topics with playwrights, poets, statesmen, and legal minds. When with the lowly they danced the black bottom. Flitting in and out of the circle were other writers of the Renaissance—George S. Schuyler, Countee Cullen, Jean Toomer, and Arna Bontemps. Standing off at a short distance were its friendly critics—Alain Locke, Benjamin Brawley, Charles S. Johnson, Du Bois. The inner circle expended a good deal of energy debunking Locke, Brawley, and Du Bois— the rear guard. It was Locke, Brawley, and Du Bois who entertained the fancy that a true renaissance was in the making. The inner circle scoffed at them and their idea, secretly wishing it were true, knowing it was not.[10]

If any one word can be said to characterize this group it is the word "nonconformity." Its members were consciously breaking away from the old modes of thought—consciously striking out in search of new ways of understanding and expressing the Negro experience. If the expression "Renaissance" wearied most of them it was because that term grew out of the old ways of thinking. They were not under the illusion that they were giving expression to the Negro "racial soul," the Negro's "peculiar genius," and the like. They understood that their various talents belonged to them as individuals—individuals who had among their important experiences in life that of being black in America.

Nonconformity, however, can be a painful experience. It was not an easy task to unlearn the beliefs that had been handed down. Perhaps the most beautifully written book of the Renaissance, Jean Toomer's *Cane* (1923), is an expression of the pain involved in casting out the old faiths. In it there is Kabnis, a weak young Negro from the North, a product of the Negro's faith in Christ. The face of Kabnis is round, broad-browed, but weak-chinned, and it gets smashed by fists belonging to square faces. Kabnis is literally afraid of his own shadow. He recognizes his weakness, and hates himself for it. He is a product of the Christian religion,

---

10 For description of Harlem's bohemia, see Hughes, *The Big Sea, op. cit.*, Wallace Thurman, *Infants of the Spring* (New York: The Macaulay Co., 1932). The first is an autobiography, the second a novel.

a religion, he believes, that has made his race weak. He hates the religion as he hates himself. Hatred is the dominant motive in his life. Not that he does not sometimes struggle to see beauty in the world—he does, but its ugliness overcomes him. He feels utterly crushed by a malignant world—a world that is the creation of a cruel, unjust God: ". . . look at me now. Earth's child. The earth my mother. God is a profligate red-nosed man about town. Bastardy; me. A bastard son has got a right to curse his maker." The special object of Kabnis' hatred turns out to be an ex-slave, blind and deaf from years of toil. To Kabnis, the old man represents the generations gone before—generations made docile and servile by white man's religion. In the old man he sees himself. He turns his self-hatred outward against the old man, the old man's God and the white Christ. Apparently the old man has guessed something of all this, for, though he can speak only with the greatest difficulty, he forces himself to mutter, "Th sin whats fixed . . . upon th white folks—f tellin Jesus—lies. O th sin th white folks 'mitted when they made the Bible lie."[11]

"Kabnis," the final story in the book *Cane*, is the most devastating attack upon "Uncle Tomism" penned by a Renaissance writer. Like the book as a whole, it is full of despair and self-doubt. But what helps to lift *Cane* above the level of the ordinary is that in it quest struggles with despair, and hope does battle with resignation.

Toomer was struck with what seemed to him the debilitating effects of Christianity as a slave religion. In consequence (in *Cane*) he rejected the religion and the type of personality he supposed it developed—the Christ-like Negro, or "Uncle Tom." But what he pushed away with one hand he drew back with the other; if his despair was expressed by the servile Kabnis, his hope lay in Dan, a Negro with a redemptive mission. Dan appears in a short story named "Box Seat." The setting of "Box Seat" is Washington, D.C., or, in other words, the large city. There one is crushed, shorn of spirit by crowding civilization. "Houses are shy girls whose eyes shine reticently upon the dusk body of the street.

---

11 Jean Toomer, "Kabnis," *Cane* (New York: Boni and Liveright, 1923), pp. 158–236; S. P. Fullinwider, "Jean Toomer: Lost Generation, or Negro Renaissance?" *Phylon*, Vol. 27 (Winter, 1966), pp. 396–403.

Upon the gleaming limbs and asphalt torso of a dreaming nigger.
Shake your curled wool-blossoms nigger. Open your liver lips to
the lean white spring. Stir- the root-life of a withered people."
Dan, hot-blooded and virile, is up from the primitive regions of
the South to restore vigor and passion to a jaded, overcivilized
people—people conquered by "zoo-restrictions and keeper-taboos."
"I am Dan More," he says, "I was born in an canefield. The hands
of Jesus touched me. I am come to a sick world to heal it."[12]

In *Cane,* Toomer fully participated in the general revolt of
the Renaissance writers—the revolt against the Christ-like mythology. But the redemptive myth—the idea of Negro mission—
held him fast. In searching for a new concept of the Negro he
succeeded merely in altering the imagery somewhat. For the patient and long-suffering Christ-like Negro he substituted a primitive man of passion. But Dan, like the earlier concept, was to be
redemptive because more human than the white man.

One point that *Cane* makes over and over is the pain and misery
out of which will be born a new creativity. The Southland is, to
Toomer, a land of agony as well as a land of beauty. It is from
the marriage of these two opposites that a new Negro will arise.
Dan, at one point, is made to admonish his girl, "Life bends joy
and pain, beauty and ugliness, in such a way that no one may
isolate them. No one should want to. Perfect joy, or perfect pain,
with no contrasting element to define them, would mean a monotony of consciousness, would mean death."[13]

Through Dan the author was giving voice to what would be
a constant, though not always dominant, theme (or, perhaps better,
mood) of the Renaissance. Accept the reality of pain, it said, and
rise above it. Yet more: pain is in its way a blessing—those who
have not experienced it miss a vital insight into life. Those who
have known only comfort will lapse into contented somnolence.
Pain and anguish can be the springboard to the creative life—
only those who have known them are motivated to overcome.
With this a new note of realism begins to be heard in Negro
thought. Its source goes back to the suffering Christ-like Negro,

---

12 Jean Toomer, "Box Seat," *Cane, op. cit.,* pp. 104–29.
13 *Ibid.,* pp. 112–13.

but it has cast off the utopian and idealized elements of the old mythology. If the Negro Renaissance had a message, perhaps this theme, or mood, was it.

With this concept (the social utility of pain?) Toomer was enabled to evince a timid and halting step into reality—an optimism that is not necessarily bound up with the myth of redemption that colors much of *Cane.* The new mood is embodied in the character Lewis, who appears in "Kabnis." The self-despising Kabnis saw in the ancient ex-slave the father of the race's degradation. Lewis, a much stronger figure than Kabnis, saw in the old man something different: "That forehead. Great woolly beard. Those eyes. A mute John the Baptist of a new religion—or a tongue-tied shadow of an old." Lewis is strong and wise, and he too is a legacy of the slave. Toomer seemed to see in Lewis a new force, but his vision was blurred. Unlike his portrait of Kabnis, which is well-defined, his portrait of Lewis is shadowy and ill-defined. Moreover, in the end Lewis was defeated. He appeared in the small southern town of the story as a possible emancipator, but he ultimately fled from the overwhelming pain he found there. Obviously, Toomer was overcome with doubt at the end. He was unable to predict victory over the misery that held the southern Negro in bondage. Toomer was unable to give meaning to Lewis' life.[14]

In the end Toomer had been unable to find meaning in being Negro, and in this his experience was the crucial experience of the Renaissance. This was the fundamental break the Renaissance made witht the old synthesis as epitomized by Du Bois's thought. This was the break which made it impossible for the older leaders to grasp the meaning of the Renaissance. A man like Du Bois drew his sense of identity and meaning of life from race. A man like Toomer did not. Toomer was forced to seek a new identity, and it was this very search that the older leaders could neither understand nor sympathize with. This was the break that isolated the Renaissance writer from the race leader as militant agitator— from the racial betterment movements of the NAACP stamp. At this point Negro art ceases to be narrow propaganda and strives to become universal. It strives, in other words, to cease being Negro expression and to become art.

---

14 Toomer, "Kabnis," *op. cit.*, p. 211.

Jean Toomer carried the tendency to disassociate himself from identity with the black race further than did any of his contemporaries within the Renaissance. While never refusing to admit his direct blood relationship with his Negro grandfather, he did refuse to consider himself in any sense Negro. Once, in 1930, James Weldon Johnson wrote to Toomer with the request that some of the poems from *Cane* be included in the revised edition of Johnson's *The Book of American Negro Poetry*. Toomer replied in the negative ". . . My poems are not Negro poems, nor are they Anglo-Saxon or white or English poems. My prose likewise. They are, first, mine. And, second, in so far as general race or stock is concerned, they spring from the result of racial blendings here in America which has produced a new race or stock. We may call this stock the American stock or race. My main energies are devoted and directed towards the building of a life which will include all creative people or corresponding type."[15]

Jean Toomer's is a story of success—at age 31 his search for an identity-giving absolute culminated in success. It is also a story of tragedy; as long as he was searching he was a fine creative artist; when the search ended so did his creative powers. So long as he was searching, his work was the cry of one caught in the modern human condition; it expressed modern man's lostness, his isolation. Once Toomer found an identity-giving absolute, his voice ceased to be the cry of modern man and became the voice of the schoolmaster complacently pointing out the way—his way.

Toomer's overriding concern for the human condition grew out of an early lack of self-esteem, a concomitant tendency toward introspection and soul-searching, and a loss of his childhood absolutes. His problem with self-esteem was a product of his early family life, particularly, his relationship with an imperious grandfather, P. B. S. Pinchback. The former Reconstruction lieutenant-governor of Louisiana had suffered political and financial reverses when the Republicans lost power in the South, and had removed to an imposing house on Washington's Bacon Street, an all-white neighborhood. There he lived a high life—the life of a social lion—while his money and prestige lasted. But a politician

---

15 James Weldon Johnson to Jean Toomer, July 4, 1930, Toomer papers, Fisk University Library; Jean Toomer to James Weldon Johnson, July 11, 1930, Toomer papers, Fisk University Library.

out of office quickly loses status and influence. As his fortunes declined, Pinchback became increasingly autocratic toward his daughter Nina and his sons. The beautiful Nina married twice, first to a young southern planter who disappeared after a year, and then to a ne'er-do-well who misrepresented his wealth. The second marriage, with its drudgery and lack of love, killed her. So Jean, a product of the first match, led a troubled young life with his grandfather.[16]

As Jean Toomer grew in childhood he turn in upon himself, away from the tyrannical grandfather, away from his unhappy mother. Slowly he created a rich inner life, but it was a life almost totally disassociated from the outside world. Pinchback's fortunes continued to decline. One day he moved the family to a house on Florida Avenue, the heart of the Negro upper class world. "With this world—an aristocracy such as never existed before and perhaps will never exist again in America—mid-way between the white and Negro worlds. For the first time I lived in a colored world." Jean liked his new life. He felt that he had found here, "More emotion, more rhythm, more color, more gaiety," than he had met in the chilling atmosphere of white society. But this was a time, too, of morbid introspection. Now 14, he became a nuisance in the classroom, an inveterate troublemaker. He became the victim of overpowering sex impulses, and seems to have concluded that these impulses were destroying his health. He turned to barbells and special diets. By then the Pinchbacks were on the verge of poverty and family relations were deteriorating. A three-year period of revolt and wandering began for the boy. His revolt first took him to the University of Wisconsin to study agriculture (this lasted a semester), then back to Washington to endure hard looks of reproach. He was assailed by self-doubt. He tried the Massachusetts College of Agriculture for almost a week, then a physical training college in Chicago. There he paid more attention to lectures at the Loop than to physical training. Men like Clarence Darrow held forth there on exciting subjects like Darwinism and the ideas of Haeckel . . . and atheism. Jean felt his intellectual world collapse. His belief in God (as he thought) evaporated. He felt "con-

---

16 Jean Toomer, "Book of Parents," unpublished manuscript *c.* 1930, pp. 17–37, Toomer papers, Fisk University Library.

demned and betrayed." "In truth," he wrote much later, "I did not want to live." His old absolutes were gone; he began a desperate search for new ones. For a time socialism seemed to serve the need. "I had been, I suppose, unconsciously seeking—as man must ever seek—an intelligible scheme of things, a sort of whole into which everything fit . . . it was the *body*, the *scheme*, the order and inclusion. These evoked and promised to satisfy all in me that had been groping for order from amid the disorder and chaos of my personal experiences."[17]

After Chicago there were further wanderings, further soul-searchings. A reading of Lester F. Ward's *Dynamic Sociology* led to a short fraternization with that subject at New York University. But he found a history course at City College more attractive. Then history became a bore and psychology took its place. The war came and he was rejected by the draft. He tried odd jobs for a year; he sold Fords in Chicago, taught physical education in Milwaukee, and did a 10-day stint as a shipfitter in a New Jersey shipyard. His contact with the construction workers caused him to lose heart with socialism. In 1920 he returned, defeated, to his grandfather in Washington. It was not a cheerful reunion. In this mood of defeat and atmosphere of rejection he turned to reading literature—Robert Frost, Sherwood Anderson, the imagists. He learned the importance of expressing one's inner image of things rather than the things themselves—one's experience rather than the things experienced. For three years he wrote incessantly, tearing up what he wrote. He learned to handle words, learned their symbolic potential. He became an artist.[18]

Toomer learned as he handled words that they had no meaning beyond what he gave them arbitrarily. He began to see that words are mere symbols of things and not the things themselves. He was traveling the road to nominalism, and as he traveled that road he felt the concrete world begin to dissolve about him. He was entering the world of modern alienated man. Apparently it was during this time that he began to experience the severing of his intellect from his emotions—the seemingly peculiar phenomenon

---

17 Jean Toomer, "Outline of Autobiography," unpublished manuscript, *c.* 1930, pp. 2, 8, 26, handwritten note on back of page 25, Toomer papers, Fisk University Library.

18 *Ibid.* pp. 27–55.

of the modern mind that has been described as the "frigidization of the self." The phenomenon has been described as an overwhelming sense of self-consciousness—a standing outside oneself, as it were; an objectification of the self. The intellect seems to overpower the emotions, making it impossible to have effective emotional relations with other people. One finds an impenetrable wall standing between oneself and those one would love. Toomer made the solution of this problem—this "frigidization of the self"—his major intellectual theme. Again and again in his later writings he reverted to his argument that the intellect must somehow be fused with the emotions: "Themosense (thought *and* emotion *and* sensing) is the inner synthesis of functions, which represents the entire individual and gives rise to complete action." Of course, in Toomer's case much of this "frigidization of the self" can be traced to his deliberate retreat from an outside world (his family life) that was too threatening—a retreat into the isolation of subjectivity. In one place he tells of wrongs being inflicted upon him in such profusion that "Finally we reached the stage where we vowed to suffer no more. Of people, of life, of the world we said, 'Don't touch me.' We resolved that no one ever would." It was while in this mood that he accepted an offer in 1921 to act as temporary superintendent of a small Negro industrial school in rural Georgia.[19]

Georgia was for Toomer a small shack in the hills. It was the whispering pines. It was the folk-singing that drifted over in the evenings from the Negro dwellings. Most of all, it was the southern Negro spirit—a spirit with which he developed a deep feeling of kinship. *Cane* was at once the joy of discovering this folk-spirit and the sadness of the realization that it was a passing thing. He wrote of the spirituals, "But I learned that the Negroes of the town objected to them. They called them 'shouting.' They had victrolas and player-pianos. So, I realized with deep regret, that the spirituals, meeting ridicule, would be certain to die out. With Negroes also the trend was towards the small town and towards the city—and industry and commerce and the machines. The folk-spirit was

---

19 Jean Toomer, "Essentials: Prose and Poems," manuscript, 1930, pp. 112–18, Toomer papers, Fisk University Library; Walter H. Sokel, *The Writer in Extremis: Expressionism in Twentieth-Century German Literature* (Stanford, Calif.: Stanford University Press, 1959), pp. 85–118; Jean Toomer, *Work Ideas I*, Mill House Pamphlets, Psychological Series, No. 2 (Doyleston, Pa., 1937), p. 13; Jean Toomer *Living Is Developing*, Mill House Pamphlets, Psychological Series, No. 1 (Doyleston, Pa., 1937), p. 14.

walking in to die on the modern desert. That spirit was so beautiful. Its death was so tragic." [20]

Toomer, suffering intensely from "frigidization of the self," appears to have entertained the idea that in the southern Negro folk-
spirit he might find emotional release—that in this spirit he might
find not only his own salvation but salvation for the modern industrial world. This, at least, is the message of "Box Seat." This
was the message Dan carried as he brought emotion and vitality as
his gift from rural Georgia to the city. Toomer could *almost* believe in Dan. For perhaps a year he convinced himself that his
identity lay with the Negro race. "Within the last two or three
years however," he wrote the editor of the *Liberator* in mid-1922,
"my growing need for artistic expression has pulled me deeper and
deeper into the Negro group. . . . I found myself loving it in a way
that I could never love the other." But this new identification—this
new absolute—lasted no longer than his socialism. He had probably broken with it when *Cane* was published in 1923. His return
to New York in 1923 ushered in a new period of "chaos": "Everything was in chaos. I saw this chaos clearly, I could and did describe and analyze its factors so well that I got a reputation for
being sort of genius of chaos." [21]

What happened to Toomer in the years between 1923 to 1925
is described by Gorham Munson, who knew him well at the time.
Toomer continued his quest for what Munson calls "unity," or
"personal wholeness," first by training his "conscious control of
the body," and then by spending a summer (1924) at the Gurdjieff
Institute, Fontainebleau, France. The Russian mystic's approach
to "unity" was through the science of psychology, in his formulation an interesting blend of Freudian and religious categories.
Toomer found what he was looking for in Gurdjieff's philosophy.
He became a disciple, spending many of his summers in Fontainebleau and his winters organizing psychological experiments. But
the crucial moment for Toomer came one summer evening in
1926. It happened at the end of one of those humdrum days of no
special significance. Toomer was waiting on an El platform in New
York City, minding his own business, when suddenly he tran-

---

[20] Toomer, "Outline of Autobiography," *op. cit.*, pp. 58–59.

[21] Jean Toomer to editor of *Liberator*, August 19, 1922, Toomer papers, Fisk
University Library; Toomer, "Outline of Autobiography," *op. cit.*, p. 63.

scended himself: "I was born above the body into a world of psychological reality . . . In my private language I shall call this experience the Second Conception."[22]

That was it for Toomer; he had his absolute; his search was over. From that time he began to proselytize in the age-old tradition of religious converts. He wrote novels, he wrote philosophic works, he wrote descriptions of psychological experiments, and he wrote volumes of material that defies classification—all with the purpose of persuasion. The publishers were not buying. His literary life after 1926 became a dreary round of rejection slips. The fault was not his; nor his publishers'. He had come up with an answer to the troubles that plagued the age. He had an answer for Van Wyck Brooks's cry of "externalization"; for Waldo Frank's plight of being "objectified." He had an answer for modern man's agonizing sense of incompleteness. His answer was disconcertingly couched in half-psychological, half-mystical language ("Our center of gravity is displaced. Our essence is passive; and we lack essential self-activating energies. . . . We have no being-aims and purposes."), but what he was doing, in essence, was putting into his own symbols an age-old experience—religious conversion. Following willy-nilly behind Gurdjieff, he had gotten himself completely at cross-purposes with the whole thrust of American intelligence in the 1920's. Van Wyck Brooks, Charles S. Johnson, Alain Locke—all were asking that man, through his creative art, to turn to experience. The answer found by these modern critics lay in creating beauty and meaning out of the living contact with the world of reality. Toomer was saying just the opposite; turn for beauty and meaning to your inner essence: "An artist," he wrote, "is able, by effort to contact his own essence, wherein exist common universal symbols." Toomer was asking his age to adopt another absolute; the age was not buying.[23]

---

22 Gorham B. Munson, "The Significance of Jean Toomer," *Opportunity*, Vol. 3 (September, 1925), pp. 262–63; Jean Toomer, "From Exile into Being," unpublished manuscript, 1938, p. 1 of Prescript, Toomer papers, Fisk University Library.

23 Unpublished novels of Jean Toomer: "The Gallonwerps," *c.* 1927; "Transatlantic Crossing," *c.* 1930; "Eight-Day World," *c.* 1932; "York Beach," *c.* 1928. Unpublished philosophic works of Jean Toomer: "Essentials: Prose and Poems," *op. cit.;* "Essentials: Definitions and Aphorisms," 1931. Unpublished psychoogical experiment of Jean Toomer: "Portage Potential," 1931. Toomer, "Essentials: Prose and Poems," *op. cit.,* pp. 64, 46.

Toomer's artistic expression lost something once he had found his answer—it became didactic, it became unconvincing. His unpublished novel, "Eight-Day World" (*c.* 1932) is a case in point. It pictures a group of people aboard a transatlantic liner escaping from their unsatisfactory lives in America. The critique of life in America was the one expressed by a hundred writers in the 1920's. Life had become materialistic, commercial, and unfulfilling. The group escaping from this life aboard the liner was no sooner at sea than infighting and backbiting began. The people felt inadequate to themselves, and yet strove for independence from others. It was Toomer's early experience being retold. Hugh was the one man of the story who understood something of what was going on, but he was in the same predicament as the others, trying to break down the barriers his own inadequacy built up between him and them; trying, without success, to find an answer to the frigid self. Finally, Hugh found his answer in the beautiful Vera, and at the same time crystallized a philosophy of it all. He had come to understand that each person must attain a satisfying independence and yet give of self. That is the goal. But in order to achieve it, one must transcend oneself: "This means," said Hugh, "that we must recapture our full *being. Being* is the base of everything."[24]

"Eight-Day World" ended as Toomer had ended, with all problems solved, with everyone satisfied. The artist could no longer express modern man's restlessness and lostness. His work had become smug—and dead. Toomer had been modern in *Cane*. There the author had confronted his readers with the pain of reality unmitigated by the pleasant knowledge of having in hand The Answer. After writing *Cane*, Toomer fled from reality, found his absolute and clung to it. He talked about finding "being," but he would have been horrified at the modern definition of being—the "being" of Heidegger or of Sartre. He turned from experience of outward reality to an inner thing he called "essence" or "being," thinking that the thing he was camouflaging with the symbols of psychology was newly discovered. By 1940 he realized it was not new. He requested admittance to the Society of Friends, saying: "For some time we have shared the fundamental faith of the Friends...." His "essence" had been none other than the Quakers'

---

24 Toomer, "Eight-Day World," *op. cit.*, pp. 324–25.

"inner light"; his 1926 experience of the "Second Conception" had been the experience of religious conversion. Toomer had gone full cycle from his childhood faith in God, through total rejection in *Cane,* and then back again to God. Meanwhile the Negro Renaissance passed him by, continuing the course Johnson and Locke had laid down for it—the coming to grips with painful reality. The sadness of it all was that in losing Toomer the Renaissance lost the one man who had come to terms with modern art and who had the talent to symbolize so beautifully the inner experience of that reality.[25]

That the plunge from the safe world of mythology into modernity was most difficult is the lesson gained by looking at another of the Renaissance writers, Countee Cullen. In his poetry, which was the best produced by the Renaissance, is the drama of thrust and counterthrust; the struggle between myth and modernity made for the ultimate prize—a man's soul. Woven into the fabric of this basic drama were other themes: the struggle against his much beloved foster father's fundamentalistic faith, a heartbreaking love affair—all this heaped on the slight shoulders of this gentlest of men.

Cullen was of a too-retiring nature to fit in with the bohemian group that made Wallace Thurman's studio its headquarters. "Though he had firm friendships with many of us," wrote one of the Thurman group, "he was not, by temperament, inclination, or choice, our leader. . . . But Countee had already arrived, due to his greater talent and application. We play at being writers, while he wrote." Indeed he did. By the time he graduated from New York University with Phi Beta Kappa honors his first book of poetry, *Color* (1925), was on the presses, and he had already won the Witter Bynner Undergraduate Poetry Prize after twice being runner-up. He had long since been getting high praise in the Negro magazines, and by 1923 his poems were appearing in *Harper's, Century, Nation, The American Mercury.* The literary circle in which he felt most at home was that amorphous one including Walter White, Charles S. Johnson, James Weldon Johnson, Carl Van Vechten, Alain Locke, and (when Walter White was

---

25 Jean Toomer to Overseers, Buckingham meeting, Lahaska Pa., August 28, 1940, Toomer papers, Fisk University Library.

absent) W. E. B. Du Bois. This was a circle which stood slightly apart from the Harlem bohemians of Thurman, often criticized the Thurman group and, in return, was the object of much bohemian raillery. This was the circle of race leaders, the intellectuals, the high upper class of black society—men whose interest was on a theoretical level or propaganda basis. Listening to them could have turned Cullen either toward or away from modernity, depending on who impressed him most. But theirs was an intellectual level of debate, carried on in a rarefied atmosphere far removed from the black masses and their lives. He could not follow the main thrust of the Renaissance toward finding self-definition in the cultural experience of the masses. Before him lay two roads: one back into the sheltering embrace of the old mythology, the other into Darwin's universe and fatalism.[26]

Cullen was educated for this difficult choice by that fine old slum institution, the broken home. As a welfare child he was boarded out to a woman—possibly his grandmother—who earned her livelihood through him, and others. Age 13, he was taken in by a kindly and well-to-do minister. The new home in the 14-room Harlem church pastorage brought security, both physical and emotional—for there was an abundance of love, and faith in God. Just how and why doubt entered the boy's thoughts are things that cannot be known. But it did. It became the drumbeat of his poetry.[27]

Cullen had an exquisite sense of the fitness of things, a sense he could transmit to paper in delicately drawn lines. Who can doubt that his fine sensitivity was burdened to the limit by oppression?:

> Once riding in old Baltimore,
>   Heart-filled, head-filled with glee,
> I saw a Baltimorean
>   Keep looking straight at me.

---

[26] Dorothy West to Sister Margaret, n.d., quoted in Beulah O. Reimherr, "Countee Cullen: A Biographical and Critical Study," (unpublished M.A. thesis, University of Maryland, 1960), pp. 56–57; see Countee Cullen, "The Horizon," *Crisis*, Vol. 23 (March, 1922), p. 219; Reimherr, "Countee Cullen," *op. cit.*, p. 55.

[27] There are two biographies of Countee Cullen: Blanche E. Ferguson, *Countee Cullen and the Negro Renaissance* (New York: Dodd, Mead and Co., 1966), and Beulah O. Reimherr's "Countee Cullen . . ." *op. cit.* Where the two have differed on Cullen's early life I have chosen to go along with the more complete and challenging Reimherr work.

> Now I was eight and very small,
>   And he was no whit bigger,
> And so I smiled, but he poked out
>   His tongue and called me, "Nigger."
>
> I saw the whole of Baltimore
>   From May until December;
> Of all the things that happened there
>   That's all that I remember.[28]

Cullen did not react to prejudice by rushing out to join the NAACP; he reacted instead in a quiet inward crisis of faith. How could this world of hatred and oppression have been the work of a benevolent, all-powerful God?:

> I doubt not God is good, well-meaning, kind,
> . . .
> Yet do I marvel at this curious thing:
> To make a poet black, and bid him sing![29]

Where was God, he wondered in another place, when a man was lynched last night?[30]

Cullen's poetic statement of his struggle with faith began during his student days with "The Shroud of Color" (1924). In it he described the travail of a young black man who, beginning in despair and resignation, is presented with visions of the true nature of life, comes to an understanding, and, ultimately, takes up the struggle. The first vision that comes to the young man is the world of remorseless struggle:

> I raised my burning eyes, beheld a field
> All multitudinous with carnal yield,
> A grim ensanguined mead whereon I saw
> Evolve the ancient fundamental law
> Of tooth and talon, fist and nail and claw.

But why the everlasting struggle? Why do not the living creatures, seeing what kind of world they are condemned to, give up like

---

28 Countee Cullen, "Incident," *Color* (New York: Harper & Bros., 1925), p. 15. Reprinted by permission of Harper & Row, Publishers.

29 Countee Cullen, "Yet Do I Marvel," *Color* (New York: Harper & Bros., 1925), p. 3. Reprinted by permission of Harper & Row, Publishers.

30 Quoted in Benjamin E. Mays, *The Negro's God, as Reflected in His Literature* (Boston: Chapman & Grimes, Inc., 1938), p. 219.

the young man and renounce life? One must not ask why—it is just a brute fact of nature: "And no thing died that did not give/ A testimony that it longed to live." In the end, the young man adopts a sort if vitalism—not a very satisfying solution in itself, but Cullen has given it larger implications. The later visions stated in the poem concern a struggling race—a race caught in the toils of oppression but struggling on; building on its pain; creating a nobler people out of its travail.[31]

In "Heritage," the major poem of the following year (1925), the same nagging skepticism is evident; the struggle for a faith is renewed, but the terms are somewhat different. The note previously struck of finding meaning in the fact of struggle itself gives way to militancy, the *refusal* to endure. Into "Heritage" creep also elements of myth. The Christ-like personality—meek, humble—is rejected for the sort of primitivism that was being made popular among white novelists in such works as Carl Van Vechten's *Nigger Heaven* (1926) and Sherwood Anderson's *Dark Laughter* (1925). First, he feels the primitive within him:

> So I lie, who find no peace
> Night or day, no slight release
> From the unremittent beat
> Made by cruel padded feet
> Walking through my body's street.
> Up and down they go, and back,
> Threading out a jungle track.
>   . . .

Then the Christian image is introduced, and the two do battle:

> I belong to Jesus Christ
> Preacher of humility;
> Heathen Gods are naught to me.

> Father, Son and Holy Ghost,
> So I make an idle boast;
> Jesus of the twice-turned cheek,
> Lamb of God, although I speak
> With my mouth thus, in my heart
> Do I play a double part.

---

31 Countee Cullen, "The Shroud of Color," *Color* (New York: Harper & Bros., 1925), pp. 26–35. Reprinted by permission of Harper & Row, Publishers.

> Ever at thy glowing altar
> Must my heart grow sick and falter,
> Wishing He I served were black,
> . . .

And the sense of militancy and anger is introduced to struggle with Christian patience and humility:

> Lord, I fashion dark gods, too.
> Daring even to give You
> Dark despairing features where,
> Crowned with dark rebellious hair,
> Patience wavers just so much as
> Mortal grief compels, while touches
> Quick and hot, of anger, rise
> To smitten cheek and weary eyes.[32]
> . . .

The sense of security that Cullen so needed had begun to erode by the time "Heritage" was written. The sense of fading security seems evident in the son's lasting attachment to his foster father. The two spent most of their time together throughout Countee Cullen's early manhood. Each summer for 12 years (1924–36) they traveled together to Europe, unable to relinquish each other's company. But the security he found in his father was being lost in other areas. His religious faith was strained to the breaking point. Then, in concert wtih the rest of the Renaissance writers, Cullen became rebelliously impatient with the Christ-like Negro. In "Heritage" he tried to see in primitivism a substitute identification, but that was a white man's concoction and was never more than a passing attraction for the Negro writers.

As if all this were not enough, Cullen got involved in a disastrous marriage. As early as 1923 the young poet began to get emotionally involved with a beautiful fellow student at New York University—the daughter of W. E. B. Du Bois. Being a poet, he began to write poetry. "Timid Lover," set the tone and others followed in profusion—"One Day We Played a Game," "In Love's Way." The poems told the story of a shy admirer bending his knee

---

[32] Countee Cullen, "Heritage," *Color* (New York: Harper & Bros., 1925), pp. 36–41. Reprinted by permission of Harper & Row, Publishers.

in reverence. One thing led to another until one day in April of 1928 3,000 people found themselves fighting their way into Harlem's Salem Church for the social event of the year—the Cullen-Du Bois wedding. A month later the Cullens, father and son, set off on their usual trip to Europe—without the bride. Countee Cullen remained the next two years abroad, while his bride remained in Baltimore, teaching school. Divorce came in 1930. Cullen's poetry of 1928 registered the shock and chagrin he felt at being deserted: "Be still, heart, cease those measured strokes;/ Lie quiet in your hollow bed;/ This moving frame is but a hoax/ To make you think you are not dead."[33]

We find, then, throughout Cullen's rather brief period of poetic creativity (a period coinciding with the decade of the 1920's) a note of quiet desperation: "I would my life's cold sun were setting/ To rise for me no more." Behind that note lay his childhood insecurity, his sensitivity to prejudice, the crisis of faith in religion and racial myths, and finally his tragic marriage. But despite these things he had a certain buoyancy. Charles S. Johnson, who worked with Cullen for two years on the staff of *Opportunity*, called him "restful, stimulating, whimsical, and gay . . ." It was, perhaps, this buoyancy or resiliency that drove him while in Paris, in that disastrous year, 1928, to seek another major resolution of faith in a new poem, "The Black Christ." By now the artificial primitivism was gone. Gone also was the proud, defiant mood of "The Shroud of Color," in which he had been moved to write, "And somehow it was born upon my brain/ How being dark, and living through the pain/ Of it, is courage more than angels have." What was left in "The Black Christ" was the struggle between fatalism and the Christ-like mythology. With the scene set in the South, two black boys, brothers, are told by their mother to keep the faith: "Whom God has made shall He not guide?" But her words had little effect on the boys, whose eyes saw only the desert of oppression. Again, we hear the refrain: "God, if He was, kept to His skies,/ And left us to our enemies." The day came, as it had to, when the oppression struck home—struck the rebellious brother Jim. He killed a man, his lynching followed. In horror the narrator watched his

[33] Countee Cullen, "The Foolish Heart," *On These I Stand: An Anthology of the Best Poems of Countee Cullen* (New York: Harper & Bros., 1947), p. 88. Reprinted by permission of Harper & Row, Publishers.

brother die. But it was Christ who died that day—a black Christ. Following Jim's resurrection, faith returns in final triumph: "Knowing He can at will confer/ Magic on miracle to prove/ And try me when I doubt His love."[34]

"The Black Christ" did not end the struggle for Cullen. The next turn of the wheel found fatalism gaining the upper hand. The main evidence for this is his last attempt to do an important work—a revision of *The Medea* in 1935, to which he gave the title, "Byword for Evil." For Cullen the original version lacked the needed plethora of murder and revenge, a lack which he remedied while the chorus intoned: "Immortal Zeus controls the fate of man, decrees him love or grief; our days the echo of his will resound in fury or pass in nothingness away."[35]

In any case, less important for Cullen than the ending was that bright middle, when, like Toomer, he broke free from the mythology for a brief moment to a tougher, more honest vision. Like Toomer, he had gone a long way toward carrying out the program laid down by Charles S. Johnson and Alain Locke—that of finding beauty and meaning in experience.

One of the tragic things that can befall a black man in America is the experience of self-hatred. Investigations have shown that Negroes of the middle and upper classes are unusually subject to this malady because often they live by values they can never attain. They value the lightness of skin color, straight hair, the culture of the white upper class, but no matter how light their skin, no matter how cultured they become, they are forever excluded from the white world by a word—"Negro." There follows a loss of self-esteem. This "self-hatred" had a devastating effect on the lives of at least two of the Renaissance writers. Their experience shows how naked were those who had suddenly lost their mythology and

---

34 Countee Cullen, "Requiescam," *Color* (New York: Harper & Bros., 1925), p. 108. Reprinted by permission of Harper & Row, Publishers. Charles S. Johnson to those gathered at the formal ceremonies for the renaming of the 13th St. branch of the New York Public Library to the Countee Cullen Branch Library, September 12, 1951; quoted in Reimherr, "Countee Cullen," *op. cit.*, p. 44; Countee Cullen, "The Black Christ," *On These I Stand* (New York: Harper & Bros., 1947), pp. 104–37. Reprinted by permission of Harper & Row, Publishers.

35 Countee Cullen, "Byword for Evil," manuscript, 1941, Cullen papers, James Weldon Johnson Collection, Yale University Library.

with it their ability to identify with their race. Self-hatred probably destroyed them. Their experience shows the urgency involved in the Renaissance search for a new means of identification with the Negro race. It also shows that the identification could no longer come through idealization of the race (the Christ-like image)—the way, for instance, of James Weldon Johnson. The new generation of writers was far too skeptical (often cynical) to idealize anything.[36]

Nella Larsen mixed cynicism with naïveté. Her idea of a good joke was to play the primitive exotic before a group of unsuspecting whites. But her real understanding of her race was small. She seems to have seen her first southern Negro on a visit to Nashville in 1930: "And the Negroes themselves!" she gushed in a letter, "I've never seen anything quite so true to what's expected. Mostly black and good humored and apparently quite shiftless, frightfully clean and decked out in the most appalling colors, but somehow right." Nella, herself, was short and brown, married to Professor Elmer Imes of Fisk University (a specialist in spectroscopy), and thoroughly discontented with life. Her origins are obscure (apparently a product of a mixed marriage); histories of the period invariably pass her over with brief mention. The first concrete view of her comes in 1926 when an extensive correspondence with author Carl Van Vechten was begun. In 1926 she lived in Jersey City, but was dissatisfied and wanted to open a bookstore in Harlem. She did get to Harlem next year (no bookstore), and got her first novel, *Quicksand* (1928), written. By 1930 she had become both bored with Harlem and estranged from her husband. October found her in Mallorca, Spain, having an affair with a tall young Englishman, a polo player. By early 1931 she was bored again. "All the amusing people are gone," she wrote from Mallorca, "and really I've never been so lonely in my life. I could almost weep from boredom. I do hope I'm not going to be quite so forlorn in Paris." In 1933 she returned to her husband in Nash-

---

[36] Possible references to self-hatred among the Negro middle class are legion. The best are probably the following: Abram Kardiner and Lionel Ovesey, *The Mark of Oppression: A Psychological Study of the American Negro* (New York: W. W. Norton & Co., Inc., 1951); E. Franklin Frazier, *Black Bourgeoisie, The Rise of a New Middle Class in the United States* (New York: The Free Press, 1957).

ville for a while and found life "pretty terrible." The arrangement did not last. We lose track of Nella Larsen in 1940; so did her husband.[37]

The inspiration for Nella Larsen's first novel was apparently Carl Van Vechten's *Nigger Heaven*. Van Vechten's is the story of a bright young Negro college graduate who is consumed and destroyed by self-hatred. Larsen's *Quicksand* is a novel of a young woman similarly consumed and destroyed. But there is too much pain in her novel for it to have been wholly borrowed—it told her story. Her portrait of the utter desperation that can be the lot of the mulatto with social pretensions is unsurpassed in Negro literature. Helga Crane, heroine of *Quicksand*, is a young woman of Danish and American Negro extraction (like Miss Larsen herself). Helga dreamed the American dream of material security, gracious living, and happiness. She was well-educated and cultured, had the beauty to make a good marriage, but happiness was forever to elude her. As the story of Helga Crane unfolds, we are carried into a penetrating study of self-hatred. Helga's white mother, after being deserted by her husband, married a white man. So, at an early age, Helga was thrown in among white stepbrothers and stepsisters who despised her for her color. The resulting self-hatred drove Helga to project her hatred onto those about her—especially those who were Negro. She was antagonistic and superior to all Negro acquaintances. Always she was on the lookout for someone who could live up to her standards, but, of course, no such person existed.

So far this was good psychology. But Nella Larsen was also working at another level: the saga of Helga Crane is above all a search for a sustaining myth—a myth that will enable her to escape from her self-hatred. She simply needed to like herself; that meant liking her race. Her first flight was to Harlem to be "among her own," but it was no good; she was soon hating the dark faces around her. She escaped from the dark faces to Copenhagen and her mother's family. Her built-in self-hatred followed her, of course. Copenhagen was fine until suddenly she discovered her

<hr />

37 Nella Larsen to Carl Van Vechten, June 15, 1929, Van Vechten papers, James Weldon Johnson Collection, Yale University Library; Larsen to Van Vechten, May 22, 1930, Van Vechten papers, *ibid.;* Larsen to Van Vechten, July 22, 1930, Van Vechten papers, *ibid.;* Larsen to Van Vechten, May 12, 1933, Van Vechten papers, *ibid.;* Elmer Imes to Van Vechten, February 24, 1940, Van Vechten papers, *ibid.*

true primitive, exotic nature. Then back to Harlem, the world of wild color, of dark laughter, to glory in her primitivism. "How absurd she had been," wrote Nella Larsen, "to think that another country, other people, could liberate her from the ties which bound her forever to these mysterious, these terrible, these fascinating, these lovable, dark hordes. Ties that were of the spirit." But primitivism was a delusion and Helga found no escape in it from herself. One night, driven to desperation, she walked into a storefront church; into a mad scene of shouting and singing. She felt herself caught up in the madness of it—she was "saved." Again she felt release—release in the simple grandeur of Christianity. In a desperate attempt to strengthen her newfound sense of security she married the pastor, a "rattish yellow man," and removed with him to his pastorship in the South. The children began to arrive, year in and year out. The preacher was a self-righteous, ridiculous creature. Life became a misery . . . again.[38]

Nella Larsen's message was simple and direct—it was the futility of trying to escape from oneself. Helga Crane tried all ways of escape: into middle-class respectability, into racial identity through primitivism, and finally into religion. All ways were equally futile, but the last was least satisfying of all. The final attempt at escape ended in her ripping away all illusion until only the uncomfortable reality remained. Of God, Larsen wrote, "He wasn't there. Didn't exist. Into that yawning gap of unspeakable brutality had gone, too, her belief in the miracle and wonder of life. Only scorn, resentment, and hate remained—and ridicule. Life wasn't a miracle, a wonder. It was, for Negroes at least, only a great disappointment." Helga's rejection of God was extreme because he was the white man's God—a hoax perpetrated on the black man. Her attitude toward the Christ-like image of the Negro is implicit in this passage: "How the white man's God must laugh at the great joke he had played on them! Bound them to slavery, then to poverty and insult, and made them bear it unresistingly, uncomplainingly almost, by sweet promises of mansions in the sky by and by."[39]

---

38 Nella Larsen, *Quicksand* (New York: Alfred A. Knopf, Inc., 1928), pp. 213–14, 255, 271 ff.

39 *Ibid.*, pp. 290–91, 297.

Quicksand, for all its faults, gave expression to a profoundly wounded soul. In it we read Nella Larsen's alienation from white civilization, from the Negro race and its mythology, even from life itself. The author discovered her problem—her self-hatred—but found no way to escape from it. Every such effort was an exercise in self-delusion.

Like Jean Toomer, Nella Larsen and Countee Cullen spent little time upbraiding the whites. It was not a matter of being happy with their oppressors; naturally, they were thoroughly alienated from the whites and from white culture. It was a matter of turning away from the outside world—of turning inward. Their search was for identification and it led to a probing of the inner being. It should occasion no surprise, then, that their concern centered on the problems of the psyche—the conflicts and tensions that arise from being Negro in white America. Their concern led them to look upon their psychological problems as paramount and basic—the problems that must be solved *before* turning attention to the alien environment. They were looking for the inner resources with which to conquer themselves individually. Jean Toomer thought for a brief period that he had found it in his character Lewis, but then he turned away. Countee Cullen found it in the fact of life itself; life as manifested in his race's conquest over pain and despair. Nella Larsen looked and discovered no inner resources with which to cope with the overwhelming fact of self-hatred. The same can be said of the most tragic figure of them all, Wallace Thurman.

At the center of the Renaissance, and of Negro bohemia, stood the figure of Wallace Thurman, brooding and magnetic. He was the catalyst whose presence set the mood for the rest. He was capable of the most violent shifts in mood, at one moment exuberant, the next gouging at his own vitals in masochistic delight ("But what I do feel is an immense discouragement, a sensation of unbearable isolation, a perpetual fear of some remote disaster, an utter disbelief in my capacity, a total absence of desire, an impossibility of finding any kind of interest."). He literally ached for fame and greatness—to attain the heights of a Joyce or a Proust. Failing that, he plunged himself into hackwork for Hollywood and the pulp magazines—work that he did with utter cynicism ("The morons should eat that up especially in the movies, if

given a deal of darky dancing, nigger comedy, and coon shouting."). He ridiculed the Renaissance and scorned himself for being a part of it. He had the talent, or so he thought, but greatness
of theme and expression escaped him—why?[40]

To explain the reason for his failure Thurman pointed to his
identity as a Negro and to the necessary consequence of it—self-
hatred. To free his talent he must overcome this debilitating infirmity. But how? He grappled with this problem in two novels.
In his first, *The Blacker the Berry* (1929), he wrote of a young
girl whose extreme blackness made her socially unacceptable in
her middle-class society. Wherever she went, whether it be to a
Western university or to Harlem, she found herself held in contempt by members of her own race. She was too black. She tried
the various expedients—the skin cream, the hair straghtener, etc.—
but all failed her. It finally dawned on her (as it apparently had
dawned on Thurman) that her problem lay not with her color
but with her psyche. The only viable solution was to accept herself for what she was: "What she needed to do now was to accept
her black skin as being real and unchangeable, to realize that
certain things were, and would be, and with this in mind begin
life anew, always fighting, not so much for acceptance by other
people, but for acceptance of herself." In time of extremity she
had remembered the words of a friend, "everybody must find
salvation within one's self, . . ." That statement, which may be
taken as the core of Thurman's philosophy, pretty well sums up
the movement of the Renaissance.[41]

In his novel, *Infants of the Spring* (1932), Thurman pursued
his theme. The book is a devastating attack on the Harlem Renaissance. To Thurman's mind the literature was bad, the attitudes were bad, the foundations it laid for future Negro literature
were rotten. He found the Renaissance to be a charade, an exercise
in fantasy. He was almost overcome with disbelief at the things
that had transpired: a noted Negro college professor, Dr. Parks
(i.e., Alain Locke), trying to persuade the assembled writers to

40 Wallace Thurman to Jordan Rapp, *c.* 1929, Thurman papers, James Weldon
Johnson Collection, Yale University Library; Thurman to Rapp, August 1, 1929,
Thurman papers, *ibid.*

41 Wallace Thurman, *The Blacker the Berry: A Novel of Negro Life* (New York:
The Macaulay Co., 1929), pp. 257, 256.

go back to their African roots; Raymond, the central figure, trying to maintain some contact with reality, answering: "Is there
any reason why *all* Negro artists should consciously and deliberately dig into African soil for inspiration and material unless they
actually wish to do so?" The answer of Dr. Parks: "I don't mean
that. I mean you should develop your inherited spirit." Paul (another Renaissance writer) interrupts: "I ain't got no African
spirit." Failure of communication between generations was complete.[42]

In another scene Thurman pictured a dance gotten up by
members of his clique at "Nigaratti Manor" during which members of both races clung together in sweaty embrace; each somehow believing that such behavior meant emancipation. It was
really little more than a drunken orgy with no meaning beyond
its meaninglessness. And that, Thurman was led to suspect, was
the essence of the Harlem Renaissance. Its "creativity" was an
exercise in self-delusion. It was not necessarily that the Negro
writers were barren of talent, but that they were so busy posing
at being literary that there was little time left for writing. The
posing was an escape: if one was an "author," a "bohemian" character, an unrecognized "singer," then one need not face up to
being a black man. Beyond that there was the self-hatred, always
central in Thurman's thought. The characters of *Infants of the
Spring* were afraid to put themselves to the test. One cannot fail
if one does not try. So not trying becomes an escape. "That ninety-
nine and ninety-nine hundredths per cent of the Negro race is
patently possessed and motivated by an inferiority complex,"
Raymond said in answer to a question. "Being a slave race ac-
tuated by salve morality, what else can you expect?"[43]

Raymond, a young Renaissance writer (Wallace Thurman),
felt that he could rise above this; that he could free himself from
identity with any race or group and become pure individual,
identifying himself only with his own created values. This was
a philosophy of individualism which Thurman himself identified
as Nietzschean. By creating his own identity he would rise above
the self-hatred that comes from identification with the black race.

---

42 Thurman, *Infants of the Spring, op. cit.*, p. 237.
43 *Ibid.*, pp. 186–87, 140.

But was this not really another type of posing—another self-deception?—this attempt at disassociation? Was this not just another way of refusing to confront that powerful reality, self-hatred? These questions immobilized Thurman. At one point Raymond was asked by a friend to recall a previous conversation: "You pronounced yourself a Nietzschean. I pronounced you a liar. I still admit I'm at sea. I don't know whether you are or not." "Neither do I," said Raymond. The friend then continued: "You'd like to be. You try hard to be. But after all, something holds you back and that something hinders your writing."[44]

Thurman directed his hard gaze inward, but all certainties dissolved before it. No myths remained to give him comfort. As with the others of his generation the "Uncle Tom" type connoted only servility (characterized by the groveling Pelham). The suggestion that the Negro writer had a mission was met with incredulity. Race leaders were scorned. Communism was a matter of indifference. He could not even identify with the Negro race: "Yes," Raymond's friend told him, "race to you, means nothing. You stand on a peak. . . . Propaganda you despise. Illusions about Negroes you have none." Thurman died shortly after writing *Infants in the Spring*, emancipated from everything but himself, liquor, T.B., and despair.[45]

III

Part of the story of the Negro Renaissance of the 1920's was the strong tendency to turn inward, toward introspection and self-analysis. Behind this tendency was a crisis of identity caused not only by the conflicts inherent in the Negro's situation in American society, but also by the loss of absolutes. The absolutes that were crumbling were not only the 19th-century faiths, common to all Americans, but also the myths peculiar to the American Negro of middle-class origins. Wallace Thurman and Nella Larsen, with overwhelming sense of self-hatred, could find nothing to sustain and support them; they consequently plummeted to the depths of despair. Jean Toomer in *Cane,* and Countee Cullen, al-

---

44 *Ibid.,* pp. 58-59.
45 *Ibid.,* pp. 143, 60.

though they rejected the suffering, Christ-like Negro, nevertheless borrowed from him the idea of the social utility of pain, and evolved a kind of hard realism that saw value in the confrontation with reality. At this point another element enters into the picture: the sturdy realism of the uprooted Negro folk—the spirit that was expressed in the blues.

The blues arrived in the big cities in the early 1920's. In November of 1920, a faltering record company recorded the first blues as a sort of last gasp attempt to stay alive. The song OKeh Records recorded was the "Crazy Blues," the songwriter, Perry Bradford, the singer Mamie Smith. OKeh Records refused to identify Mamie's race on the record label—the company was embarrassed in its extremity. Also, OKeh was unhappy with the recording. The band—the Jazz Hounds—had been asked to play sweetly and quietly in the background. The Jazz Hounds did not know how, so they belted it out in the usual manner. So did Mamie. By the end of the first month, 75,000 records had been sold. By the end of the year, Perry and Mamie had turned the blues into a multimillion dollar business.[46]

The blues became a craze . . . for about four years. It was just another fad for the songwriters on Tin Pan Alley, and for the white audiences. The writers turned out blues *en masse*, the recording companies followed suit, and the white audiences loved it. They loved it until about 1925, then something else came along. It wasn't that way in Harlem. In Harlem it wasn't a fad, it was an expression of life. In Harlem, the blues did not arrive in 1920 and disappear in 1925. Mamie Smith had been singing them in Harlem cabarets for years. Bessie Smith had been singing them in her big, sad voice since she was a child, singing them on the road with carnivals, circuses, and tent shows. "Ma" Rainey had taught her how to hold a tough, pugnacious audience by sheer power and depth of expression. The less-celebrated Clara Smith was Bessie's equal. Clara's voice was soft and sweet, and she sang the blues with sympathy and understanding. There were many others—dozens who were professionals, thousands who were not. The blues were no fad—not for the Negro masses.

---

[46] Charters and Kunstadt, *op cit.;* Paul Oliver, "Blues to Drive the Blues Away," Nat Hentoff and Albert McCarthy (eds.), *Jazz* (New York: Rinehart & Co., 1959), pp. 85–103.

It would be futile to attempt here to capture the variety and the richness of the blues. Others have done it with some degree of success.[47] A few lines, however, may give some indication of the moods developed by the blues. Hope and realism were mingled:

> I'm gonna quit worrin' and will stop grievin' 'cause the
>   bad luck will change someday, (*twice*)
> It's hard to walk in that straight and narrow way.[48]

Or, there was a mixture of realism and wry humor:

> Well, I'm broke and hungry, Dulcie, you got the feast for
>   me, (*twice*)
> My stomach's filled with nothin', nothin' else but grief.
>
> My friends don't see me, no, they just pass me by, (*twice*)
> I wouldn't mind it so much, but they hold their heads so high.[49]

There was the weary determination shown by this singer headed away from the Southland toward the northern city:

> I've been tramping this lonely road, night after night and
>   day after day, (*twice*)
> If your prayers don't help me, you know I'll die trying
>   to make my way.[50]

There was sadness, there was trouble, but there was no flight from reality:

> People, if you hear me humming on this song both night and day,
> People, if you hear me humming on this song both night and day,
> I'm just a poor boy in trouble, trying to drive the blues away.[51]

The Renaissance writer thus had an alternate heritage to look to, should he be inclined to turn from an upper class to a lower class tradition. This was not the easiest thing for him to do, however. Negro critics held strongly to the Christ-like tradition and angrily denounced the attempts to deviate. Du Bois, Benjamin

---

[47] Most notably Paul Oliver in his *The Meaning of the Blues* (New York: Collier Books, 1963).

[48] *Ibid.*, p. 80.

[49] *Ibid.*, p. 81.

[50] *Ibid.*, p. 82.

[51] *Ibid.*, p. 338.

Brawley and many of the newspaper editors looked askance at the intrusion of the blues and jazz into Negro culture. The argument between the critics and the writers centered on the question of whether or not literature should be propaganda. Du Bois maintained that it should, that the Negro should present himself in the best light by portraying himself as upper class and cultivated. Brawley added his affirmation in unambiguous terms. These were the two most strident voices among many in opposition. In fact, Du Bois gave everyone a chance to air his opinion in *The Crisis*. Brawley, who went as far as anyone in idealizing the Negro into a Christ-like figure, used the opportunity to wish "that so many artists would not prefer only what is vulgar. There is beauty in the world as well as ugliness, idealism as well as realism." In a study of Negro literature, Brawley went further and denounced the new trend: "Introspection and self-pity," he wrote of the Renaissance, "ran riot . . ." He was not at all happy with jazz ("that filled the popular demand for the exotic") or the blues ("so-called art"). It was not a happy time for those who had once looked to the literary movement to express the Negro's racial soul.[52]

Sometimes with more heat than light the younger writers rallied around the spirited manifesto of Langston Hughes in the June, 1926, issue of the *Nation*. The Negro masses, wrote Hughes, are free from American standardization, commercialism and similar values. They are free to be themselves. It is time that the artist should look for distinctive material. He meant, in particular, the blues. "To these," he said concerning the themes of the common black man, "the Negro artist can give his racial individuality, his heritage of rhythm and warmth, and his incongruous humor that so often, as in the Blues, becomes ironic laughter mixed with tears." It is the duty of the Negro writer, he said, to revolt against that old whisper, "I want to be white,"—to overcome it by turning to the music of the masses, to jazz, to the blues.[53]

Hughes, in effect, asked for a second emancipation of the Negro mind. The first, already largely accomplished, had been the eman-

---

[52] Benjamin Brawley, "The Negro in Art: How Shall He Be Portrayed," *The Crisis*, Vol. 32 (June, 1926), p. 72; Benjamin Brawley, *The Negro in Literature and Art, in the United States* (New York: Duffield & Co., 1929), pp. 115–16.

[53] Langston Hughes, "The Negro Artist and the Racial Mountain," *The Nation*, Vol. 122 (June 23, 1926), pp. 692–94.

cipation from the slave psychology—the resignation, the repression of anger, the longing for heaven in the hereafter to escape this world. Largely through the Christ-like mythology the Negro intellectuals and leaders had channeled anger that previously had been repressed into a militant creed. Still, that creed was not based on the Negro of reality, because the race leaders had been unable to identify with the common man. Hughes was saying that the intellectual no longer needed to be ashamed of his race; that he no longer needed to idealize the race into an abstraction; that the masses have given the race a heritage valuable in itself—a heritage it can be proud of. The second stage in the emancipation of the Negro mind was only partially successful. What success it had it owed to the blues writers—Langston Hughes, Zora Neale Hurston, and Sterling Brown. The vital difference between the blues writers and the others cannot be understood in terms of class, of conscious revolt against one's elders, or in terms of middle-class writers versus intellectuals. Especially, it cannot be seen in terms of assimilation versus cultural pluralism. The vital difference was simply this: the blues writers did not feel lost, did not feel a lack of identity. They were emotionally secure people; which means they had no problems of identity—they identified with the Negro race easily and satisfactorily without having to idealize it. When the old myths died they simply turned to the masses to get their bearings. All the others, whether they accepted the Christ-like image or revolted against it, felt lost without an idealized image of the race. Once deprived of the mythology, they were thrown into a search for identity which was seldom satisfactorily fulfilled. They could not accept the blues because they could not accept their race as it really was.

It was the fate of perhaps the most brilliant of the Renaissance writers to fall into the latter category. Rudolph Fisher, try as he might, just could never come to terms with the ghetto proletariat. He wrote about them. He filled his pages with jokes about "niggerness":

"Now you gettin' bad, ain't you? Jus' 'cause you know you got the advantage over me."
"What advantage?"
"How could I hit you when I can't even see you?"

"Well if I was ugly as you is, I wouldn't want nobody to see me."
"Don't worry son. Nobody'll ever know how ugly you is. Yo' ugliness is shrouded in mystery."[54]

But his novel and his short stories without fail turned out to be requiems for the dying order—for the Christ-like Negro come to the big city only to lose his purity. His heroes were people who sang spirituals, his villains sang and played jazz. His heroes were usually done in by his villains because he felt that the city-slicker, the con man, was being created by the new environment, and it made him sad. Fisher, who won honors all the way through high school, Brown University and Howard University medical school, was as isolated from the black masses of the ghetto, whom he liked and tried to understand, as he was from the white man, whom he hated.[55]

Fisher's case illustrates how difficult it was for the middle-class Negro, hedged about by myths and by the prejudices of his peers, to successfully appreciate his people. But it was not impossible. Sterling Brown, when a student at Williams College, found it necessary to wait until everyone else in the dormitory was asleep, then found himself a secluded corner, before he dared to defy the current canons of sensibility by listening to Mamie Smith sing the blues. Later, when a professor of English at Howard University, Brown tried to organize a jazz concert for the students. The music department would not hear of it. Brown, who was to become the best of the blues poets, had to fight this kind of thing all his life, this middle-class estrangement from the proletariat. His own success at breaking down the psychological barrier between himself and his people is probably due to the fact that, for him, the barrier never existed to begin with. Never, as he says, was he troubled by the problem of identity.[56]

54 Rudolph Fisher, *The Conjure-Man Dies: A Mystery Tale of Dark Harlem* (New York: Convici-Friede, 1932), p. 33.

55 For a short sketch of Fisher's life, see Pearl M. Fisher, "Biography, Rudolph Fisher, 1897–1934," biographical sketch prepared for the Schomberg Collection of Negro Literature, May 9, 1951, Fisher papers, James Weldon Johnson Collection, Yale University Library.

56 From an interview with Brown, July 15, 1965; LeRoi Jones, "Philistinism and the Negro Writer," Herbert Hill (ed.), *Anger and Beyond: The Negro Writer in the United States* (New York: Harper & Row, Publishers, 1966), p. 52.

When Brown wrote a poem it was very often about a person he had met and liked. He was, among other things, a folklorist—a folklorist who recorded the lore of his people in poetry. The result was that his characters emerge from his poems as concrete individuals. Gone are the abstractions that haunted the pages of Charles W. Chesnutt and Du Bois, gone even the innocents and con men of Fisher's work. Once Brown met an old woman of Virginia who was about to die alone:

> Boy that she suckled—
>   How should he know,
> Hiding in city holes,
>   "Sniffing the 'snow' "?
>
> And how should the news
>   Pierce Harlem's din,
> To reach her baby gal,
>   Sodden with gin?[57]

At another time, Brown's students brought a vagabond guitarist to his office. The guitarist became the singer of Brown's version of "When de Saints Go Ma'ching Home":

> Deep the bass would rumble while
>   the treble scattered high,
> For all the world like heavy feet
>   a-trompin' toward the sky.
>   . . .

There'd be—so ran his dream:

> "Ole Deacon Zachary
> With de asthmy in his chest
> A-puffin' an' a-wheezin'
> Up de golden stair.
> Wid de badges of his lodges
> Strung across his heavin' chest
> An' de hoggrease jes' shinin'
> In his coal black hair. . . .[58]

---

[57] Sterling Brown, "Maumee Ruth," *Southern Road* (New York: Harcourt, Brace & Co., 1932), pp. 10–11.

[58] Sterling Brown, "When de Saints Go Ma'ching Home," *Southern Road* (New York: Harcourt, Brace & Co., 1932), pp. 12–18.

Deacon Zachary is no saint—not a disembodied Christ-like saint, anyway. He is hardly the man to redeem civilization. He is just a little puffed-up and pompous. But he is human and we like him. Brown did, too.

Brown was never (sociologically speaking) any closer to the masses than was the Du Bois group or the other Renaissance writers. His whole career has been devoted to teaching English in college. If we speak in psychological terms, however, there is a world of difference between the Du Bois group and Brown. The trend of the Renaissance was always to decrease the psychological distance between the writer and the common man of his race. It was less a case of the writer becoming common than of the common man emerging as a distinct individual. The race ceased to be a vast category and became people—or, one might say, the race tended to disappear leaving only individuals. The category "race" (with all its racial traits) as a barrier between the writer and the black masses began to dissolve. And, as the barrier began to fall, it became more and more possible to put the experience of the people into the form of art. The result, when Sterling Brown turned to protest poetry, was protest from the angle of vision of the low-down looking up, not the distant race leader looking paternally down. The result, also, was poetry full of heartache and trouble and indignation that was stronger for the absence of the self-righteous superiority that ran through the Christ-like mythology.

> O Ma Rainey,
> Li'l an' low,
> Sing us 'bout de hard luck
> Roun' our do':
> Sing us 'bout de lonesome road
> We mus' go. . . .[59]

It is fitting that Langston Hughes should have written the manifesto for freedom of expression that appeared in the 1926 *Nation*. It was Hughes, more than any other, perhaps, who injected the spirit of the blues into the literature of the Renaissance. In 1958 he recalled his introduction to the blues 50 years in the past. He

---

[59] Sterling Brown, "Ma Rainey," B. A. Botkin (ed.), *Folk-Say: A Regional Miscellany, 1930* (Norman, Okla.: University of Oklahoma Press, 1930), p. 277.

heard them first on Independence Avenue in Kansas City, then on Chicago's State Street, then "Harlem in the twenties with J. P. and J. C. Johnson and Fats and Willie the Lion and Nappy playing piano—with the blues running all up and down the keyboard through the ragtime and the jazz. House-rent party cards. I wrote *The Weary Blues:*"

> Droning a drowsy syncopated tune,
> Rocking back and forth to a mellow croon,
> I heard a Negro play.
>
> . . .
>
> I heard that Negro sing that old piano moan—
>
> "Ain't got nobody in all this world,
> Ain't got nobody but ma self.
> I's gwine to quit ma frownin'
> And put my troubles on the shelf." [60]

Langston Hughes was not himself of the lower class, at least not as it is reckoned among Negroes. It is true that as a boy he knew poverty, was from a broken home, and his mother at times made her living as a waitress. On the other hand, his mother had a college education, and his grandmother's memories went back to her marriage with Sheridan Leary, one of John Brown's men at Harpers Ferry. Her second marriage had been to the brother of John Mercer Langston, congressman from Virginia during Reconstruction. So an air of tradition and pride had permeated the atmosphere of Langston Hughes's boyhood home in Lawrence, Kansas.

Hughes moved to Cleveland with his mother in time to attend a rather good high school, and to know a wonderful English teacher who discovered Carl Sandburg for the boy; also Amy Lowell, Vachel Lindsay, and Edgar Lee Masters. At the age of 14, Hughes was already something of a poet in the Sandburg tradition:

> The mills
> That grind and grind,
>
> . . .

---

[60] Copyright 1926 by Alfred A. Knopf, Inc. and renewed 1954 by Langston Hughes. Reprinted from *Selected Poems*, by Langston Hughes, by permission of the publisher.

> They belch red fire.
> The mills—
> Grinding new steel,
> Old men.[61]

As a freshman in high school Hughes worked behind a soda
fountain and, for the first time, really came into contact with the
migrants from the South. It was, according to his later recollection,
love at first sight: "They seemed to me like the gayest and bravest
people possible—these Negroes from the Southern ghettos—facing
tremendous odds, working and laughing and trying to get somewhere in the world." [62]

When Hughes was 20 and a student at Columbia University
the wanderlust caught up with him. In his autobiography he recorded his adventures on a tramp steamer to Africa, his life in
Paris, his attempts finally to get a scholarship to Howard University in Washington. By that time he had become widely known
for his poems in *The Crisis* and in *Opportunity*. But no scholarship. He took a job in a Washington laundry and became quite
bitter toward the Negro social elite, Howard, and upper class
"culture." His experience made his identification with the masses
that much stronger. He became a poet of the masses. The southern
atmosphere of Washington's Seventh Street inspired him to try
to write poems—"poems like the songs they sang on Seventh Street
—gay songs, because you couldn't help being sad sometimes. But
gay or sad, you kept on living and you kept on going. Their songs—
those of Seventh Street—had the pulse beat of the people who
keep on going." [63]

So Langston Hughes decided to sing the song of the black
masses. He was not a great poet; at times he sang with but in-
different success. But at times he managed to capture the spirit of
the blues—the realism, the strength:

> Well, son, I'll tell you:
> Life for me ain't been no crystal stair.
> It's had tacks in it,
> And splinters,

---

[61] Hughes, *The Big Sea, op. cit.*, p. 29.
[62] *Ibid.*, p. 55.
[63] *Ibid.*, p. 209.

And boards torn up,
And places with no carpet on the floor—
Bare.
But all the time
I's been a'climbin' on.[64]

. . .

This poem sums up Hughes's philosophy. It was nonideological and nonintellectual. It was a mood stripped bare of all nonessentials. As a young man he had read Schopenhauer and Nietzsche; he was familiar with various socialist publications and once listened to Eugene Debs. None of these affected him greatly. He seems to have been immune to doctrine. This was an aspect of his character that disturbed the Russians whom Hughes came to know during his trip to their country in 1932. They asked him why he did not join the Party. His answer, far from being cast on an ideological plane, was that in Russia jazz was taboo: "It's my music," he told them, "and I wouldn't give up jazz for a world revolution."[65]

Hughes did not, in his published works, attempt the kind of self-analysis that is associated with Nella Larsen and Wallace Thurman. No shadow of moodiness crosses the pages of his two autobiographies. This suggests a lack of profundity (and that was probably the case); it also suggests that he needed to make no search for identity; that he felt complete in himself and in his identification with the masses. In adopting the spirit of the blues, moreover, he was accepting reality in a way that did not (as he interpreted them) permit despair or self-pity:

Homesick blues, Lawd,
'S a terrible thing to have.
Homesick blues is
A terrible thing to have.
To keep from cryin'
I opens my mouth an' laughs.[66]

---

64 "Mother to Son." Copyright 1926 by Alfred A. Knopf, Inc. and renewed 1954 by Langston Hughes. Reprinted from *Selected Poems*, by Langston Hughes, by permission of the publisher.

65 Langston Hughes, *I Wonder as I Wander: An Autobiographical Journey* (New York: Rinehart & Co., 1956), p. 122.

66 "Homesick Blues," from *The Dream Keeper*, by Langston Hughes. Copyright 1932 by Alfred A. Knopf, Inc. and renewed 1960 by Langston Hughes. Reprinted by permission of the publisher.

Hughes wrote only one novel, *Not without Laughter* (1930). It avoids penetration being satisfied with moods. There is a mood of bitterness towards white people. There is a mood of rebellion against the "Uncle Tom" Negro. But, paradoxically, the strongest character of the book, Aunt Hagar (the hero's grandmother), is just such a person. Born in slavery, strong in her Christianity, she believes in the Christ-like virtues: "Honey, don't talk that way," she told her rebellious daughter, Harriet, "It ain't Christian, chile. If you don't like 'em, pray for 'em."[67]

This seeming paradox, this ability to view the slave generation and its supposed submissiveness in diametrically opposed ways, gets us to the core of what the blues writers were trying to say. The Renaissance writers had become thoroughly alienated from white society and its *mores*. The alienation was doubly directed against those who had passively submitted to the whites—they were the race's traitors. In *Not without Laughter* the alienation and fury were characterized by the hero's wayward (but loved) aunt, Harriet. It was Harriet who proclaimed her hatred for the whites and her disgust for the "Uncle Toms." She manifests the trend toward alienation that turned the Christ-like image into the "Uncle Tom" stereotype. And Hughes was clearly in deep sympathy with Harriet—she was a part of him. But Hughes's greatest sympathy was reserved for Aunt Hagar. As he develops her character it is not the alienated part of him that is speaking—it is another part, admiring what Harriet could only reject. The side of Hughes that admired Hagar needs to be considered. Hagar was not set up as a paragon, an ideal that will save humanity. The mythology of the Christ-like Negro has been cast aside by the alienation—there are no utopias, nor are there virtuous ones to lead us there. But there is in Hagar the everyday confrontation with reality; a confrontation that was made with a grace that Hughes had to admire. Seen in this light, Hagar was not submissive to the white man any more than she was a savior of mankind. Though she raised the white man's children, scrubbed his floors, did his laundry, she never submitted to him; never allowed him to turn her from her ideals and her faith. Though he controlled her body he could not enslave her heart and mind. Hughes could not believe in her

---

[67] Langston Hughes, *Not without Laughter* (New York: Alfred A. Knopf, 1930), pp. 46, 76.

God, but he could admire her courage and her faith. She had, after all, made the best use of what tools and knowledge she possessed in her confrontation with life, and she had refused to be borne down. She had overcome—not by transcending herself into a state of perfection as Du Bois would wish, but by plugging away.

When the Renaissance revolted against it the Christ-like mythology simply evaporated leaving nothing, no racial essence, no mission. Identity and meaning could no longer depend on myth. But the revolt cleared the air. If they so wished, the writers could begin to look at the Negro masses with something like objectivity. When they turned their attention in that direction they heard the blues come wafting up to them—out of their record machines, out of the cabarets and speakeasies. The masses did have a lesson for those who would listen: they said that the singers of their songs were struggling human beings, and were to be accepted as such.

So when Hughes looked at Hagar he looked through the medium of the blues and saw neither sycophant nor saint. This was a new way of seeing the Negro past, and it was something upon which a new cultural tradition could be built. It was to be, in fact, the starting point for both Ralph Ellison and James Baldwin. Beyond this, however, it had another significance for the future. It marked a long, long step away from Du Bois's humanism—the demand he made for perfection through self-transcendence. The "talented tenth" was replaced by the man on the street as the racial ideal. The humanist pull, that operated so strongly on Du Bois's generation, was no longer present to work against the pull of the emotional and the irrational.

When the Negro author was beginning to come of age in the early 1920's, a blithe young spirit could frequently be seen on the streets of Harlem buttonholing startled passersby and measuring their cranium capacities with tape measure and calipers. No record exists to tell us how well their Christ-like natures bore up under this new indignity, we do know that it helped Dr. Franz Boas collect his cephalic indices, and it helped his favorite student work her way through graduate school at Columbia University.

Zora Neale Hurston was a rare plant whose struggle toward the sun had its roots in the impoverished soil of a small Negro community near Jacksonville, Florida. Rare because the soil was bitter and the struggle hard. Her father had been an itinerant preacher

—one of those who had learned the secret of moving the hearts of his listeners toward God while moving their offerings toward the collection plate. He had kept his wife poor and burdened with children, while he used his power to capture his female listeners' minds as the key by which he gained access to their beds. Incessant bickering was the mark of the Hurston household until Zora Neale's mother died. Zora Neale had never received her father's love, always she had been her mother's child. Her father had bowed resignedly to the white man's ways. Her mother encouraged rebellion and hope: ". . . jump at de sun."[68]

Zora Neale was her mother's child—she aimed at the sun. She was sassy and rebellious; her father said she would hang. Among the neighborhood children she was leader and instigator; but she could also at times hide away by herself, overcome by a "cosmic loneliness." At 15, Zora Neale became lady's maid to a singer. That was more pleasant than home, but she was aiming at the sun, and that meant school; it meant high school in Baltimore and, after that, Howard University. Then it was Barnard College where she became the "sacred cow" of the social set. Finally, it was Columbia University because Franz Boas had gotten her a scholarship.

Zora Neale Hurston's autobiography is free of self-pity and self-doubt. Her mind (a better one than that of Hughes) ranged freely and without agony. "I take no refuge from myself in bitterness," she wrote. "To me, bitterness is the under-arm odor of wishful weakness. It is the graceless acknowledgement of defeat. . . . I am in the struggle with the sword in my hands, and I don't intend to run until you run me." This was Zora Neal's personality: free of cant, free of recrimination, free of apathy.[69]

All this is not to say that Zora Neale Hurston was unmindful or unmarked by the pain of her childhood years—years spent as one of the lowly. When she turned to writing her first novel. *Jonah's Gourd Vine* (1934), those were the years of her life that she drew upon. The novel is a recapitulation of her early life in Florida. It is peopled by the proletariat. No whites, no upper class Negroes enter into it. Of special interest is her attitude toward her people—her race and class. She neither idealized nor scorned

---

68 Zora Neale Hurston, *Dust Tracks on a Road: An Autobiography* (Philadelphia: J. B. Lippincott Co., 1942), p. 29.

69 *Ibid.*, p. 228.

them. At times she described actions that she reprobated—the backbiting among her father's flock, for instance. But it is description; it is clinical; there is no moral indignation, no wrath. She was telling about the world as it was—her world, and also *the* world. *The* world because there is no ingroup feeling about it. She does not distinguish between "us" and "they." She is not split into two parts: one part identifying herself with her race, the other part rejecting it. She was never split apart by the conflict between the two worlds of white and black. She was black— that was her world.

Jonah's Gourd Vine is basically the story of Zora Neale's father and his journey through life. It takes him from the beginning when he was the son of a Virginia sharecropper to the end, when he was a preacher somewhat fallen from respectability because of his numerous illicit love affairs. The story ends when her father was struck down by a railroad train. There is absolutely no moralizing about the end, nor is there a moral implicit in the story. The author was saying only that this is the road of life; it begins when it begins and ends when it ends. One does one's best while traveling it, but do not try to get a lesson out of it; do not search for a meaning where there is none. The denouement with the railroad train was a matter of pure chance, it made no sense, it meant nothing more than the end.

VII

Another country

The 1930's marked a crisis in Negro thought in the sense that the forces that had been at work to destroy the old consensus—the Christ-like mythology—had by then completed their work. The sociological imagination reigned supreme among the emerging race leaders. In the context of the sociological imagination the irrational, racist elements of the Christ-like mythology had no place. The humanist element in that mythology had been transformed from the idea of perfection to the idea of the integrated personality, and with this came the shift from the ideal of the individual lifting himself above society to the idea of the individual adjusting himself to society. It was the sociological imagination that was to have its day in the 1930's as the social scientists moved into the position of potential leadership, and as the blues writers, pushed by the logic of the depression, turned to social protest in the tradition of economic radicalism. But the significant thing about this period for the sociological imagination was that though it called for personal adjustment, assimilation, and integration, it wanted none of these things with the capitalist social structure. The social scientists went beyond civil rights to fundamental social change. Their program was tied up with the Renaissance movement toward identification with the black proletariat. The social scientists began to think of themselves less as middle-class professionals than as spokesmen for the proletariat. The Christ-like mythology had done its work well in one regard—it had left an indelible impression on the Negro mind that American civilization, as it stands, is a rather hopeless affair. The depression simply reinforced the impression. The problems of the thirties—because the sociological imagination was supreme—were approached from within the context of science. That is to say, the approach was rationalistic. But when the rationalistic approach was blocked at every turn during the decade the other heritage left by the Negro Renaissance emerged to become dominant—the turn inward, the idealization of the masses, the rejection of a rationalistic idea of mission. From these elements a new ideology began, in the 1940's and 1950's to emerge; an ideology free of the rationalism that humanism had imposed on the Christ-like mythology.

II

The Great Depression brought incredible hardship for the Negro masses, always the first to be fired. Not yet organized in their new urban communities they fell prey to the further disorganizing effects of nationwide unemployment and inadequate relief programs. The pitifully threadbare and hopeless antique furnishings of families being dispossessed from their dismal tenement flats began to clutter the ghetto streets. Such sights became the rallying points for black nationalist street orators and Communist party agitators. Instead of sending in relief the white power structure sent in the police. The pattern for the ghetto was set: desperation checked by police power. The law became the enemy.

Into the void swarmed the pedlars of dreams. The numbers racketeers, the pushers of dope, the panderers, the hustlers swarmed in. Money equals status, so these parasites got the status. Small boys emulated them. The police took their cut; the white community ignored it all.

Other pedlars of dreams were abroad. When reality gets too cruel people have a way of turning their thoughts to visions of another, better world. It was a time for saviors. In the Eden Street Baptist Church of Baltimore there emerged the prophet Samuel Morris, whose title "Father Jehova" reflected the fact that he was immersed in the "supreme spirit." In Washington, D.C., John Hickerson, pastor of the "Church of the Living God," came to the hair-raising conclusion that his wife was God. Bishop Charles Manuel ("Daddy") Grace organized 50 branches of his House of Prayer for the worship of himself. "Never mind about God," he warned, "Grace has given God a vacation, and since God is on His vacation, don't worry Him. . . . If you sin against God, Grace can save you, but if you sin against Grace, God cannot save you." Grace's organizations were in constant competition with each other to see which could raise the most money for Grace. Better than that, however, was the special dispensation given Prophet F. S. Cherry, to whom God had given exclusive right to profanity.[1]

The greatest of these was Father Divine, the man people called God. Divine's (George Baker) apprenticeship in his chosen field was long and trying. When a child of 9 or 10 in the Savannah River rice plantation area, he and his people were visited one night by a white man proclaiming himself Christ and them his chosen people. Apparently the white man, before jailed, had the community pretty well stirred up; at least the seed was planted in the young mind of George Baker. The South had a way of sending its Messiahs off to prison or institutions for the insane, so for Baker it was often touch and go as he plied his trade. Just before the turn of the century he heralded himself as "The Son of Righteousness" and opened a meetinghouse in which he told of his supernatural powers. This earned him six months on the chain gang. In 1913, during a return visit to Georgia as "The Messenger," he persuaded many that he was God. He left one jump ahead of the authorities.

Divine next turned up in the small Long Island community of Sayville. There he opened a free employment agency and when the destitute came he fed and clothed them. In 1932, after 10 years in the rather tolerant Sayville, he was forced to remove his operations to Harlem, a community now sunk in the mire of depression.

The story is told of an ancient black hag living in the gutters of Newark, New Jersey, whose stomach burned from drink, who slept in alleys and who robbed garbage cans for her sustenance. Divine put her in charge of a restaurant (15 cents a meal), then a dormitory for homeless old women, then, within 19 months, nine dormitory extensions, a fleet of automobiles and buses.

---

[1] See Robert A. Parker, *The Incredible Messiah: The Deification of Father Divine* (Boston: Little, Brown and Co., 1937), pp. 94 ff; and Arthur Huff Fausett, *Black Gods of the Metropolis: Negro Religious Cults of the Urban North* (Philadelphia: University of Pennsylvania Press, 1944), pp. 25–32.

Divine, Grace, and the others, were simply filling a leadership void left by the inability or the unwillingness of the middle class to reach the masses. However much the established churches might have cast their venom at the head of Divine they did nothing to fill the void. There were a very few exceptions to this. Adam Clayton Powell, Sr., pastor of Harlem's largest Baptist church set up a free food kitchen that remained open until mid-1931. But when he suggested the idea of a community house in Harlem to be financed by the Baptist denomination his colleagues accused him of wanting to dilute Baptist doctrine. The idea was voted down 92 to 8.[2]

The story of the National Association for the Advancement of Colored People during the decade is the story of how the middle-class militants failed to fill the void. It is also the story of the frustration of the sociological imagination in its attempts to work out a solution. Success, by its criteria, would have been a mass movement of the proletariat to effect a radical, but thoroughly rational, restructuring of the American economy. Failure left the way clear for less-rational movements.

Throughout the better part of the decade the NAACP found itself in the throes of a crisis in leadership. Du Bois had been shunted aside (1934) to a professorship at Atlanta University for his unyielding opposition to the tight control and halfhearted policies of the small group that ran the organization. To him the times cried out for the Negro to break free from dying capitalism and decadent American culture. The times called for separatism, economic and cultural. NAACP policy called for assimilation and no rocking of the economic boat. But times were perilous and traditional policy came under constant fire from those outside the Association. Under pressure, the NAACP leadership decided on a reevaluation of its policies. An economist, Abram L. Harris of Howard University, was called in to recommend a new program. He did, and for a brief moment it looked as if the Association would meet the challenge.

The crisis within the NAACP had been set off by Du Bois's announcement of new policy in the pages of *The Crisis*. As the crisis

---

2 Adam Clayton Powell, Sr., *Against the Tide: An Autobiography* (New York: Richard Smith, 1938), pp. 208–09.

gathered momentum Association president, Joel E. Spingarn, called for a meeting of the race's younger intellectuals to be held at his country estate for three days in August, 1933. Tents were put up on the lawn for the sociologists, economists, lawyers, and others who assembled for debate. Ira De A. Reid, sociologist and chief researcher for the National Urban League was there. He had replaced Charles S. Johnson at the Urban League but would soon be going to Atlanta University. Ralph Bunche, head of Howard University's political science department, was there. Abram L. Harris, Howard University economist, Charles H. Houston, vice dean of the Howard University law school, E. Franklin Frazier, Howard University sociologist—all were there and soon in hot debate. There was general excitement and expectation that the time had come for a new departure. Walter White, William Pickens, and Roy Wilkins, the Association's executives, took the brunt of a three-day attack. The executives were for civil rights. Du Bois, who hovered always near the center of debate, was all for civil rights, but was tired of knocking on the white man's door only to be kicked in the face. Here were the two alternatives, what did the younger generation think of them?

The younger generation thought very little of them. In fact, the younger generation made an important break with the past. Always before the black man had made his appeal to the white man's conscience. Always it had been a call for moral reform, or, at the very least, for understanding. There was no divergence on this between Du Bois and the executives. They asked only that the white man live up to his ideals—the ideals found in the country's historic documents—the Declaration of Independence, the Bill of Rights. This was the civil rights approach. Up the Hudson River on the manicured lawns of the Spingarn estate the younger generation told the older men that the national ideals were irrelevant. They told the old-line fighters that the fight had been an exercise in futility. They said that economic self-interest comes first in the real world, not ideals. They pointed out that in the present economic system most of the nation's economic pie goes to the fortunate few and that the masses get only the crumbs. It is only through the exercise of power that the process might be reversed; the power of the capitalists and their middle-class allies would have to be met by the power of the masses. The Negro must see himself in terms of economic class not in terms of race. To the younger men it was economic reorganization, not civil rights, that was the goal; the means was to be massed power.[3]

The effect of the debate at the Second Amenia Conference, as the meeting came to be known, was to introduce a hard realism into the picture. The whole thrust of the sociological imagination was summed up in the rejection of the moral issue. There is no right or wrong, good or bad, in the sociological outlook, only social forces. In saying that economic self-interest should be accepted as the basis for the Negro's movement to gain power the sociological imagination was asking that the Negro become exactly like the hated white man, that he give up all pretentions of being better. In asking that the Negro do this the young intellectuals were asking that the Negro forget his whole experience in America; more than that, it was asking the Negro to accept the fact that his American experience has been utterly devoid of meaning. This was hard realism, but it was hardly realistic.

On its part, the NAACP procrastinated for a year before allowing itself to confront the issues raised at the Second Amenia Conference. Or, rather, there were certain difficulties that the Association had to face which the younger generation of intellectuals, less practised in running an organization, did not grasp. First, there was the problem of the law. The younger men wanted integration and would brook no compromise on the matter. But the Association lawyers could only work within a system of law as they found it, and there was nothing in the American system of law that made integration a right. For years the lawyers had been working for equal accommodations under the *Plessy* v. *Ferguson* "separate but equal" doctrine (1896). Under this doctrine the segregated "Jim Crow" facilities for Negroes were legal if they were equal to the corresponding facilities provided for whites. Of course, they never were. Throughout the South rest rooms were labeled "white ladies," "white men," "negroes." Railroads would provide one car of a train for Negroes, usually the most dilapi-

---

[3] E. Franklin Frazier, "The Status of the Negro in the American Social Order," *Journal of Negro Education*, Vol. 4 (July, 1935), pp. 293–307; Ralph J. Bunche, "A Critical Analysis of the Tactics and Programs of Minority Groups," *Journal of Negro Education*, Vol. 4 (July, 1935), pp. 308–20; Louis L. Redding to Roy Wilkins, September 2, 1933, Joel E. Spingarn papers, Moorland Collection, Howard University Library; Ira De A. Reid to Joel E. Spingarn, September 2, 1933, Spingarn papers.

dated. Most appalling were the schools. An NAACP report covering 11 southern states in the year 1930 showed that 82.6 percent of
all Negro schools were of the one- or two-teacher type. The median
teacher of the one-teacher schools (63.8 percent of the Negro
schools) received an annual salary of $314. For this sum she taught
six months. Her education covered about two years and six months
above elementary school. The average expenditure per pupil per
year for all schools throughout the United States was $87.22; the
11 southern states expended $12.57 on each Negro pupil per year.
The figure for Mississippi was $5.45.[4]

Obviously segregated facilities were an intolerable burden for
the Negro to bear. But how carry out the legal fight? The logical
answer was integration, but that was not the legal answer. The
14th Amendment, as interpreted by the courts, had two loopholes
through which racial discrimination might enter: first, it restrained states, but not individuals, from discrimination; second,
the provision for equality of rights, of life, liberty, and property,
did not cover "social rights"—the right to intermingle with the
rest of the population. This meant that such "individuals" as railroads had the right to discriminate; it also meant that states could
segregate if the facilities were kept equal. The NAACP lawyers
therefore had no body of law to support a fight for integration, or,
in large areas, for equal facilities.

For years the NAACP had maintained a publicity campaign
against the terrible school conditions with no results. On the local
level Association branches had lawyers working on the problem,
with no results. So, in 1932, Nathan R. Margold, head of the Association's legal defense committee, announced a "bold" new program: fight inferior facilities by attacking the principle of "separate but equal" on the grounds that never in practice had that
principle worked. On the face of it this was purely a pragmatic
approach. No longer, said Margold, would the "separate but
equal" doctrine be fought on the basis of principle, that is, on
the basis that it infringes on the Negro's rights as citizen and
human being. Margold was exactly following the philosophy ar-
ticulated by Oliver Wendell Holmes that law is not abstract prin-

---

4 "Notes on Negro Schools," NAACP Administrative File, General Correspondence, NAACP papers, Library of Congress.

ciple, it is what the courts decide. Margold's pragmatism was compounded by his statement that the aim was not desegregated facilities but equality of facilities. He was going to fight for "separate but equal" by threatening a fight for desegregation. The idea of fighting for "separate but equal" by fighting against it might worry some nonlegal minds, but it worked. The new legal program, by winning a series of cases on the basis that separate facilities are inherently unequal, built up, over a period of years extending through the 1940's, the legal precedents from which to attack successfully segregation itself. Philosophies and ideologies were one thing, the logic of the law quite another.[5]

The second difficulty confronting organized Negro leadership was that of money. In July, 1967, after having just declared whites unwelcome in their organization, the Congress of Racial Equality received a $175,000 grant from the Ford Foundation. The financial report of Martin Luther King's Southern Christian Leadership Conference states cash received between September 1, 1964 and June 30, 1965 was $1,582,792.39. Throughout the 1930's the NAACP limped along on a budget of less than $50,000 a year. Between 1931 and 1936 the salaries of the national staff were cut three times. Field Secretary William Pickens forlornly asked that he at least be paid the salary he had received his first year with the Association, 15 years before. A desperate plea to the Budget Committee from Walter White was alone able to save Assistant Secretary Roy Wilkins's salary from being halved. The entire national staff of 16 (including 10 office secretaries and 1 janitor) was working a seven-day week. In 1933 they were able to count 11 donors who gave $200 or more (none above $1,000). Only two funds, The Christian Social Justice Fund and the New York Foundation, could be persuaded to give anything.[6]

---

[5] Nathan R. Margold, address to 23rd Annual Conference of the NAACP, Washington, May 30, 1932, NAACP Administrative File, Annual Conferences, NAACP papers, Library of Congress.

[6] *Newsweek*, July 24, 1967, 27; "Annual Report, Dr. Martin Luther King, Jr.," delivered at SCLC's Ninth Annual National Convention, Birmingham, Alabama, August 11, 1965; William Pickens to Walter White, March 19, 1935, NAACP, Board of Directors Correspondence: Budget Committee, 1935, NAACP papers, Library of Congress; "Report of Committee on Budget for Fiscal Year Beginning January 1, 1933 and Ending December 31, 1933," NAACP Board of Directors Correspondence: Budget Committee 1933, NAACP papers, Library of Congress; Walter White to Mark S. Knapp, August 1, 1933, NAACP Administrative File, Financial, General, NAACP papers, Library of Congress.

The NAACP national staff, working to exhaustion and on the verge of personal privation, was publishing a magazine (*The Crisis*), organizing a legal campaign against separate facilities, conducting a campaign of propaganda and lobbying for the Costigan-Wagner antilynching bill in Congress, organizing annual conferences, organizing NAACP branches throughout the country, carrying on a campaign against discrimination by the New Deal, and trying to dig up money with which to function. In July, 1934, Secretary White began trying to pry loose some money from the newly opened Rackham Fund of Ann Arbor, Michigan. Many letters and several interviews were expended on the amiable and sympathetic Dr. Mark S. Knapp, who was in charge of the fund. In desperation White described to Knapp the horrors of lynching: "Having had the experience of investigating forty-one lynchings and eight race riots, many of them exceedingly bestial, I thought I was almost immune to further shocks. The Mariana lynching, however, so sickened me that I was actually ill for several days." The money went to the Detroit Museum of Arts.[7]

Most of the Association's operating expenses came from the poor themselves in the form of members dues and donations. During the depression it was not easy for the poor to give. The Akron, Ohio, branch wrote to the national office that as much as they would like to contribute to the legal defense fund, they could not. Eighty-five percent of Akron's Negroes were on charity.[8]

So, while the young intellectuals were calling on the Association to organize the vast black proletariat and lead them on to a structural transformation of American society, Walter White must have felt that he was moving in molasses; to overcome the most rudimentary obstacles took extraordinary exertion. Lynching in the United States over the years had been steadily diminishing from a peak of over 250 in 1894 to 10 in 1929. Then in the early depression years there seemed to be a recrudescence of the evil— 28 men were lynched in 1933. White, who, because of his white skin, had been sent to investigate many lynchings, had developed

---

[7] Walter White to Dr. Mark S. Knapp, November 27, 1934, NAACP Administrative File, Financial, General, NAACP papers, Library of Congress; Ira W. Jayne to Walter White, November 5, 1934, NAACP Administrative File.

[8] Elmer M. Lancaster to James W. Johnson, January 20, 1935, NAACP Administrative File, Financial, General, NAACP papers, Library of Congress.

a horror reaction to them. To stop lynchings became almost an obsession with him. The Association attacked the problem on two fronts. It tried to get legislation passed specifically outlawing lynching, and it tried to get the Justice Department to prosecute lynchers under existing laws. The hope for legislation rested with the Costigan-Wagner antilynching bill, first introduced in 1933. White made superhuman efforts. He got the backing of church, labor, women's, civil rights, fraternal, professional, and other organizations with a membership that totaled 53,720,593. Some years this tremendous backing was not even enough to get the bill out of the southern-dominated House committees. White awoke to the fact that his numerous pleas to the President were not getting by the presidential secretary, Marvin McIntyre. Finally, Mrs. Roosevelt got White an interview with the President himself. Nothing came of it—Roosevelt told White he dared not alienate his party's southern leadership. In 1938, a seven-week Senate filibuster killed the antilynching bill for all time.[9]

Equally frustrating was the attempt to get the Justice Department to act. In August of 1933, Alabama sheriff's deputies turned three boys accused of murder over to 12 armed men to be riddled with bullets. Two died, one was critically wounded. Charles Houston, NAACP Special Counsel, joined with members of the Civil Liberties Union, the International Labor Defense, and others in arranging an interview with someone in the Justice Department. All arrived at the appointed time only to find their Justice Department official out of town. Their outraged protests brought Attorney General Homer Cummings himself to the scene. Cummings agreed to study a brief of the case that Houston proposed to write. Houston delivered the brief on October 13. Four months came and went with no word from Cummings. When Houston finally called in he was told that the Justice Department had long ago decided it had no jurisdiction. On October 26, 1934, Claude Neal was kidnapped from jail in Brewton, Alabama, by a mob. He was taken across the state line into Florida and lynched. Houston, feeling that now he had an airtight case of a crime punishable under the kidnapping statutes, began to prepare his brief. The amended Lindbergh Act, generaled through Congress with

9 See Walter White, *A Man Called White: The Autobiography of Walter White* (New York: The Viking Press, Inc., 1948).

the aid of Cummings himself, stated that the federal government should have jurisdiction to prosecute in interstate kidnappings where the victim was held for "reward, ransom, or otherwise." This time Cummings was too fast for Houston. Before the NAACP counsel could act the Justice Department issued a statement that the Claude Neal case did not come under the meaning of the law— "otherwise" did not include lynching. In the United States lynching was lawful, and, apparently, supported by the government from the local sheriff's deputy to the U.S. Justice Department.[10]

Oppression had worked its way into the nooks and crannies of American institutions becoming the cement of a way of life. To stand against it, and to do it with a tiny staff and minuscule budget, was a job that soon made for a degree of cynicism. Field Secretary William Pickens, who in his organizing activities across the country was constantly confronted by antagonistic whites ("Once in a long while, when they attempt a smile, it is more terrible still,—a gorgon-like mockery,—strange, unbecoming."), advised White emphatically that "The Negro will get only what he *takes*. . . ." In a similar frame of mind Charles Houston wrote White: "I don't think one could expect a solution from the Democratic or Republican party. With all due respect we have not worked out a solution, nor has any of the other organizations best known in the field. . . . Nothing but the Socialists and Communists [are] left; or perhaps I am cockeyed." A few weeks later Houston had occasion to tell White that, "All along I've been telling you that your President [Roosevelt] had no real courage and that he would chisel in a pinch."[11]

Staggering from crisis to crisis, drunkenly running just to stay even, the Association executives had little time to ponder philosophies of reform. They lived at a level where pragmatism (opportunism, if one likes) was imposed on them. The question they had to ask was what would work in a given situation, any questions beyond that were futile. In this way the NAACP became an organization without ideology.

---

10 See NAACP, *Memorandum Brief for the Attorney General of the United States,* New York, November, 1933; Charles H. Houston, "Justice for All," manuscript, December 19, 1934, NAACP papers, Library of Congress.

11 William Pickens to The Gang, May 5, 1932, NAACP Administrative File: Special Correspondence, NAACP papers, Library of Congress; William Pickens to Walter White, July 28, 1932; Charles H. Houston to Walter White, May 23, 1935; Charles H. Houston to Walter White, July 3, 1935.

It was at this time that Du Bois began agitating for a new and unbelievably far-reaching program and for leaders in the Association who would carry it out. The struggle between Du Bois and White created bad blood all around. Then, when Du Bois finally resigned on June 11, 1934, there was widespread wrath throughout the branches. The rank and file of the Association were not too much concerned with abstract debate on the finer points of the integrated versus the segregated economy. They knew only that Du Bois had for years been their most militant and devoted champion.[12]

It was at this critical hour that the Association's Board of Directors decided to set up a committee, with Howard University economist Abram L. Harris as chairman, to create for it a new program. This was July 9, 1934. By mid-September, Harris had his report ready. Harris was one of the younger generation intellectuals who had held forth at the Second Amenia Conference; his report embodied the thought of that group.[13]

Harris began with a statement that the "principles of 18th-century liberalism" on which the Association program had always been based are outdated. The old philosophy, he wrote, dealt only with political rights, coupling those with economic freedom. That was fine in its time, but the new age of industrial capitalism, he thought, has put the nation's wealth into the hands of the few leaving the masses propertyless and powerless. Civil rights for the Negro will do little good because even complete political and social equality will leave the masses of Negroes—industrial labor all—propertyless and destitute.[14]

From that statement of premises Harris went on to outline a fundamental program for economic change based on the proposition that the Negro masses must identify themselves with the masses of white workers in a class struggle with the capitalist class. He called for collaboration with the trade union movement, a cooperative movement among Negroes based on the experiences of

---

12 William Pickens to Walter White, June 8, 1934, NAACP Administrative File: Special Correspondence, NAACP papers, Library of Congress; William Pickens to Walter White, June 15, 1934; William Pickens to Roy Wilkins, June 24, 1934.

13 Committee on Plan and Program of the Association and the Future of *The Crisis*, "Preliminary Report," NAACP Board of Director File, NAACP papers, Library of Congress.

14 *Ibid.*, pp. 2–3.

similar movements in Denmark, England, Russia, and Austria, and, most important, he called upon the various NAACP regional branches to create workers' councils. The workers' and farmers' councils—the heart of Harris' proposal—would be the agencies that would work to end racism in the unions, work to create the cooperative movement, and work to create a third party—a workers' party. They would be educational, political, and economic organs for the creation of a new and equitable society. The society he envisioned was one of complete racial integration.[15]

There is no evidence that Secretary White showed either shock or amusement when he received the report. He seems to have received it with the aplomb of a man who really did have several million dollars and hundreds of organizers for such a campaign. In any case, he got the gears of the bureaucracy (small as it was) to grinding. The report was duly mailed out to the various members of the Board of Directors for consideration. Some, like Joseph Prince Loud of Boston, rejected the idea of the NAACP getting in on the class struggle on the wrong side (all of the board members were distinctly middle class). Some, like Mary White Ovington, thoroughly approved of having the workers engage in a class struggle, but could not envision the NAACP as the organization to lead it. Most just shrugged it off as a dream. Other than Harris himself, there is no record of any enthusiasm for the program.[16]

The board began meetings in late September, 1934 to take up the report. On the 24th, the board approved it in principle. On October 8, the board specifically approved Harris' central idea— the workers' and farmers' councils. At the meeting of December 10, the board progressed to the point of approving the second key point of the report—that segregation per se should be fought in the area of transportation. To all outward signs the Board of Directors was complying with the recommendations as best a deliberative body might. But Harris must have seen something that lies hidden from the historical record; he resigned from the board. The gears of bureaucracy ground on. At the board meeting of

---

15 *Ibid.*, pp. 4 ff.

16 Joseph Prince Loud to Walter White, September 22, 1934, NAACP Board of Directors File, NAACP papers, Library of Congress; Mary White Ovington to Walter White, September 21, 1934; Daisey E. Lampkin to Walter White, September 22, 1934; Isadore Martin to Joel E. Spingarn, September 24, 1934; William H. Hastie to Walter White, September 24, 1934.

June 10, 1935, the idea of the workers' and farmers' councils was dropped from the program. From that point onward discussion of the new program ceased. But the last word had not been spoken, the mills of the gods grind slow. On December 9, 1935, the board met to consider a program for the coming year. Embodied in 12 points, the program was a simple restatement of what the Association had been doing for a decade, with an added vague reference to "Efforts, as outlined in the New Plan and Program [the Harris report] for a more specific, more sustained and better integrated program of activities by the branches." Such was the influence of the younger generation of intellectuals upon the Negroes' one functioning militant organization.[17]

Finding no home in the NAACP, the young intellectuals had to look elsewhere. Many of them participated in a conference held in May of 1935 at Howard University to discuss the economic crisis. Papers were read by Ralph Bunche, Abram Harris, E. Franklin Frazier, and others. The New Deal was attacked by Bunche as a compromise program between big business and the middle class to save capitalism from the chaos engendered by class war, the desperate situation of the Negro was discussed, spokesmen for the Socialists and the Communists were heard (apparently with more appreciation than was given the spokesman for the New Deal), and a decision was made to create a new organization capable of mobilizing the mass power of the race. The upshot was the National Negro Congress.[18]

The National Negro Congress would last but a few years; it would be big with promise and little with results. But during its life the Negro intellectuals had large hopes for it. It was to be an attempt to coordinate all of the Negro organizations with all their memberships into one vast, mass movement. At the organizing meeting held in Chicago, February 14 to 16, 1936, were delegates from churches, fraternal societies, trade unions, professional

17 "Minutes of the Special Meeting of the Board of Directors," September 25, 1934, NAACP Board of Directors File: Minutes of Meetings, NAACP papers, Library of Congress; "Minutes of the Meeting of the Board of Directors," October 8, 1934; "Minutes of the Meeting of the Board of Directors," March 11, 1934; "Minutes of the Meeting of the Board of Directors," June 10, 1935; "Minutes of the Meeting of the Board of Directors," December 9, 1935.

18 For the several addresses delivered at "The National Conference on the Economic Crisis of the Negro," May, 1935, see *Journal of Negro History*, Vol. 6 (1936).

groups, educational societies, business groups, and others. The dream was massed power. It was resolved that the Negro build a mass consumers' organization, that an independent working-class political party be supported, that a drive to get Negroes into the white labor unions be made, and that a powerful and inclusive civil rights organization be created.[19]

Ralph Bunche, who had helped organize the Howard University conference, was enthusiastic. He saw an end to the "crooked, reactionary and prostituted leadership that traditionally has misled the Negro." He saw the Congress' fundamental purpose as that of making the Negro conscious of his proletariat status and of leading him into the labor movement. Seeing a unity that probably did not exist, he said that no one doubted that the Negro's salvation lies in working-class unity and mass-pressure.[20]

But unity was not to be. Too many diverse groups with too many diversive philosophies were involved. John P. Davis, the national secretary, was a Communist; A. Philip Randolph, the president, was an old-line Negro militant from the early 1920's as well as the leading Negro labor unionist. Randolph made it clear at the 1937 meeting that he was in the camp of the moral reformers: "Be it also known that the Congress does not seek to change the American form of government, but rather to implement it with new and rugged morals and spiritual sinews to make its democratic traditions, forms and ideals more permanent and abiding as a living force." Randolph would, at the third meeting of the Congress, refuse to stand for reelection when he learned that Davis was getting most of his funds from the Communist party. As they watched the party get control and as they listened to the radical resolutions being passed at the several meetings, the conservative church and business groups withdrew. By the time of the 1940 meeting few besides party members remained.[21]

After the National Negro Congress faded from the picture dur-

---

19 Wilson Record, *The Negro and the Communist Party* (Chapel Hill, N.C.: University of North Carolina Press, 1951), pp. 153–56.

20 Ralph Bunche, "Triumph? or Fiasco?" *Race*, Vol. 1 (Summer, 1936), pp. 93–96.

21 A. Philip Randolph, "The Crisis of the Negro and the Constitution," in Second National Negro Congress, *Official Proceedings* (Washington, D.C., 1937), address to the Congress; Lester B. Granger, "The Negro Congress—Its Future," *Opportunity*, Vol. 18 (June, 1940), pp. 164–66; Record, *The Negro and the Communist Party, op. cit.*, p. 161.

ing World War II, several things had become apparent. The rationalist approach had failed. The depression had seemed to afford the best chance to get the class struggle under way and to make racial lines give way to class lines. With the lonely exception of the CIO, nothing of the sort had occurred. Labor unions remained, next to the churches, the most racially exclusive organizations in the country. Capitalism and the capitalist power structure had, with the help of the New Deal and the war, managed to survive. Labor emerged from the ordeal without its hoped for larger slice of the economic pie. For the intellectuals who had come of age during the 1930's all roads were blocked.[22]

III

The sociological imagination, blocked at every turn during the depression, had yet one more shock in store for it. Assimilation into American culture had always been its accepted goal. In the end this idea, too, had to be questioned. To sociologist E. Franklin Frazier, looking at the Negro middle class, assimilation, in practice, began to appear to lead to mimicry, to the aping of American society. Such Negroes, he came to believe, became "exaggerated" Americans—exaggerated in the sense that like other Americans they went after status, wealth, and power but, unable to get any of these, they had to make believe. "The black bourgeoisie," he was to write, "suffers from 'nothingness' because when Negroes attain middle-class status, their lives generally lose both content and significance." When the sociological imagination turned to the Negro lower class, as it did when Richard Wright wrote *Native Son*, it perceived something more terrible still—it perceived a monster.[23]

During the depression, when the intellectuals were observing things from the seclusion of their ivy-enclosed campuses, Richard Wright was walking the streets of Chicago observing things from

22 For an analysis of the national distribution of wealth after the New Deal and the War, see Gabriel Kolko, *Wealth and Power in America: An Analysis of Social Class and Income Distribution* (New York: Frederick A. Praeger, Inc., 1962).

23 E. Franklin Frazier, *Black Bourgeoisie: The Rise of a New Middle Class in the United States* (New York: Collier Books, 1962), p. 195.

the breadline. As he walked the streets or worked at odd jobs that came his way this Mississippi boy rubbed elbows with the flotsam and jetsam of the black ghetto. It was an experience that struck him deeply. It struck him that the people he met were lost and terrified, that what lay at bottom of their anguish was empty lives. Those jobs that brought him into contact with white people convinced him that they were just as lost, their lives just as empty as any forgotten black man.[24]

Wright was in the process of trying to discover himself and his relation to the world. He had come to feel that he was one of the suffering masses, that he was one with these people who drifted by around him. He came to feel the need of breaking through his isolation to find communion with other suffering people. But his shock of recognition was that these people around him, black and white, were incapable of communion—incapable because they were empty. Black or white, it made no difference, each was absolutely absorbed in one thing, the "lust for trash." Each was so busy pursuing material things, the symbols of status, that no time was left for breaking through his isolation. It was during these dreary days that Wright was made aware that American society offered nothing save trash. The people that he met were the way they were because America gave them no other values. American society was as empty as those people were empty.[25]

One day, when the depression was at rock bottom, the relief agency sent Wright to work at the South Side Boys' Club. This began a new period of his life. Working with the slum boys started the germinating process in Wright's mind from which was to evolve Bigger Thomas. These boys were nothing special except that they were products of the slum and Negroes, and they were, thought Wright, sent to play ping-pong in the boys' club in order to keep them off the streets and out of trouble. They were dangerous. American society had made them empty, then hid them away. The boys were frustrated, a menace to law and order. The boys' club was the gift of philanthropists, good and benevolent trustees for the downtrodden, who out of their wisdom and graciousness

---

24 Richard Wright, "Early Days in Chicago," Edwin Seaver, (ed.), *Cross Section, 1945: A Collection of New American Writing* (New York: Book Find Club, 1945), pp. 306–42.

25 *Ibid.*

offered the boys ping-pong to fill their empty lives. At least, so thought Wright. In his mind it was a bribe made by the oppressors, a pitifully inadequate bribe.[26]

In a pamphlet describing "How Bigger Was Born," Wright ranged back over the development of his thoughts as they took shape to produce the final Bigger. He told how as a child in Mississippi he had been impressed and awed by certain black men who seemed to care nothing about their final destruction. Their hatred for the white man was so overpowering that certain death could not deter them from flaunting their contempt before the white faces. They were known as "bad niggers." Their lives were likely to be short and their ends violent. Wright thought about these people and wondered how to explain them. And as he wondered Bigger Thomas was born. The character that finally evolved in Wright's mind would change the course of Negro literature. His had little in common with the harmless and lovable characters who sang the blues in the literature of the Negro Renaissance.[27]

Bigger Thomas of *Native Son* was a monster who found his sense of self-fulfillment in killing. Bigger's defense attorney described the monster in court:

It has made itself a home in the wild forests of our great cities, amid the rank and choking vegetation of slums! It has forgotten our language! In order to live it has sharpened its claws! It has grown hard and calloused! It has developed a capacity for hate and fury which we cannot understand! Its movements are unpredictable! By night it creaps from its lair and steals toward the settlements of civilization! And at the sight of a kind face it does not lie down upon its back and kick up its heels playfully to be tickled and stroked. No; it leaps to kill!

Nor was Bigger an exception to the rule. He was, in Wright's mind, a symbol for the whole Negro population in America:

Multiply Bigger Thomas twelve million times, allowing for environmental and temperamental variations, and for those Negroes who are completely under the influence of the church, and you have the psychology of the Negro people. . . . Taken collectively, they . . . constitute a separate nation, stunted, stripped, and held captive

---

[26] Richard Wright, *How "Bigger" Was Born* (New York: Harper & Bros., 1940), p. 28.

[27] *Ibid.*, pp. 4–5.

within this nation, devoid of political, social, economic, and property rights.[28]

This image of the Negro was an absolute rejection of the Christ-like image or the image as the blues writers of the Renaissance imagined it. Instead of being more human than the white man he was subhuman, or, as Wright often described Bigger, a corpse. In creating this image of the Negro, Wright was also robbing the Negro experience in America of meaning. The centuries of suffering have gone for *nothing.*

But, for Wright, Bigger was more than just the image of the Negro; he was the symbol of modern man. "Your honor," said Max, the defense attorney, "is this boy alone in feeling deprived and baffled? Is he an exception? . . . There are others, Your Honor, millions of others, Negro and white, and that is what makes our future seem a looming image of violence." Wright was writing when Fascism seemed to be the wave of the future. The Biggers throughout the world, festering in the industrial slums, in the modern wastelands, greedy for things that glitter but with no chance of getting them, starved of human values and human communication in a civilization dedicated to grab—these Biggers were poised for the attack.[29]

While Wright was still at the South Side Boys' Club, and Bigger was yet a blurred outline in his mind, he joined Chicago's John Reed Club. His hope was to write for the club's periodical, but he was also stirred by a quickening interest in the Communist movement of which the club was an integral part. Here was, as he thought, the one movement in America that represented the community of the suffering. It was a way of joining into that sense of community he had been searching for since he arrived in Chicago. It was possibly (though it turned out otherwise) a way of breaking down the barrier of self-distrust that separated him from others. Though his involvement with the Communist party turned into disaster, and though he became the butt of party smear tactics, he always retained the sense that here was the community for which he longed.[30]

---

28 Richard Wright, *Native Son* (New York: Signet Books, 1963), pp. 361–62, 364.

29 *Ibid.,* p. 368.

30 See Richard Wright's chapter in Richard Crossman (ed.), *The God That Failed* (New York: Harper & Bros., 1949), pp. 115–62.

This longing for community was made a basic theme in *Native Son*. Bigger was simply a product of his environment, no more. He was filled with a self-hatred that was made manifest in a hatred of everyone else. More than that—and here is where Wright went beyond the sociologists—he was empty of human values because American culture was empty of human values. He was a monster. But he was also human. His humanity made him feel the need for some kind of self-fulfillment. He found this in murder. He was thus a monster; he was thus human. Murder gave him a feeling of being somebody, he had done something on his own, for the first time he had exercised choice. And after he reached this new level of existence, grotesque as it was, he began to grope toward a new thing, toward communication, toward human relations. He had been the victim of "the frigidization of the self"—a wall existed between himself and others. It was though Mr. Max, the Communist defense attorney, and Mr. Max's Communist vision of a community of the suffering that Bigger was first given what American society had always denied him—an inarticulate desire to have relations with someone on the human level. In his jail cell this feeling came over him: "If he reached out with his hands, if his hands were electric wires, and if his heart were a battery giving life and fire to those hands, and if he reached out with his hands and touched other people, reached out through these stone walls and felt other hands connected with other hearts—if he did that, would there be a reply, a shock?"[31] Wright was postulating the existence of a community of souls of which American society knew nothing.

Much of what went into Bigger Thomas had gone into the making of Richard Wright himself. Boyhood emotions crushed by a cruel environment. Human relations little more than a confusion of shame and hate. The dim vision of a different kind of life. As a boy Wright had steeped himself in the writings of the American naturalists—Dreiser, Anderson, Lewis, Masters—had gained from them a vantage point from which to view his own struggles. *Native Son*, not surprisingly, was to carry naturalism into Negro literature. It began something of a school of Negro writing. But the school he started was rather short-lived. Wright's real importance lies with those who reacted against him. In reacting against the subhuman Bigger a later generation of writers would have to react

---

[31] Wright, *Native Son, op. cit.*, p. 335.

against the sociological vision—and the rationalism—that produced him. In reacting against Bigger the younger writers could never ignore him. They would have to grapple with him—to use him as their starting point. The creation of Bigger Thomas marked a new departure for Negro literary thought.

But in writing *Native Son*, Wright had done more. Prior to him the sociological imagination had rejected the moralistic approach to the Negro's problems in favor of a redistribution of wealth and of assimilation. The sociological imagination had conjectured the necessity of a structural change in American society—from capitalism to socialism perhaps—but had taken the realistic approach to values. American values—wealth and status—were functions of industrial society and not to be wished away. But, even beyond that, the sociological imagination knew (or thought it knew) that social structure, values, and everything else belonging to the superstructure of a society have their roots in the economic organization. Change must begin with the redistribution of wealth, for with wealth goes power and the ability to make fundamental social change take place. Wright went along with the sociological imagination to a point, but when that point was reached he was forced to go beyond. Part of the problem was social disorganization and the brutalizing effects of the ghetto—this he recognized. That much would account for Bigger's self-hatred; his disorganized behavior. But to account for Bigger the monster Wright had to go on to postulate a society that creates monsters. Such a society does not possess the values which make a man human. For Wright it was a matter of values. American society creates dead men because it is dead. American society must therefore be rejected in its entirety. This thought led Wright to take the first tentative steps toward an intellectual position that was to become a widespread assumption and to have the most far-reaching consequences for Negro thought in America. This position assumes the existence of an almost mystical community—an ideal that is placed in absolute contrast to American society. Wright's contention that American society is soulless, dead, lacking in human values, and destructive of the humanity in its people would become generally accepted. His search for a human community in contrast with and in opposition to this soulless society would be carried on and its implications developed by others. It is as if the old Christian dualism between body and soul, between the earthly city and the heavenly city, was being resurrected. Only the heavenly city, in the resurrected version, was to become distinctly racial.

In almost classic dialectical response Wright's image of the Negro generated its opposite. In Negro literature the reaction against the subhuman Bigger and his meaningless existence led to the recreation of the more human Negro with his redemptive mission. The unfolding of the dialectical process, the reemergence of the more human image of the Negro, began almost before Bigger Thomas himself appeared. It began when a young friend of Wright's read *Native Son* in manuscript and had discussions with the author on the subject. The young friend was Ralph Ellison, who would later become famous as the author of *Invisible Man*. But the man who would be the leader in the rebellion against Bigger was to be Wright's most ardent young admirer, James Baldwin. Both Baldwin and Ellison would struggle with Wright's image in order to develop their own. Baldwin later wrote, "I had used his work as a kind of spring-board into my own. His work was a road-block in my road, the sphinx, really, whose riddles I had to answer before I could become myself."[32]

Ellison saw Bigger as the product of the sociological imagination; Baldwin saw him as the product of white liberal thought; for both men Bigger was the white man's creation, not Wright's. Bigger is the white man's attempt to understand the Negro from his vantage point outside of him—the result is a superficial and dehumanized picture, an abstraction. The sociologist can see only statistics and conditioned responses to environment, not the humanity within. The white liberal sees in the Negro only what his guilt and his fears allow him to see. Neither can get beyond their own constructions to see the reality. The result is a Bigger. The environment was monstrous, so a monster must, *ipso facto*, have been produced.[33]

---

32 James Baldwin, "Alas, Poor Richard," *Nobody Knows My Name: More Notes of a Native Son* (New York: Delta Books, 1961), p. 197; For his part Ellison denies Wright's influence, but his frequent references to Wright's work makes it clear that he gave *Native Son* a good deal of thought.

33 James Baldwin, "Many Thousands Gone," *Notes of a Native Son* (Boston: Beacon Press, 1955); Ralph Ellison, "The World and the Jug," *Shadow and Act* (New York: Random House, 1953).

Both writers attempted, in their critiques, to show that Wright, in his abstraction of the Negro, had left out the human element. To resurrect the human element it was felt necessary to throw out the sociological imagination, to abandon the rationalistic explanation of man. The tendency of the modern mind is to reject the idea of innate or a priori truths and to define reason as one of two things: it is either the scientific method or it is rationalization. Baldwin saw Bigger as the embodiment of the white man's rationalizations concerning the Negro—defense mechanisms that spare the white ego from feelings of guilt. Ellison saw Bigger as the result of the scientist going about with a tape measure trying to measure the human soul. Both men threw out reason as a means of coming to grips with the humanity of the Negro. In the process they helped create a new more human image of the Negro. But in doing so they threw out the restraints involved in the rationalistic approach.

Thus there was begun a swing away from the sociological imagination that had reigned supreme for a time during the 1930's. It was to be a swing back to the moralistic approach: the idea that the Negro embodies the finer values and that he has a redemptive mission. In a sense it marked a return to the more human ideology of W. E. B. Du Bois. But there are crucial differences between the Du Bois image of the Negro and the image that began to emerge in the late 1940's in reaction to Bigger.

The Christ-like image, so dear to Du Bois and others of his generation, appears to have satisfied several emotional needs: the need for status, the hatred of the white man, and the need for community. The need for a sense of status, denied him as a Negro by white society, was met by the knowledge that he was more human than the white man. The hatred he felt toward whites was expressed in the invidious comparison the more human ideology made. For the cold and isolated Du Bois the need of a sense of community was of necessity most compelling. The idea of the racial soul that was embodied in the Christ-like mythology gave one membership in an ingroup—it gave a sense of belonging. Acting together in an ideology that made for invidious comparison of the races, the inner dynamic created by these three emotional needs was toward racism. Du Bois every so often lapsed into racism, but there were important restraints holding him back. The restraints may be listed as follows: a humanist belief in self-perfection; his psychological separation from the masses; a rationalistic approach to the understanding of man; and, a 19th-century tendency to look for meaning in a cause outside of himself. His humanism warred with racist tendencies by setting the goal of individual excellence above identity with the masses. His sense of distance from the masses worked the same way. His rationalistic approach to the understanding of man—his sociological imagination—constantly led him to question the reality of race. This questioning of race, when combined with his need to work for a cause outside of himself, led him to embody his racist tendencies in the very rationalistic cause of Communism.

In the thought that came after Du Bois the four restraints against the tendency toward racism were broken down. The Negro Renaissance revolt against myth broke down the 19th-century tendency to look outside oneself for a cause. The Renaissance turned the search for meaning inward. The blues writers of the Renaissance broke down the psychological distance between the writer and the masses. Negro writers became free to enter the realm of the irrational when the revolt against Bigger brought about the rejection of the rationalistic approach to the understanding of man. And, finally, the humanist faith of Du Bois, which idealized the isolated hero lifting himself above common mortals, was dissolved in the solvent of community. The hunger for human relations replaced the hunger for excellence. What emerged after the four restraints were broken down was to be a more human Negro who finds self-realization in his emotions, in community, in separatism (the Negro community as opposed to white society), and in revolt.

What is at work here is not a sudden flocking to the banners of an irrational ideology but a tendency. We must see Du Bois as swimming very hard against the currents of rationalism to maintain his racial vision; we must see the post-Wright writers as swimming very hard (sometimes not so hard) against the currents carrying them toward racism.

The problem facing the post-Wright writers was this: given Wright's assumptions about American society, how does one find a way to selfhood for the Negro different from Bigger's self-fulfillment in murder. The social-scientific approach, given the premise that American society is empty, leads almost inevitably to Bigger. Science must be shown to be inadequate, but how? Bigger was a corpse because society, the only source of values to the sociological imagination, was empty. Another source of values must be found, and here, of course, the blues writers had prepared the way: the Negro past, the Negro experience, the Negro psyche.

In *Invisible Man*, Ralph Ellison managed to say both what it is like to be a Negro in America and what it is like to be a modern man. To be a Negro in America is to have had one's humanity under attack through more than 300 years of history. This because the Negro's humanity is a threat to society—it is the threat of chaos. To be a modern man is to be conscious of living in a society which so fears man's humanity that it has created a vast network of self-deception to enable and to force man to deny that humanity. Modern man has begun to realize this, but knows not where to turn. Ellison felt that one's humanity lies somewhere in the dark and fathomless recesses of the Id—in the psychic depths where true passion, hate, and love, lurk in chaotic confusion. Modern society has chosen the course of order, the course of repressing the inner chaos in favor of the Superego. Having the Superego rule makes for an ordered, predictable course of events; it also destroys true feeling, true emotional commitment between people, true community. The rule of the Superego ends in the sort of isolation and detachment—the "frigidization of the self"—that separates man from man. Ellison's search in *Invisible Man* was the search for his humanity in both senses: as a black man in America and as a modern man.

In his search for selfhood Ellison, in *Invisible Man*, tried three paths: first, the path of the Superego, the "Great Tradition" in America; second, the path of the Ego, the way of Communism; and, finally, the way of the Id, the way of chaos. Each path, in its turn, he found to be an exercise in self-deception.

The Superego, in *Invisible Man*, was the power structure of society, both black and white. Its embodiment was found in two characters, the "benevolent" white Mr. Norton, millionaire trustee of a Negro college, and Dr. Bledsoe, president of the college. The task of both men was to encase the Negro in the cold customs and traditions of white society—to educate him in the "Great Tradition"—because, to the mind of the white man, the Negro, not so educated, is the embodiment of unrestrained passion, chaos. To the white mind the Negro is the Id of American society. Schools are established with the announced ideal of "advancing" the Negro which, in reality, are institutions of social control. The college president, Dr. Bledsoe, was in the tradition of Booker T. Washington. Outwardly gentlemanly and courteous, he was inwardly the crafty and cold Superego in pursuit of ruthless repression. He was a manipulator, manipulating whites by his suave, outward "Uncle Tom" demeanor, manipulating his Negro students with calculated coldness. The novel's hero was well on his way to following in the footsteps of Bledsoe when one day, quite by accident, he was exposed to chaos. A tenant farmer who had committed incest and a group of insane Negro doctors, lawyers and other professionals introduced the hero to life uninhibited by the Superego. Once exposed to chaos he was unfitted for the "Great Tradition" and life in the Negro college. He was expelled.

After that experience, with its aftermaths, and beginning to understand the nature of the self-deception involved in the capitalist society of the "Great Tradition" where ruthless power and greed rule supreme in the guise of humane enlightenment, the hero ventured into the Communist party. Having given up on the Superego, he was turning to the Ego, to reason, to Freud's reality principle. The Communist party provided both a cause (the overthrowing of the "Great Tradition" with its hypocrisy) and a way of life structured by reason. The Communist party embodied the sociological imagination—it saw people as being determined by their environment; it saw history as being determined by economic causes. It was a mechanistic interpretation of the world that was optimistic in its hope that the future can be brought under scientific control.[34]

For a time the book's hero was well satisfied with the party (the "Brotherhood"). It enabled him to strike out at the oppressive way of life embodied in the "Great Tradition." But there were problems here also. In the first place, his emancipation from the "Great Tradition" had started him on the road to the discovery of his emotions: "Somewhere beneath the load of the emotion-freezing ice which my life had conditioned my brain to produce,

---

[34] Ralph Ellison, *Invisible Man* (New York: Signet Books, 1953), pp. 436–37.

a spot of black anger glowed and threw off a hot red light of such intensity that had Lord Kelvin known of its existence, he would have had to revise his measurements." For the first time he had discovered true emotion, he had begun to *feel*. And it was this, as much as the rationalism of the party, that made him seek out the Communists. The party promised the way of controlled anger—of emotion controlled by reason. Then, in the second place, he sensed in the party a feeling of "we-ness," of the breaking down of barriers between himself and others—the feeling that Bigger Thomas vaguely sensed near the end. The feeling came over him while giving a speech to a party rally: "My voice fell to a husky whisper, 'I feel, I feel suddenly that I have become *more human*. Do you understand? More human. . . . With your eyes upon me I feel that I've found my true family! My true people! My true country! . . .'" Here was a sense of community—another country than impersonal American society. But party officials attacked the speech as unscientific.[35]

The hero in *Invisible Man* soon learned that reason, too, was the enemy of emotion. The scientific temper of the party mind, harnessed as it is by dogma rather than by love of individuals, saw people as depersonalized objects to be manipulated for the sake of the cause. Scientific reason was impersonal, emotionless. He began to sense that the party was simply one more form of self-deception; that he was getting his sense of selfhood for a cause little related to him as a personality. More and more he felt forced to turn to the final alternative—the Id.

The novel's apostle of the Id was Rinehart. Pure chaos, restrained neither by morality nor by reason, marked Rinehart's career. He was the con man of Harlem—at once a renowned preacher of the gospel, a leading numbers racketeer, and the community's most venerated pimp. He was the unsentimental manipulator of people for self-gain. To one disgusted with self-deception Rinehart held a definite appeal. Why not be truly cynical?—at least that was being honest with oneself. By this time the hero was in a state of desperation.

Then, during a Harlem riot instigated by the party for its own ends, the hero began to understand. He began to understand that

---

35 *Ibid.*, pp. 226, 300.

all three ways of life he had found in America are based on the manipulation of others for selfish ends. The result of this arrangement is the self-deception of the manipulators and the depersonalization of the manipulated. America is the castrating society, because in each case, whether one be manipulated or a manipulator, one loses his manhood. Few can really be free from either side of the equation, but such a freedom is the object of the search.

Ellison's hero ended up living in an abandoned cellar in complete alienation. He had abandoned the idea of changing society. This, the approach of the sociological imagination, he abandoned when he left the party. The other side of the sociological approach, that of individual adjustment to society, he turned his back on long before when he gave up on the "Great Tradition." At this point Ellison was heading in the direction of humanism, toward the idea of the individual rising above society. But this was to be a new humanism that turns away from reason and embraces the emotions. When Ellison was a boy in Oklahoma, society provided him with two kinds of examples: one kind, the "respectable" people, he found to be hypocrites; the other kind, the jazz musicians of the Negro community, men outside the pale of respectability, men who defied convention, Ellison found to be free. The leading citizens—the judges, ministers, and politicians—had usually been "crooks, clowns or hypocrites." But not the jazzmen: ". . . despite the outlaw nature of their art, the jazzmen were less torn and damaged by the moral compromises and insincerities which have so sickened the life of our country." Jazz set the standard. It defied convention, it embraced chaos and from it created its own forms.[36]

Ellison's ideal for the individual became that of self-definition as a way of life. He strained after a humanist vision of this, but, lacking faith in reason, achieved something more akin to a Nietzschean ideal. Art replaces reason as the means of creating forms. The jazzman replaces the thinker.

James Baldwin's *Go Tell It on the Mountain* is the gem of Negro fiction. It is the answer to Bigger; the agonized affirmation that man can climb out of the valley of his self-imposed degrada-

---

[36] Ellison, *Shadow and Act, op. cit.,* p. xiv.

tion up the long steep mountainside into grace. Baldwin's people were ground down in their pain, their bitterness and hatred, and above all, in their sense of sinfulness. As individuals they were isolated, inward-turning, helpless to love. Desperately they wanted to love and to be loved, but too often their only emotion was hate. They were Protestants thrown back in upon themselves; standing naked in their sin before an angry and merciless God. Throughout, Baldwin hinted at a different condition, the condition of pagan innocence. The pagans, unacquainted with the concept of sin, were emotional and passionate people. They had the ability to unashamedly and unself-consciously love. It was those who had religion, who called themselves saints, who were incapable of love. Ordinarily—if Baldwin had followed a thousand other American writers—the message would have stopped at that point and would have rung in its clarity: forsake your Puritan heritage and learn to make love again. But for Baldwin things were not all that simple. He would not say that a false sense of sin lies at the bottom of modern man's "frigidization of the self," that the authentic life lies in the direction of laughing away one's superego. For him sin was too real, the wickedness of man too awful. Here was a burden man could not lay down.

The pagan innocents, though they were the warmest characters of Baldwin's book, were not the heroes. Baldwin's message was to pick up your burden and start up the mountain. The pagans refused to recognize any burden. Contrasted with the pagans was the hero's father, Gabriel. This man, an evangelical minister, had self-consciously picked up his burden and made life hell for everyone else. Gabriel, like Bigger, was a product. He was the product of white society and of his own uncontrollable lust. His lust he translated into a self-hatred-producing sense of sin and guilt. His response to the white world was a depthless hatred which fear made him turn against his black brothers. His world was an iron bed of hate, fear and guilt, not at all unlike the world of Bigger Thomas. But Baldwin's was not a world controlled by forces before which men are powerless. In Baldwin's world people were responsible for what they were. If Gabriel's burden was too heavy to bear, that is tragic, but we know that he was not without guilt; he had volunteered to bear it. Here lay the riddle that Baldwin had to solve. The burden—the weight of the white man's inhumanity together with the power of one's own lust—that was a given, it was something one could not escape. How then was one guilty for failing to bear up under it? How was one guilty if one became a Bigger Thomas? Baldwin's answer was that one can, like the pagans, avoid the burden by refusing to admit its existence, or, one can admit of the burden but blame others for it. These are the ways of escape. Neither way was acceptable to Baldwin who demanded that each man not only admit of the burden but accept his own responsibility for it. The burden is one's own humanity.

In the novel, John, the young hero, tried hard to avoid confrontation with his own humanity, but found that impossible. It came to him during a religious experience—the sort of experience that brings one to his knees in trancelike anguish:

> This sound had filled John's life, so it now seemed, from the moment he had first drawn breath. . . . Yes, he had heard it all his life, but it was only now that his ears were opened to this sound that came from the darkness, that could only come from darkness, that yet bore such sure witness to the glory of the light. And now in his moaning, and so far from any help, he heard it in himself—it rose from his bleeding, his cracked-open heart. It was a sound of rage and weeping which filled the grave, rage and weeping from time set free, but found now in eternity; rage that had no language, weeping with no voice—which yet spoke now, to John's startled soul, of boundless melancholy, of the bitterest patience, and the longest night; of the deepest water, the strongest chains, the most cruel lash; of humility most wretched, the dungeon most absolute, of love's bed defiled, and birth dishonored, and most bloody, unspeakable, sudden death. Yes, the darkness hummed with murder: the body in the water, the body in the fire, the body on the tree. John looked down the line of these armies of darkness, army upon army, and his soul whispered: *Who are these? Who are they?* And wondered: *Where shall I go?*

John's vision that night, *and his humanity*, was the Negro's experience in America. This was the burden that John had to consciously pick up, and start up the mountainside.[37]

In picking up the burden John reaffirmed the faith that the

---

37 James Baldwin, *Go Tell It on the Mountain* (New York: The Dial Press, Inc., (1968), pp. 200–01. Reprinted from *Go Tell It on the Mountain* by James Baldwin. Copyright © 1953, 1952 by James Baldwin and used by permission of the publisher, The Dial Press, Inc.

Negro's experience in America has not been in vain—the faith that there is meaning in life. At the roots of this faith is the desperate hope that man can make himself human.

Baldwin brought back the more human Negro that both the Renaissance writers and the sociologists had rejected. But this was to be an image of the Negro entirely different from the perfectionist ideal held by Du Bois. Excellence through self-transcendence had meant for Du Bois seeking out the eternal truths that lie outside of history and, by their aid, lifting oneself up to transcend the imperfections of the social environment. Baldwin turned inward, not outward. Man is not to reach out beyond history but to sink himself into history, grasping history to him, accepting what history has made of him and finding his humanity in what he is. Not self-perfection, is the goal, but the acceptance of responsibility for one's imperfection. Baldwin had no recourse but to accept what the sociologists said about the Negro—to accept Bigger. But he turned Bigger into an affirmation. Bigger is the burden that the Negro must bear. To deny him is to deny responsibility for oneself. To simply blame him on society is to allow the white man to define oneself. To blot him out is to blot out the race's history in America and to desire only to become a white man in black skin. For Baldwin that would be the ultimate horror.[38]

In his novel *Another Country* (1960), Baldwin developed the radical opposition between community and society that Wright had strongly hinted at. In *Another Country*, American society was painted as it had been countless times by novelists and poets, as T. S. Elliot painted it in *The Waste Land*. In it lives are routinized, mechanized and the people have become mechanical dolls. It is institutionalized greed—life revolves around the fast buck. It is also institutionalized escapism—in it life is so structured that one need never come to terms with one's true self. It is a never-never land in which the agonies of pain and sorrow have been forever banished—except for the Negro. It substitutes ennui for experience because experience is painful. Such is American society.

Contrasted with society is the community—another country—which everyone in the novel seeks. Community is the ability to

---

[38] For Baldwin's critique of Bigger see his "Everybody's Protest Novel," and, "Many Thousands Gone," *Notes of a Native Son* (Boston: Beacon Press, 1955).

love, to have true emotional relationships with others. In society human relationships are manipulative. In society one relates to another on the basis of ego gratification. Community is the ability to relate on a higher plain. But the search for community is a painful one; it requires coming to terms with oneself, assuming the responsibility and accepting the guilt for what one is. True emotion, true community, because it threatens the make-believe world, is dangerous to society, and one who dares try it courts ostracism or worse. In America it is a crime to love.

By adding *Another Country* to *Go Tell It on the Mountain*, one begins to get the drift of Baldwin's thought. For the white American the road to escape from one's own humanity is all too easy to travel. Society had been made for him. But for the Negro it is different—for him there is no escaping. Like John of *Go Tell It on the Mountain* the pain and burden are thrown up at him, he must confront them. Society in America is structured so that the white man may evade his guilt—one needs only money and status. But the Negro is denied these things. In a real sense, the Negro is the product of the white man's evasion. The white man, in pursuit of money and status, brought the Negro here, enslaved and exploited him, then made him into a Bigger, both in reality and in stereotype, as a way of rationalizing the exploitation, the guilt. For three centuries or more the black man has borne the white man's guilt. Again and again black men, like John, have been confronted with this burden. Again and again, like John, they have lifted and carried the burden. And each confrontation, each lifting has been a reaffirmation of the black man's humanity. The social process in America, as painted by Baldwin, has been for the white man to reject his own humanity by shifting his guilt to the black man, while the black man has built a tradition of bearing the burden of his own humanity. This was Baldwin's more human Negro.

Baldwin had no illusions about the Negro being a Black Christ; the experience of oppression did not, in his mind, make for Christ-like people. As a result, the mission he assigned his people was less a mission than a bare possibility. It was the possibility that the black man, by confronting the white man with his humanity, may be able to make the white man confront *his* own. "The goal of the student movement," he wrote, "is nothing less than the liberation of the entire country from its most crippling attitudes and habits. . . ." Whites must "see the Negroes as people like themselves . . ." if they ever hope to see themselves as they are. Only then can the white man come to grips with his guilt and take responsibility for it. Only then can the white man grapple with the reality of himself and cease his escape into innocence. In an open letter to his nephew, Baldwin wrote that despite everything the black man must accept the white man—accept him and love him—for he has no other hope. Integration, he continued, means above all, "that we, with love, shall force our white brothers to see themselves as they are, to cease fleeing from reality and begin to change it." The Negro could achieve the emancipation of the white man from his superficial existence because he, the Negro, had earned the right to be teacher. He had suffered the rope, the fire, the torture; he "is forced each day to snatch his manhood, his identity, out of the fire of human cruelty that rages to destroy it. . . ." At this point in Baldwin's thought a minor theme of the Renaissance—the vision of strength through suffering that was glimpsed by Toomer and Cullen—becomes dominant. Suffering enables one to confront "with passion the conundrum of life." Suffering enables one to rip away the "totems, taboos, crosses, blood sacrifices" with which we imprison our minds in order to escape life. Suffering, and its conquest, makes for freedom.[39]

Baldwin emerged as the prophet of a new more human Negro who, because he is in communion with his own being, is capable of communion with other beings. Communion replaced Du Bois's lofty isolation; the search for authentic emotion and feeling took the place of Du Bois's austere rationalism. In short, Du Bois's aristocratic ideal was giving place to the ideal of the lowly, the underclass.

This shift away from the rationalism always associated with the aristocratic temper to the emotionalism and irrationalism associated with the masses becomes of utmost importance in understanding the direction taken by Negro protest in the 1960's. Negro thinkers and spokesmen more and more associated themselves with the proletariat. The Renaissance writers ended in complete identi-

39 James Baldwin, "East River, Downtown," *Nobody Knows My Name,* (New York: Delta Books, 1961), p. 75; James Baldwin, "My Dungeon Shook," *The Fire Next Time* (New York: Delta Books, 1964), pp. 22, 23–24; James Baldwin, "Down At the Cross," *The Fire Next Time* (New York: Delta Books, 1964), pp. 113, 105.

fication with the "blues people." The sociologists and economists of the 1930's identified the Negro in America with the industrial proletariat. Richard Wright created a character that subsequent writers were forced to recognize as *the* Negro. In order to prove the Negro's humanity Baldwin had to work not with the "talented tenth" but with Bigger Thomas of the Chicago slums. Rationalism came to be identified with the mechanized, sterilized civilization created by whites, and with integration into that civilization. As Baldwin wrote: "Do I really *want* to be integrated into a burning house?"[40]

The post-Richard Wright writers were in full revolt against a style of thinking (rationalism) and a civilization that all too apparently denied the individual his autonomy as a free human being. As such they were in the humanist tradition. But humanism—an aristocratic, rationalistic tradition that seeks to lift the individual above society to self-perfection—was definitely not what they had begun to preach. Theirs was a humanism turned inside-out, in which the individual was to find autonomy not in isolation but in community. Theirs was a humanism in which the authority of human reason gives way to the authority of human emotions. In a sense theirs was a humanism for the masses, and it carried with it a very definite transvaluation of values.

In his writings James Baldwin's heart was not with the "talented tenth," not even with the rural "folk," but with the underclass in the ghettos—the pimps, whores, and racketeers. He tells of his childhood horror of street life and his flight to the bosom of the church to escape it. But later he realized that the people he had so feared were beautiful. They were free and authentic people. They were "present" in all they did. The songs they sang—blues, jazz, gospel songs—reflected their freedom and authenticity. He contrasted them with the joylessness and sterility of white America. He even contrasted their straightforward criminality with the hypocritical immorality of white America. The pimps, whores, and racketeers knew how to live and to feel. More and more in the post-Richard Wright literature it was these people that supplied the model for the more human Negro and the new humanism. It is to them that we must turn.[41]

---

[40] Baldwin, *The Fire Next Time, ibid.,* p. 108.
[41] *Ibid.,* pp. 55–57.

VIII

The moral equivalent
of blackness

The tendency in Negro thought to search for and develop a new humanism that shifts from the ideal of lonely perfectionism to community was complemented and reinforced by an ideal growing out of the city ghettos—the ideal of a community of soul-brothers. The key to the new social ideal appears to be found in the development of Negro humor and the humorous con man as a social ideal.

The Negro writer, spokesman for the black middle class, began his search for a new social ideal in the 1920's. The search led him in many directions, through various ideologies, but inevitably to the lower class, the folk. While the search continued the nature of the folk was undergoing profound change as the people found their way to the big cities and the ghetto. The Black Christ ideal had begun with the field hand and got embodied in the spirituals before it became the ideal of the intellectuals. As an ideal it was irrelevant to the ghetto, so a new social ideal, like the first originating at the bottom of the social ladder, was slowly developed. Its expression in music was jazz. The black middle class was aghast. They stopped up their ears. But in the end they had no place else to turn.

Sociologists describe the social life of the ghetto as pathological, the product of disorganized society and unfulfilled desires. White society, standing off at a distance from the ghetto, beckons invitingly from every television set and shop window with the promise of things. Things are the ideal. With things goes status, prestige, wealth, leisure, and more things. White society does not absolutely withhold things from the Negro, but it sets up difficult ground rules for their attainment; rules that must be rigidly followed. The ground rules are these: conformity, respectability, and a periodic statement of such phrases as delight the white middle-class ear. These are not different from what is required of the white man seeking success, but the white man is trained in them from birth; they become second nature. Such training for the ghetto child is difficult to come by. In two chances out of three he will be from a broken home. It is likely that his mother works during the day and has little but frustration left for the child in the evenings. The school he will attend is even less capable of equipping him. In Chicago and New York City, for instance, 90 percent of the teachers in the ghetto schools are either new (and waiting to get to the suburbs), "problem," or probationary. Should the child, despairing of school, attempt to gain some sort of skill he will find the labor unions shut to him. In 1965 there were more Negro Ph.D.'s than there were licensed Negro plumbers and electricians combined. The schools offer more opportunity than the labor unions. Were the ghetto child to have relatively easy access to the prestige, wealth, and leisure offered but withheld by white society he might not question so readily the ground rules for their attainment. But for the child of the black ghetto these goals are distant, the road to them long and gruelling beyond imagination. To him the conformity, the respectability, and the appropriate phrases tend to ring false and artificial. Over the years his search for the true and the real has led in another direction.[1]

The opposite to conformity, respectability, and the appropriate phrases is clownishness, laziness, ignorance, and emotional spontaneity—all the attributes that white society has deemed it fitting to label "nigger." It has become popular to protest that there is

---

[1] The view that what emerges from ghetto life is not a true subculture but rather a pathological "contraculture" is expressed by J. Milton Yinger, "Contraculture and Subculture," *American Sociological Review*, October, 1960), pp. 625–35; for the situation on ghetto schools, see Whitney M. Young, Jr., *To Be Equal* (New York: McGraw-Hill Book Co., 1964); for the situation in the labor unions, see Herbert Hill, "Racial Inequality in Employment: The Patterns of Discrimination," *The Annals of the American Academy of Political and Social Science*, Vol. 357 January 1965), pp. 30–47.

no such thing as "nigger," that the word represents nothing more than the white man's prejudices and wish fulfillment. But the truth is that "nigger" represents a possible alternative social role for the ghetto child. It is a possible life-style—the style of a person who consciously chooses to live by the values white society proscribes simply because white society proscribes them. It is a way of life that suggests revolt. It is a thumbing of the nose, a raucous laugh at white society. It is a transvaluation of values. It is also a big laugh. Out of the humor and the pathology of the ghetto streets there developed a new life-style—the "con man" style—and a new social ideal widely known as "soul." It is because this life-style partly represents a joke against white society that Negro humor needs to be considered.

There are several things that come to light in a study of the Negro's rural folk humor: hidden aggression, the Sambo mask, the development of ingroup feeling, and the development of a style—the "cool cat" as folk hero. It is generally recognized (since Freud first introduced the idea) that all humor has an element of aggression; Negro humor is no exception. The theologian Howard Thurman related a story that brought laughter from a Negro audience. An almost destitute Negro was one day walking in Chicago's Loop when he spotted a white beggar in a pitiful state. The beggar had lost both legs and an arm. One eye was blind and opaque. The Negro gave the beggar four quarters, telling him that it was all the money he had in the world. The beggar asked why someone would give his last cent and received this answer: "You are the first white man I have ever seen that is cut up the way a white man deserves to be cut up that the least I can do to show my thanks, is to give you my last dollar."[2]

Traditionally the aggression in Negro humor has been more carefully cloaked than it was in Thurman's story. The "Uncle Remus" stories are a case in point. It has been shown that Brer Rabbit was indeed a malevolent critter. He had an astonishing ability to involve his enemies—Brer Fox, Brer Bear—in violent deaths. And, if Fox and Bear had an equally amazing ability to recover for the next episode . . . well, the white folks are always

---

[2] Howard Thurman, *The Luminous Darkness* (New York: Harper & Row, Publishers 1965), p. 44.

around. Brer Rabbit was a means of expressing hostility at a time in the Negro's history when any overt expression meant condign punishment. It was the cry of the oppressed in the form of humor.[3]

In the white man's humor concerning the Negro, the black man emerged as a "Sambo"—a stereotype that involved the black face, broad, happy but vacuous grin, an abundance of white teeth, a shuffling gait not hidden by outrageous clothes. The white man's Sambo was a dull-witted black whose attempts to imitate white culture were considered outrageously funny. One storyteller told this tale back in 1835: " 'Ben, how did you like the sermon to-day?' I once inquired of one, who for pompous language and high-sounding epithets, was the Johnson of the Negroes—'Mighty obliged wid it, master, de 'clusive' 'flections werre destructive to do ignorum.' "[4]

In the Negro's own version of Sambo there was a marked difference. Sambo was a mask—hidden behind that mask was a cunning wit. The idea of it being to play dumb for the white oppressor (avoiding his wrath) while outsmarting him. The result of this little drama was a *modus vivendi:* the white man would allow the Negro great latitude of behavior so long as the black man wore his Sambo mask, thereby giving the white man his accustomed laugh, bolstering his ego, and renewing his rationalizations for slavery. Apparently both parties came out of this degrading game with a sense of superiority. Richard Wright saw the less-humorous side of it when in his autobiographical *Black Boy* he described an episode in which a Negro elevator operator in St. Louis invited a white passenger to kick him in the seat of the pants. The white man complied, and in gratification tipped the Negro; all parties were happy—except Wright.

One element of Negro folk humor, then, lay in the "Malevolent Rabbit" tradition—the expression of aggression and the feeling of superiority when the weak (hiding behind the Sambo mask) outwitted the strong. The second element involved almost the opposite: this was the tradition of the innocent in the hands of

---

[3] Bernard Wolfe, "Uncle Remus and the Malevolent Rabbit," *Commentary*, Vol. 8 (July, 1949), pp. 31–34.

[4] Carl Wittke, *Tambo and Bones: a History of the American Minstrel Stage* (Durham, N.C.: Duke University Press, 1930), p. 8; J. H. Ingram, *The Southwest*, Vol. II (New York: Harper & Brothers, 1835), pp. 247–50.

fate. Fate in this case was often the white man's society, pictured as an implacable, impersonal set of forces in which the innocent victim was immersed. It does not sound humorous as first glance; but, then, all Negro humor walks a tightrope above the hard floor of tragedy. This tradition comes down in folklore from the South Carolina Congaree River region. In one such story, "Judge Fool-Bird," the Negro victim was fined $100 for getting beaten over the head by an enraged white man. This was too true to form to excite comment from the listeners, but they were flabbergasted to learn that the judge had also fined the white man:

> VOICE: 'Fore God! What made he fine ole man Hall fi' Dollars? Ain't he white folks?
> PERK: Jedge Foolbird is de law, an' he goin' do what he goin' do. He de law, and de law is de law.[5]

In a second story the victim was again pitted against the law—white man's law. Scip told the story of Primus' recent troubles. Primus had stolen two tires from an abandoned car. Since the owner could not be found, Primus was fined $25 and dismissed:

> VOICE: Wuh dey do wid de tire if dey ain' know who dey b'long to?
> SCIP: De judge put one on he car, an' de police put one on he car.
> VOICE: An' Primus pay de twenty fi dallahs?
> SCIP: Ain't Primus stole de tires?[6]

On one plane of logic Primus was innocent. On another, guilty. A comic effect comes when the two planes suddenly intersect with Primus the victim. The result is irony—irony directed at the logic of the oppressor. If Primus was innocent, who was guilty? Not the judge so much as all the forces that caused those two planes of logic to suddenly intersect. The two stories would have been tales of tragedy and woe had not the victims (they were all victims) pretended to accept both levels of logic as reasonable. That made it comedy, but only because the victims voluntarily put on the

---

5 Edward C. L. Adams, "Judge Fool-Bird," *Congaree Sketches: Scenes from Negro Life in the Swamps of the Congaree and Tales by Tad and Scip of Heaven and Hell with Other Miscellany* (Chapel Hill, N.C.: University of North Carolina Press, 1927), pp. 12–13.

6 Edward C. L. Adams, "Primus," *Congaree Sketches, op. cit.*, pp. 87–88.

Sambo mask. By playing dumb they got their ironic point across—then the mask was removed and the white world stood naked before their accusing fingers. Sambo, it turned out, wasn't so dumb as he had seemed. The white man finds humor (if he finds it at all) in the irony of the situation. The black man finds it in wearing the mask; in the fact that he, who appears so obtuse, is making the white man indict himself. And so, who is the real fool? One's answer depends on one's color. The thing that needs to be stressed is this: the Negro world, as Professor Sterling Brown points out, is constantly immersed in a flood of humor, far more so than the white world. For every bit of prejudiced behavior against the Negro, every act of discrimination, has its ludicrous side. When a Negro walked into an Atlanta, Georgia, courtroom and was forced to swear on a segregated Bible he could either laugh or cry. The Sambo mask, so long taken as proof of Negro inferiority, was in fact a standing indictment of American society.

A third element in the rural Negro's tradition of humor was that of poking fun at the swelled-up, the pompous. Of course, this is the province of all humor, but in the Negro's case it took on a special significance. For a generation or two after emancipation, virtually the only way a Negro American could get ahead—gain status—was through one of his religious organizations. Not only did the would-be big shots get ahead by becoming preachers and, hopefully, bishops of the church; the little people got status by having influence in the local congregation. One might become a deacon or an elder, or one might be a leading sister of established grace. The result was that pomposity became associated with religiosity and an important category of humor developed around religious hypocrisy and incompetency. Booker T. Washington used to disturb the militants to the point of distraction by larding his speeches with anecdotes that seemed to reflect on the race. One he used to tell (probably one of the milder ones) was a story of the time he was called into settle an argument that had split the congregation of a church situated near Tuskegee Institute. The elders were refusing to pay the minister his contracted salary, which was supposed to be based on the number of sermons he had preached during the year. The indignant preacher gained Washington's sympathies, and the Tuskegee president confronted the elders: "We don't *owe* him nuthin," said one old deacon with heat, " 'cause we done paid him for dem *same* sermons las' year!"[7]

In spite of some pretense of learning, most of the old-time preachers were unlettered men. Naturally, humor was directed at this pretense. In this class is a story of an old-time preacher teaching Sunday-school class. The story has the preacher asking what dog licked Lazarus' sores. One student volunteered, "Rover." Not Rover, said the preacher. "Moreover." "Fer de scripture sez: 'Moreover de dog cam and licked his sores.' " The story goes on to have the preacher inquire, "Boys, don't you know it's a sin ter play marbles? Scripture sez: 'Marble not.' " These digs at pretended learning are rather gentle. One gathers that the Negro folk could forgive the preachers their meagerness of learning if it were compensated for with emotional power. In fact, there was a sort of admirable audacity in the unlettered preacher. One story, long since consecrated by usage, is that of the preacher who was given a particularly difficult passage of Scripture to interpret. He rose to the occasion: "Brothers and sisters, this morning—I intend to explain the unexplainable—find out the undefinable—ponder over the imponderable—and unscrew the inscrutable."[8]

A much more devasting strain of humor in this third tradition has to do with hyprocrisy. The attempt to gain status by being saintly can lead to backstabbing. The "holier-than-thou" individual is more than a bore when he spreads malicious gossip in order to destroy the reputation of rivals. This type was the subject of the "Old Sister" stories of Congaree River folklore. "Old Sister" was one of the congregation's elderly saints who spread dirt about people in the name of the Lord, and, as she claimed, to save the souls of her victims. The stories pictured the trouble she made on earth for her supposed friends, then took her to heaven. Her entrance into heaven was purely by accident—during a raging storm St. Peter forgot for a moment to guard the gate. Once there, she soon had God and the angels in a fit. She harassed Peter and Michael to the point of desperation, "an' she had de tall angel worried up so till he spend most er he time settin' on de top of

---

7 William Pickens, *American Aesop: Negro and Other Humor* (Boston: The Jordan and More Press, 1926), pp. 14–15.

8 *Ibid.*, p. 21; James Weldon Johnson, *God's Trombones* (New York: The Viking Press, 1927) p.5.

a barn by he self, an' Gabel say he mind tangled up so he mighty nigh forget how to blow he horn." God gave Peter the devil for his absent-mindedness, and, thoroughly chastened, Peter said nothing would ever get him away from that gate again.

Finally, the angels succeeded in throwing Old Sister out of heaven and down the long flight of steps to hell, her hardness sending sparks flying all the way down. The devil kept a special pen for old sisters to keep them from terrorizing his domain. Especially bad villains were from time to time thrown into the old sister pen to be worked over. Old Sister, however, got to hell unannounced and lost no time running amuck. "When our Ole Sister hit hell," went the tale, "the first thing she do been to try and make sheself satisfied. She start messin' in everybody business, carrin' news on dis un dat. . . ." Shadrach, Meshach, and Abednego jumped into the fiery furnace seeking a haven, but the Old Sister went right in after them. "De devil say she had 'im so nervous he can't sleep. He say he think he nerves is 'stroy. . . ."[9]

Here, in Negro folk-humor, we find a tradition that stands in stark contrast to the Christ-like mythology so esteemed by the pre-Renaissance militants. It is the Christ-like Negro turned inside-out—become a vicious hypocrite. The old aunties and uncles, whose saintliness became a legend, apparently did some backbiting on the side. Neither this, nor any humor ever broke through the solemnities of the Du Bois group—it had no place in their idealization of the race. The militants, for all their honorable intent, for all their love of justice and their courage, were after all, a self-righteous group. They set themselves just a little above ordinary, garden-variety mortals. While the leaders and intellectuals were serving myths, the folk were doing their best to shoot the myths down. They were poking fun at the ways of status-climbing, at the hypocrisy of those who imitated whites, at those who pretended to be saintly, and at white society. They were laying the foundations for a life style which used a deadpan mask as a symbol and instrument for the rejection of the white man's ways.

The three elements of Negro humor set forth here reflect the same emotional needs served by the Christ-like mythology. In a

---

9 Edward C. L. Adams, "Old Sister in Heaven," *Congaree Sketches, op. cit.*, pp. 21–25; "Old Sister in Hell," *Congaree Sketches, op. cit.*, pp. 25–29.

sense they served to supplant the mythology. The "Malevolent Rabbit" tradition syphoned off and directed aggression just as did the invidious comparison between the races that the mythology made. The tradition of being an innocent caught up in the impersonal white world was like the Christ-like mythology in that it made the Negro out to be a more human, more lovable person than the cold, impersonal white man. It provided the Negro with a sense of self-esteem denied him by American society's refusal to give him status. The third tradition—the tradition of poking fun at the self-righteous—was the opposite of the Christ-like tradition in that it was an indication of emotional stability. Once the individual could indulge in the humor of the third tradition, he had lost the need to idealize the race in order to identify with it.

There are many strange customs in the South. It was rumored in some circles, for instance, that in the segregated motion-picture houses of Atlanta, Georgia, the Negroes had to wait to laugh until the white folks were finished. That was only a rumor, but it made sense because of what happened to Slim Greer when he went down to Atlanta. On arriving in town Slim learned of a law making it illegal for Negroes to laugh in the streets. Telephone booths were to be used in emergencies:

> Hope to Gawd I may die
> If I aint speakin' truth
> Make de niggers do deir laughin
> In a telefoam booth.

As things would have it, the first thing Slim saw in Atlanta was a telephone booth with a hundred Negroes waiting outside it:

> Slim thought his sides
> Would bust in two,
> Yelled, "Lookout, everybody,
> I'm coming through!"

Slim hauled the other fellow out of the booth, shut the door and laughed for hours. When he was done at last he got ready to leave:

> Den he peeked through de door,
> An' what did he see?
> *Three* hundred niggers there
> In misery.—

> An Slim gave a holler,
>   An' started again;
> An' from three hundred throats
>   Came a moan of pain.

The authorities saw this couldn't go on, hospitals were filling with Slim's victims, ambulances were working overtime. Slim was run out of town so things could get back to normal.[10]

Slim Greer was the creation of Sterling A. Brown, but his roots lie in Negro folklore. In fact Slim Greer sums up several of the folk-humor traditions; more important he points the way to their further development in the ghetto. Slim's adventures continue through several poems, and his character as "con man" is developed. Once he met a good-looking cracker woman he liked so much he decided to pass for white. It was a difficult thing because he was black as dark midnight, but as con artist he was able to get by with it unsuspected until he started playing the blues on the woman's piano—that gave him away; no white man could play blues like that. Slim was thrown out, but not before he got in some considerable loving. Slim wore the deadpan mask and behind it perpetuated the joke on white society, but his inner nature came out when he played the blues. Both these aspects of Slim, the outer mask and the inner "soul," became important in the "con man" ideal of the ghetto.[11]

Sterling Brown struck his blow against religious pomposity and self-righteousness when he had Slim become a bishop of the church. This came at a time in Slim's career when he was so down and out that he decided to play the religious game. The thing that convinced him was a chance meeting with an old gambling friend who was now living in a mansion, sporting a beautiful wife, an even better looking secretary, and had a whole congregation to support him. It was obviously a first-rate racket, so Slim decided to get in on it:

> I kin be a good bishop,
>   I got de looks,
> An' I ain't spoiled myself
>   By readin' books.

---

10 Sterling A. Brown, "Slim in Atlanta," *Southern Road* (New York: Harcourt, Brace & Co., 1932), pp. 88–90.

11 Sterling A. Brown, "Slim Greer," *Southern Road, op. cit.,* pp. 83–85.

> Don't know so much
>   'Bout de Holy Ghost,
> But I likes de long green
>   Better'n most
>
> I kin talk out dis worl'
>   As you folks all know,
> An' I'm good wid de women,
>   Dey'll tell you so. . .[12]

The con artist takes the squares for all they are worth, he milks the social structure with its artificial values, but beyond that he stands as a symbol of ridicule of those values—proof that they are values of form and not of substance.

The case of Slim Greer shows how the "con man" type tended to emerge out of Negro folk-humor. Slim wore the mask—but behind it was a wit that outshone the whites and turned the joke around against their society. Behind his mask Slim was a cool cat, taking advantage of the white man's sense of smug superiority, and providing in the bargain that the white man was not superior at all. The white man, incased in his smugness, turned out in reality to be a square. The urban Negro was to make full use of the "con man" type. The result was a transvaluation of values.

Rural folk-humor ran on the fine line of tragedy. City humor, on the other hand, always threatened to explode into violence. Here again, humor was a type of aggression. It grew directly out of the disorganization of family and community life in the ghetto. Ego psychology tells us that the individual, as he develops in youth, must go through several crises of identity; the crucial one being that which occurs in adolescence. If the adolescent ego is to mature the individual must be provided with a life plan that will give him an identity in an unfolding and structured future. Society must provide the adolescent with either an ideology or an institutional arrangement in which he will count for something. If society fails in this respect, as it usually does in the young Negro's case, the ego will very likely not mature, the individual will not have the capacity to confront the world in a realistic way,

---

[12] Sterling A. Brown, "Slim Hears the Call," reproduced in Jean Wagner, *Les Poètes Nègres des Etats-Unis: Le Sentiment Racial et Religieux dans la Poesie de P. L. Dunbar a L. Hughes (1890–1940)*, (Paris: Librairie Istra, 1963), pp. 596–600.

and we will have a case for pathology. Psychology suggests that in such a case the superego (society's admonitions) may overwhelm the ego, and convince the youth that he is truly deficient in all the things that society demands from him. It will tell him that he is ignorant, lazy, bad—all the characteristics that define the stereotype "nigger." In short, the individual begins to know the torments of self-hatred, and in an effort to escape these torments may find relief in simple acceptance of his seemingly evil nature. He will find identity in his badness, his "niggerness," and, finding identity therein, he will rationalize his shortcomings into positive values. In this way the transvaluation of values is consumated.

The disorganized family life of the ghetto made the identity problem acute. As the child tried on identities he announced them; the family sat in judgment of his latest pretensions. The effect of family life in the ghetto is to rip these healthy pretensions to shreds as the following example given by psychologist Lee Rainwater shows. This was the case of a family argument that ended in a knifing and the police court. The older sisters of the family, who were pregnant, accused their mother of being a prostitute and their half brother of being a bastard. The mother pointed out to them that they were both pregnant and predicted that neither of their boy friends would support them. When the 13-year-old sister laughed at all this she was admonished that she would be pregnant within the year. The words "black-assed," "bitch," "black bastard" were frequently used.[13]

The point is that ghetto family life tends to be a continuous contest to rip away the other person's pretensions (and so deny him or her an identity), crush that person's self-esteem and at the same time reduce the tensions caused by one's own self-hatred through the aggression committed. Add to this the fact that the average slum boy grows up in a female dominated family, where men are considered shiftless, unreliable, and worthless. All the boy's attempts to build illusions about himself are destined to be thwarted by women who harbor no illusions about men.

Urban Negro humor appears to have been largely an extension of this sort of contest into the city streets among one's own peer

---

13 Lee Rainwater, "Crucible of Identity: The Negro Lower-Class Family," *Daedalus*, Vol. 95 (Winter, 1966), pp. 172–216. I rely on his analysis of identity problems of ghetto youth.

group. The "dirty dozens," as the most extreme form of this humor was called, was an institutionalized process of tearing down the other fellow's self-pretensions. The dozens, played out in stereotyped form between two boys, had one open with a formalized attack upon the sexual proclivities of his opponent's mother. The second boy, to save face, and to show his glib street wisdom, had quickly to counter with an equally obscene attack on the mother of the first party.[14]

The dozens, so far, have made their way into literature only in Richard Wright's realism, and then only once or twice and in attenuated form. In *Lawd Today* he had two characters, Al and Jake, pitted in such a contest of wit. Beginning with each other's mothers, they worked backwards through their ancestry until, in utter mental exhaustion, the regression stopped with Al's alleged "greatgreatgreatgreat grandma" who was a Zulu queen.[15]

Basically, the dozens were a systematized attack on the sexual promiscuity of the victim's mother, combined with an exaggerated account of one's own sexual prowess. In an important sense this humor was an adolescent revolt against the female-dominated home, and a search for masculine identity. Beyond that, however, it was the rejection of the values and moral standards of the dominant society—white America—as embodied in the standards set by one's mother. Richard Wright somewhere gave an example of an extreme form of the dozens in which God was depicted as having created elephants for the purpose of having sexual relations with them, much to the indignation of the elephants. As Wright commented, this went beyond atheism. The dozens were a means of learning the verbal skills essential to one who must one day live by manipulating others; they served also to create an ingroup based on pride of verbal ability and wit. Unfortunately, just below the surface there was always tension and latent violence. The dozens, when practiced between grown men, usually led to a fight.

In his intensive study of the black ghetto folklore of Philadelphia, Roger Abrahams described the transformation of the Brer Rabbit tale as it had evolved in the ghetto. In the ghetto version Brer Rabbit was chagrined at being excluded from a party being

---

14 Roger D. Abrahams, "Playing the Dozens," *Journal of American Folklore*, Vol. 75 (July–September, 1962), pp. 209–20.

15 Richard Wright, *Lawd Today* (New York: Avon Books, 1963), p. 95.

given for his fellow animals. After getting his shotgun, he broke into the party, ate all he could, forced the lion's wife to dance, violated the ape's wife, fouled the floor, made some obscene remarks, and left.[16]

The impression given by this version of Brer Rabbit that agression had become overt in ghetto folklore is reinforced by Abrahams' finding that the "trickster" and the "badman" had become the two dominant heroes of ghetto tales. The Uncle Remus Brer Rabbit had been a trickster in the sense that he "signified" (fast-talked) to save his own skin; but the ghetto trickster was the monkey who signified for purely sadistic reasons—to get the lion in trouble with the elephant. Sadism similarly motivated the badmen of ghetto lore.[17]

These findings are clear evidence of the pathology that entered into ghetto lore to make it what it became. Abrahams also emphasized another element that was most important—that of style. The badmen, the tricksters did their work in style. In the tale of "The Signifying Monkey," we find the hero dressed in a one-button roll and a two-button satch—"one of those boolhipper coats with a belt in the back." The monkey, so the tale went was dressed " 'bout sharp as hell."[18]

The style, the humor, the aggression—all blended into one in ghetto subculture to form a most notable product, the "cat" (or, less recently, the "bopper," and the "hipster"), of which the "con man" style was one aspect. The cat became the living embodiment of a great joke against white society—the society of the square. The cat was a social role, and a living joke as well. But more than that, the role of cat was seen by members of the cat subculture as offering an existence of authenticity in stark contrast to the moralistic hypocrisy and the humdrum alienation of middle-class white society.

The cat deserves some attention. His roots were definitely pathological—they lay in the disorganized society of the slum. He was a junky or a pimp, perhaps an alcoholic, and in all likelihood had a criminal record of petty thievery, pocket-picking, or one of a

16 Roger D. Abrahams, *Deep Down in the Jungle* (Hatboro, Pa.: Folklore Associates, 1964), pp. 75–76.

17 *Ibid.*, pp. 81–82.

18 *Ibid.*, p. 38.

hundred other minor offenses. To sociologists, psychologists, and welfare workers his life seemed a waste; so they planned programs to make him adjust—to make him over into a square. Such programs overlooked an important point: the "cat" had become an ideal, a life-style.

Between 1951 and 1953, psychologist Harold Finestone made a study of some 50 Chicago cats. The life of the cat as presented in this study turned out to have all the essential ingredients of Negro humor. There was, for example, the transvaluation of values: the cat placed highest value on his "kicks" and his "hustle." The kick was an emotional release of a kind proscribed by white society; it could be the kick of heroin, of a sex orgy, or a jazz session. The "hustle" was the opposite of work. The square (white middle class) was a drone who worked from nine to five (an automaton) and existed for the purpose of being relieved of his bankroll by means of the hustle—that is, by the exercise of the cat's wit. The cat was Brer Rabbit and the square Brer Bear. What kid wanted to be Brer Bear? Social science tells us that the lives of the ghetto dwellers must be one of dull drudgery, ennui, hopelessness. That is not necessarily so. Playing Brer Rabbit outwitting Brer Bear could give one a sense of excitement, could make one exult in the skill and audacity of it. The kick and the hustle were approached as the true artist approaches his canvas. Finestone wrote: "The cat seeks through a harmonious combination of charm, ingratiating speech, dress, music, the proper dedication to his 'kick,' and unrestrained generosity to make his day to day life itself a gracious work of art." The aim, he added, was to achieve a life-style at once cultivated, aesthetic and pleasant.[19]

Being a cat was a high art and difficult to master. One learned how to set off a somber business suit with dazzling shirt and tie (previously it had been the zoot suit of the bebopper or the goatee, beret, and windowpane glasses styled after Dizzie Gillespie). One mastered the language, and, since the language was in a constant state of flux, to be away from the subculture for a year was to become an outsider. Even the name given the language changed constantly. It was jive talk, bop talk, and more recently, hip talk. In

---

[19] Harold Finestone, "Cats, Kicks and Color," *Social Problems*, Vol. 5 (1957), pp. 3–13.

his autobiography, Milton Mezzrow gave as an example what a cat who wants some marijuana might have said: "And you gets it back starched and clear, solid ole man. You know one thing, I wrastled some shake-up last night with some unbooted wren, blowin' salt and pepper till my hair hurts. I ain't greased since the big bean collared a nod in the early black, and I gotta stretch my chippy's playground. I know I'm gonna call some hogs soon as I hit my roost, so pick up on this dime note and call it even-steven so's I can widen."[20]

The clothes, the language and the deadpan were all part of the ghetto's equivalent to the rural Sambo mask. But the new mask flaunted itself. It no longer hid the humor but flung it into the face of white society. The cat was a walking ridicule of the white world. The humor, its roots in pathology, made white society seem less compelling, less powerful; it gave the Negro courage to be different. And, if what its advocates said is true, it gave him the power to be different, to be free and authentic.

We may see American society as the product of a long process of rationalization that has transformed the culture of Western civilization into a highly organized, even bureaucratized, world. In contrast, the subculture of the cat grew directly out of social disorganization. Psychologist Finestone found that all his subjects were in a sense frustrated jazz musicians. Jazz is the musical equivalent of Negro humor, or, to say the same thing, it has the same emotional roots and satisfies the same needs. Louis Armstrong was a product of the New Orleans ghetto. A long succession of men lived with his mother—men he euphemistically called "uncles." He got his start in music by playing in brothels. His friends were the pimps and con men of his disorganized society. The essence of his musical style is improvization. Mezzrow, the spokesman for Armstrong's style of music, argued that jazz, pure jazz, is emotional anarchy. It is improvization—complete disregard of form. White society, with its highly developed organizational skills and its cash nexus, picked up jazz and instinctively tried to give it form. The result was swing, pop tunes, progressive jazz—insipid, sterile,

---

20 Milton Mezzrow and Bernard Wolfe, *Really the Blues* (New York: Random House, 1946), p. 219. Copyright 1956 by Milton Mezzrow and Bernard Wolfe. Reprinted by permission of Harold Matson Co., Inc.

maudlin, and conventional to the jazzman. Disorganized Negro society successively struck back with rhythm and blues, bebop, rock 'n' roll—all of them jazz derivatives, all of them disturbing, unconventional, perhaps authentic.

The complete disregard of convention, which was the mark of the cat, was thought to make for inner authenticity and freedom. Authenticity was the pride of the Negro slum culture. It came to be described by the word "soul." Soul, it was thought, gave one the ability to relate to others with empathy; to communicate directly and from the heart. Soul grew out of Negro experience. "It is the ability to survive," said one member of the cat culture. "We've made it with so much less. Soul is the Negro who has the spirit to sing in slavery to overcome the monotony." Soul was exclusively the possession of the Negro. The ideal of a community of soul brothers, which was the ideal of the cat culture, was the same ideal that theologian Howard Thurman calls Christianity, and the ideal of community that James Baldwin searched for. It is the kind of thing that, were it universal, Martin Luther King would have called the "blessed community." The ideal made its appearance in the most recent trend in blues singing, the "soul music." A study made by one student of the blues showed that the emphasis of "soul music" was as follows: *"shows solidarity,* raises other's status, gives help, reward," and *"shows tension release,* jokes, laughs, shows satisfaction." Out of the disorganized ghetto, where the very family life often ripped one's ego to shreds, there evolved the ideal of the community of soul brothers, each of whom is free, each authentic, each in communion with others, building them up, helping them with love to bear their burdens.[21]

There was, then, this other aspect of ghetto thought that needs to be emphasized. The "cool" mask of the con man was much more than a defense mechanism (as the Sambo mask had been)— it served the purpose of creating an ingroup. The wit, the verbal virtuosity, the transvaluation of values—all these things set the cat apart from white society. And so did the ideal of community. Only the chosen few have soul. And the chosen few are black. As one modern spokesman for the cat culture, LeRoi Jones, said, the

21 John Horton, "Time and Cool People," *Trans-action*, Vol. 4 (April, 1967), pp. 5–12; Charles Keil, *Urban Blues* (Chicago: University of Chicago Press, 1966), p. 73.

idea of the white man singing the blues is impossible—only the Negro has soul.[22]

This kind of idea led rather naturally to "soul jazz." "Root" music that could be sung with authenticity only by those with roots in the Negro past—Ray Charles, Mahalia Jackson, Bo Diddley and others. It was a return to the more primitive blues, gospel singing and rock 'n' roll. Of it one Negro musician said: ". . . that soul only comes from certain kinds of experiences, and only we—you know who I mean—go through what you need to have the kind of soul that makes real jazz."[23]

The social ideal emanating from the black ghetto provided the needed inspiration for those writers and protest spokesmen who, reacting against the science of the sociologists and the figure of Bigger Thomas, renewed the search for the Negro's humanity. The ghetto social ideal substituted emotion and community for the rationalism and isolation of the old more Christ-like image and thus joined with the writers in knocking out the props that kept the more human image of the Negro from sliding into irrationalism and separatism. Add to this the transvaluation of values growing out of Negro humor which opposed formlessness to form, spontaneity to social convention. In the hands of some the new social ideal would become the basis for a doctrine of revolt for the sake of revolt.

Part of the return to the roots movement of the 1950's and 1960's revolved around the word "funk." Funk was associated with the earthy phrases of the early blues and with body smells; it had to do with the unrefined, the uncouth. It brought forth images of the down home Negro untouched by the sterilizing effects of deodorized white civilization. It was to "funk" that the poet and playwright LeRoi Jones turned in an effort to get back to his roots. Jones, a product of the black bourgeoisie (his father was an elevator operator, and he, himself, once on the New School for Social Research faculty), concluded that white culture represents everything that is sick and false. Acting as an art critic, Jones made

---

22 LeRoi Jones, *Blues People: Negro Music in White America* (New York: William Morrow and Co., 1963), pp. 149, 218–19.

23 Quoted in Nat Hentoff, "Race Prejudice in Jazz: It Works Both Ways," *Harpers*, Vol. 28 (June, 1959), p. 75.

himself spokesman for the Negro artist's return to his roots, and therefore for soul music and for funk. It was in this capacity of critic that he equated funk with high art. "High art," he wrote, "first of all, must reflect the experiences of the human being, the emotional predicament of the man, as he exists, in the defined world of his being. It must be produced from the legitimate emotional resources of the soul in the world." These conditions, he continued, are found among lower class Negroes only.[24]

Jones went further. When he talked about the "soul in the world" he was not intending to speak metaphorically. He had, in fact, gone completely over from the rationalism of the humanist tradition ("the humanistic bombast of the Renaissance," he called it) to an uncritical acceptance of the irrationalism of the masses. He spoke of a creative spirit or "force" working through history which Western civilization has done its best to kill by demanding a naturalistic explanation of everything, and by valuing only artifacts rather than the creative spirit that produced them. Western civilization has, in this sense, killed God. It was to the Negro masses who, because they had never owned anything, had never learned to value material things that he looked for the reemergence of the spirit or force in the world. The Negro had become the revolutionary force in America. He would when he got "hip," rise up and destroy this society with its artifacts and all the white men in it. White folk are "devils" and are not fit to live on the same planet with "soulful human beings." Jones, in the ultimate plunge into the irrational, equated creativity with destruction. Hopefully, one supposes, funk—the armpit odor—will conquer the world.[25]

Another aspect of funk—an earthiness in sexual matters—began to exercise a powerful hold over Negro writers in the 1950's and 1960's. The reasoning went something like this: white society has a sterilizing effect, both on Negroes and on whites; the black masses, being alienated from white culture, have largely escaped from this sexual enervation, consequently the white man sneaks into the Negro cabin at night for fulfillment, but also, because of a sort of penis envy, he wants to castrate the Negro male. The

---

24 LeRoi Jones, *Home: Social Essays* (New York: William Morrow, and Co., 1966), p. 109.

25 *Ibid.*, pp. 173–78, 151, 209, 234–35, 212–15.

descriptions of whites acting to castrate blacks abound in recent Negro literature. One of the most lurid is Baldwin's short story, "Going to Meet the Man," which describes the combined barbecue and castration of a Negro. As the whites watch the castration they have a mass catharsis, and, after it is done, go home satisfied. The manhood of the white man, the story tells us, is based on the emasculation of the Negro. Similarly, to the minds of these writers, white women find black men irresistible. The sexual undertones in Jones's sadism becomes evident when he writes that the "white woman understands that only in the rape sequence is she likely to get cleanly, viciously popped. . . ." There was a good deal of wish fulfillment in the "Black Power" slogan that was to become prominent in the mid-1960's. Coupled with the widespread symbolism of the black man being castrated was the equally widespread portrayal of sexually virile black men dominating effete whites. "Most American white men," wrote Jones, "are trained to be fags. For this reason it is no wonder their faces are weak and blank, left without the hurt that reality makes—anytime." Jones was equally insistent that the white man has castrated the Negro because the white male feels that he cannot compete sexually. He believed that the Negro is " 'wilder,' harder, and almost insatiable in his lovemaking." This was almost the exact opposite of the Christ-like image which depicted the white man as hard and virile, the Negro as the softer of the races. As in the realm of humor the hidden aggression had surfaced in this new more human image in the form of sadistic fantasy.[26]

In his novel, *And Then We Heard the Thunder* (1963), John Oliver Killens faithfully reflected the tendencies that made for the new vision of the more human Negro. His hero, Solly, began as a member of the black bourgeoisie, trading in his manhood for status within the mainstream of American society. When the draft caught him Solly was in college studying to be a lawyer. The army confronted Solly with the dilemma that Killens believed confronts every Negro (and white): cooperate and be castrated, or revolt. Solly's conditioned reflexes told him to keep out of trouble (i.e., give up his manhood) in order to get ahead in the army. In

---

26 James Baldwin, "Going to Meet the Man," *Going to Meet the Man* (New York: Dial Press, 1965); Jones, *Home, op. cit.*, p. 227, 216, 221–22.

a southern army training camp this was tough going, but Solly was managing it fairly well until he met a very strange kind of savior in the person of Scotty, the incorrigible and proverbial foul ball. At first glance Scotty appeared to be little more than the usual ne'er-do-well, and Solly took him as such. But, as time passed, and Solly's manhood was constantly challenged, he began to understand Scotty's method. By his complete contempt of army regulations Scotty was able to remain a man. Scotty was the con man figure of the novel. His attitude and all his actions flaunted ridicule in the face of a white world he considered mad. Gradually the con man won Solly over, taught Solly how to save his manhood. Gradually Solly became more and more of a man; we watch him undergo a masculine metamorphosis as he becomes a war hero, a conqueror of white womanhood, and ultimately an avenging angel participating in a sort of Armageddon—a full-scale battle between white and black troops stationed in Australia. Here again, the idea of creative violence appears.

When novelist Killens was a young boy in Georgia he once had the experience of being accosted by two white men in a black Packard. The question was put to him, "Hey, boy, you know where we can get a colored gal?" Killens shouted, "Go get your dear old mother like you been doing!" and ran. Looking back on this and similar experiences Killens decided that "ever since we were brought here in chains we have been cast in the role of eunuchs in a great white harem." Killens' basic experience in America had been white society's suppression of the Negro's manhood. The strength of the Negro, he believed, lies in the fact that although the Negro has led a castrated existence in America he has been able to maintain his manhood: "To live castrated in a great white harem and yet somehow maintain our black manhood and humanity—this is the essence of the man created out of the Negro Invention. History may render the verdict that this was the greatest legacy handed to the New World by the West." This was Killens' version of Baldwin's idea that the black man has gained strength through years of shouldering the black man's burden and of LeRoi Jones's belief that pain has made the Negro strong. The paradox so explicit in Killens' version—manhood through castration—was implicit in the others. The same kind of paradox is involved in the idea that from the disorganized black ghetto there arises true creativity, true freedom, true humanity. The paradox can only be solved by making the assumption that it is white society that is pathological; that it is a case of the lunatics locking up the sane. This basic assumption had, by the 1960's, become widely held. And, of course, assimilation into such a sick culture was hardly deemed desirable. "To be perfectly adjusted," wrote Killens, "in a crazy, impractical, unreasonable society hell bent for its own annihilation seems tantamount to remaining blissful in a raging booby hatch."[27]

Killens' observation marked the point where the trend of thought growing out of the con man ideal fused with the crisis of consciousness in broader areas of American thought. Both the radical "New Left" and the *avant-garde* "anti-literature" of men like Henry Miller and Norman Mailer were attacking what appeared to be a pathologically overrationalized society. New Left idol Herbert Marcuse brought the European revolt against positivism to America, a country where positivism was almost a way of life. The "anti-literature" of the *avant-garde* writers preached Dostoevski's revulsion against society's destruction of the emotional life. There was Norman O. Brown's characterization of society as the embodiment of neurosis—the product of man's flight from death—and his plea for a return to the Dionysian consciousness or the Nirvana of early infancy. There was the apocalyptic vision of Henry Miller, and Norman Mailer's hunger for a reconstruction of personality around the orgasm.[28]

It was with Mailer's *The White Negro*, in fact, that the black movement and the white movement joined forces. Mailer prophesied the day of the "hipster," the "philosophical psychopath" or nihilist, whom, as he said, the social mechanisms of psychological repression have left unscathed. Mailer contrasted the hipster, who has tapped the life forces, with the emotionally dead square. In this view, murder becomes release, and because it is release it opens the way for the true community of love. Every category of social restraint, said Mailer, must be ripped away by the hipster—the true Dionysian man.[29]

---

27 John Oliver Killens, *Black Man's Burden* (New York: Trident Press, 1965), pp. 64–65, 21, 34.

28 For a discussion of "anti-literature," see Ihab Hassan, *The Literature of Silence: Henry Miller and Samuel Beckett* (New York: Alfred A. Knopf, Inc., 1967).

29 Norman Mailer, *The White Negro* (San Francisco: City Lights Books, n.d.), pp. 1–18.

The black writer most impressed by Mailer's logic was the 1968 Peace and Freedom Party candidate for President, Eldridge Cleaver. In his book, *Soul on Ice* (1968), Cleaver contrasted the overintellectualized and repressed white man with the virile black. For Cleaver the black man represented body, the white man mind. The white man's salvation lay with the Twist—the dance which incorporated the Negro's emotional freedom. The Twist, of course, symbolized the whole ghetto subculture—in effect, a Dionysian subculture.[30]

During the years of a long prison sentence Cleaver became a worshipful follower of Malcolm X, the most important black nationalist leader of his day. Malcolm X took Cleaver from an earlier hatred of everything white to the faith that the fight for a more human society need not necessarily be a racist fight. But Malcolm X was tragically murdered on February 21, 1965, and in 1968 the Oakland, California police began what appeared to be a systematic persecution of Cleaver's Black Panther Party for Self-Defense, so it is possible that Cleaver retreated somewhat from his unyielding opposition to black racism. In any case, by late 1968, his public rhetoric had strong revolutionary overtones. The notion of creative violence began to creep into it in the form of the Black Panther's motto: ". . . war can only be abolished through war; and in order to get rid of the gun it is necessary to pick up the gun." He had begun to believe, with Franz Fanon, that it would be necessary for the black man to "step outside of the vicious circle of the internationalized violence of the oppressed and take up arms against the oppressor. . . ."[31]

In Jones, Killens, and Cleaver the transvaluation of values involved in Negro humor and the con man ideal was consumated. Here also, in these writers, the long latent hostility and aggression surfaced. But somehow the ideal of love (the Negro is more human) and the need to aggress needed to be reconciled (which one, after all, is the black man's true nature?). The reconciliation required the idea of community. Aggression and hostility can be expressed on the social level because society is sick and needs to be either radically transformed or destroyed. But on the mystic level

---

30 Eldridge Cleaver, *Soul on Ice* (New York: McGraw-Hill Book Co., 1968), pp. 180–200.

31 Eldridge Cleaver, "A Letter from Jail," *Ramparts*, June 15, 1968, pp. 18–21.

of community the Negro's true human and loving nature can be expressed. The ultimate hope was that society can be transformed into community, but that brought up the problem of the white folk: "What are we going to do about these white folk?" asked Killens, "How are we going to get them off our backs . . . how are we going to integrate them into our New World of Humanity. . . . ? This is the enormous Black Man's Burden today." The writers were divided on the question of whether the white man can become a "soul brother." Jones believed not. Baldwin and Killens were skeptical. Thus, the question of "black power"—the slogan of the late 1960's—would involve both society and community. When it talked about society and the needed changes it spoke the language of the sociological imagination. But when it spoke of community it made the irrational assumptions—the transvaluation of values—prepared for it by the con man ideal.[32]

II

The Negro revolt that blossomed forth in the 1960 sit-ins and freedom rides, and then in 1966 seemed to shift to something called "black power," has been assigned various causes and has been dated from various first events. Some think it all began with the 1954 Supreme Court decision to desegregate schools, others believe it began with the Montgomery bus boycott and the rise of Martin Luther King, Jr. in 1956, still others think the sit-ins of 1960 ignited the spark. Whatever causes and starting points may ultimately be assigned to the revolt, the point to be made here is that the ideologies and arguments that would inform its mood had already been spelled out; the grooves along which it would ride had already been cut.

The most radical group in "The Movement"—the cutting edge —was the Student Nonviolent Coordinating Committee. As such it served as a useful weather vane for testing the winds of doctrine. As one historian has pointed out, from the time of the 1960 sit-ins to the 1966 emergence of "Black Power," SNCC made not one but several shifts. Beginning as a group of well-dressed middle-class

---

[32] Killens, *Black Man's Burden, op. cit.,* p. 150.

integrationists working for full citizenship within American society, SNCC shifted first in 1962–63 to a nonviolent guerrilla army made hard from its confrontation with Mississippi police, then, as the summer of 1964 came and passed and with it an influx of northern big city rebels, it began to shift into a stance of alienation from American society. Finally, in 1965 and 1966, culminating in the May, 1966 Nashville retreat and the election of Stokely Carmichael to its chairmanship, SNCC became separatist and nationalist.[33]

The period which opened when a small group of North Carolina Agricultural and Technical College students began their sit-ins in Greensboro, February 1, 1960, and which culminated in the well-publicized March on Washington in the summer of 1963, was a time of great hope. It coincided with the first Kennedy years, the organization of the Peace Corps, and a new flood of idealism with young people leading the way. It seemed a time of possibility. When listening to Martin Luther King tell the nation that "I have a dream" it was easy to forget certain things: that only the tiniest token school integration had taken place since the Supreme Court decision nine years before; that school integration was actually losing ground as whites in northern cities fled the spreading black ghettos; that young civil rights workers were being beaten, jailed and terrorized in Alabama and Mississippi; that churches were being bombed, crosses burned, and men, whose courage outweighed their caution, were being shot down in cold blood; that federally built housing was only one-tenth integrated; that politicians, union leaders, real estate dealers and bankers were combining to raise higher the walls that ring the ghettos; that the day-to-day police brutality that makes most Negroes feel that they are a conquered people within an alien land continued unabated. These were the rocks on which the civil rights movement would eventually founder. But for a short, golden moment it was a time of hope, and the voice of that hope was a young Baptist minister from Georgia, Martin Luther King.

For three years King spoke for the *whole* movement. This was a Doctor of Philosophy from Boston University, who had come to terms with Karl Barth, Reinhold Niebuhr, and Hegel. He had

---

[33] Jack Newfield, *A Prophetic Minority* (New York: New American Library, Inc., 1966), pp. 100–01.

come to terms with them, at least, to the extent of integrating them into the Christ-like mythology, which he clearly expressed on the day he learned of his being awarded the Nobel Peace Prize for 1964. On that day he told his followers how pleased he was with ". . . this mighty army of love, and I am sure that the entire world now looks to the Negro in America for leadership in the whole task of building a world without want, without hate, and where all men live together in shared opportunity and brotherhood."[34]

But this was a new Christ-like mythology embodying several of the important trends in Negro thought since the days of Du Bois. In a sense King's thought was to serve to reinforce the irrationalist, communitarian trend, but in another sense his thought provided the rationalist alternative to "Black Power." Three elements emerge in King's thought as the most crucial: the Christ-like image of the Negro and mission ideology, the idea of nonviolence, and the idea of the "blessed community."

The origin of King's Christ-like mythology went back, of course, to the kind of racial Christianity preached after the turn of the century by Reverdy Ransom and R. R. Wright, Jr. But there were important differences in King's thought that need to be explained. Gone were the racist overtones, the subvert aggression, the appeal to force. These were replaced by the idea of conquest through love. New, also, was the emphasis on love as the instrument of social change that replaced the old emphasis on social science. The community that Wright and Ransom hoped for was to be the socialist community, a product of scientific planning as well as of moral reform. King's shift from science to love as the instrument of change paralleled the shift from rationalism to emotion that characterized Negro literature. The best explanation for this change to love seems to be that King's analysis of his country's social ills was not, as Ransom and Wright held, a matter of the white man's immorality but of the white man's sickness. Ransom and Wright looked on white oppression as being the expression of the white man's immoral, but nevertheless rational, economic self-interest; King looking at the same phenomenon saw the white man's need for ego-gratification through the accumula-

---

[34] Martin Luther King, Jr., "A Mighty Army of Love," *SCLC Newsletter*, Vol. 2 (October-November, 1964) p. 7.

tion of things and through status, or, in other words, the white man's inability to love.

The possible influences that may have bent King in the direction of the Christ-like mythology are not far to seek. They were no further away than the milieu of a boy raised in the home of a Baptist minister and the Baptist-oriented college of the young man. The doctrine was being preached from the halls of Morehouse College to the Baptist citadels in Harlem. One need look no further than the Morehouse professor of religion and philosophy, William Holmes Borders. The Morehouse professor, who was also pastor of the Wheat Street Baptist Church in Atlanta, was, in Baptist circles, a man noted for his courage. The reporter of the *National Baptist Voice* related to his newspaper his experience at the 1948 Georgia Baptist Convention held in the small town of Pelham. Borders was the principal speaker and used the occasion to exhort militancy, telling his listeners that it was time for the Negroes to stand up to the whites. The message carried through the small town to the ears of the whites, who soon collected in a mob outside the church. Borders kept on preaching in complete disregard of the danger. The reporter, who during the speech had eased over into a secluded section behind the choir making ready to dive under a bench when the lynching began, reported all this in amazement. Yet his very strong and militant man preached that "Politeness was in the Negro's meek soul, like corpuscles in his blood," and that "I am a Christian in [Harriet Beecher Stowe's] 'Tom,' for indeed, I practiced the religion of Jesus at points better than my master from whom I learned it." [35]

As had been the case with the Methodists, the Baptists were split into two warring camps. The vast majority were uneducated and held closely to a fundamentalistic faith and the emotional camp meeting style. Only a tiny minority of the Baptist ministers held college degrees. In 1946, when King was beginning his third year at Morehouse, there were 45,000 Negro churches being served by 40,000 ministers. In Protestant seminaries that year there were only 243 Negroes studying for the Bachelor of Divinity degree. It was this very small minority, exposed in college to biblical criticism and religious liberalism, who began working for a Kingdom

---

[35] *National Baptist Voice* (December 1, 1948), 3; William Holmes Borders, *Seven Minutes at the 'Mike' in the Deep South* (Atlanta, Ga., 1943), pp. 100, 104.

of God here on earth, and who employed the mission ideology to this end. These people found their way to the faculties of such institutions as Morehouse College and Howard University as well as to some of the institutional churches in the northern ghettos. One such church was the Abyssinian Baptist Church of Harlem, whose pastor was Adam Clayton Powell, Sr., one-time student at the Yale Divinity School (1895–96), liberal thinker who inclined to sympathize with the aims of socialists and communists, and activist in the cause of the poor.[36]

The senior Powell, who liked to boast that he had once been a young tough on his way to Hell, began his New York ministry preaching in the heart of the city's most notorious red-light district. On arrival in 1908 he began a revival directed at the area's pimps and prostitutes. Finding it impossible to convert them, he waged a bitter six-month war, suffering defeat only after the harlots took to congregating outside the church door soliciting the emerging worshippers. Although he was not wholly successful in eliminating vice from New York, he was brought into contact with the problems of the ghetto people, with the city power structure, and with another tough infighter, Reverdy Ransom. In the midst of opening a free food kitchen in the early 1930's, of excoriating other Negro ministers for their neglect of the poor, and of building the largest Baptist church in the country, Powell found time to preach the Negro mythology exactly as Reverdy Ransom taught it: "Each race," he wrote, "has a contribution to make to the other. My race needs the white man's courage, initiative, punctuality, business acumen and aggressiveness. The white man needs the Negro's meekness, love, forgiving spirit and the emotional religion as expressed in his folk songs." In 1937 the elder Powell delivered an address to the Northern Baptist Convention in which he spelled out the Negro's mission in America: "I can never be moved from the opinion that the colored man was placed in America by providence of God to teach the white man the meaning of love and sympathy."[37]

When we find the same ideas coming from the pen of so worldly a man as the younger Powell, we must surmise that the Christ-like

---

[36] *National Baptist Voice*, February, 1954, p. 4.

[37] A. Clayton Powell, Sr., *Against the Tide: An Autobiography* (New York: Richard Smith, 1938), pp. 50–55, 187, 280.

mythology had become something like reflex action. When the elder Powell stepped down from his pulpit in September of 1937 the younger Powell had already emerged as something of a race leader, calling for the working peoples of the world to unite with the Negro to fight fascism. Within a year the younger man was organizing the Greater New York Coordinating Committee for Unemployment with the object of protesting the exclusion of Negroes from jobs. Already he was deep into politics. In 1941 he made it official by becoming the first black to run for the city council. By 1945 Powell was in the U.S. Congress and on his way to fame.

In 1945 Powell set down his vision of the Negro mission in America in a largely autobiographical book he called *Marching Blacks*. To his mind both the Christian church and American civilization had become dedicated to gold. Pulpits, he wrote, no longer belong to God; they belong to the "fat man" with the elk's tooth dangling from his gold chain. "The first duty of the blacks therefore," he continued, "is to Christianize religion. The religion of the slave period was probably the nearest approach to the purity of the first century church that the world has ever witnessed." Powell believed the Negro to be a natural rebel since the days of the slave revolts. So his natural tendency today is toward the more radical doctrines of communism and socialism—the brotherhood of man. "He [the Negro] will not stop until a people's democracy is born out of the rotten decaying political life of America. . . . The black man is out to save America, to salvage its best, and to take his position in the vanguard of those building an international order of brotherhood." Powell's Negro was a Christian revolutionary, a Black Christ carrying a sword. He was in the militant tradition of R. R. Wright, Jr., and Reverdy Ransom—the tradition of racial Christianity.[38]

The shift from the vision of the younger Adam Clayton Powell to the younger Martin Luther King was made possible by an infusion of love and the new diagnosis of America's ills which shifted from Powell's moralistic allegation of decadence to the more psychologically oriented idea that Americans suffer from the inability to love. The new critique took its rationale from such men as Erich

---

38 Adam Clayton Powell, Jr., *Marching Blacks* (New York: Dial Press, 1945), pp. 199–205.

Fromm and Martin Buber, who were concerned with the alienation of man from man, the one from the point of view of psycho-
analysis, the other from the point of view of religion. The man
who brought this sort of approach to bear on the problem of race
in America was the Morehouse professor of religion and philosophy, George D. Kelsey, whom L. D. Reddick, King's biographer
and friend, described as King's favorite teacher there.

Kelsey's argument was that racism is a search for meaning within
oneself; that, from the point of view of oneself, it turns other
people into objects. It sets up the "I"-"It" relationship between
people that Martin Buber speaks of—a relationship that precludes
the possibility of community. Kelsey made the case that humanism, materialism and racism are all part of the same syndrome—
they all involve competition for status and make for division between men. Racism is status-seeking in the sense that the racist
does not have to compare himself with superior men; he can,
rather, compare himself with "racially" inferior men. Putting it
another way, Kelsey pointed out that racism involves a master-
slave relationship between men: "It is through the slave that the
master exists for himself, and through the master that the slave
exists for himself. In each case, self-consciousness is derived
through the other. The one exists and can only understand himself in relation to the other." This is the sickness of our society.
It is the result of each man trying to be sufficient unto himself by
using others for one's own ego-gratification. Instead of becoming
self-sufficient, however, one becomes totally dependent on this
pathological relationship. It is an association that turns the other
person into an "It," an object, not to be related to on a personal
basis, but to be manipulated, appropriated, experienced. "The object," Kelsey wrote, meaning the slave, "is objectivized, alienated,
and depersonalized in a homogenized mass. But the consciousness
which alienates and dominates makes itself a correlate of that
which it enslaves." The master becomes emotionally dependent
on the slave.[39]

The similarity between Kelsey's critique and those of the
writers—Ellison, Baldwin, Jones—is apparent. Ellison stressed the
manipulative aspect of social relations in America; Baldwin told of

[39] George D. Kelsey, *Racism and the Christian Understanding of Man* (New York:
Charles Scribner's Sons, 1965), pp. 51, 54.

the self-deception involved in status-striving; and Jones remarked that American society is based upon ego-gratification. Each stressed the alienation of man from man that makes community impossible. Like them, Kelsey was making a radical distinction between society and community. Unlike them, however, Kelsey made no contention that suffering and pain have made the Negro strong. Being the slave of the master-slave relationship has made the black man emotionally dependent.

A most important point about Kelsey's argument was that it was anti-humanist and anti-rationalist. The striving for self-perfection and autonomy that humanism involves was for Kelsey the sin of pride, the thing that stands in the way of community. He defined man as "existence-in-love," and argued that "man is bound to man in the community of love. He can be man only in the community of love; he cannot be man by himself." For Kelsey the essence of being human lay not in reason but in love.[40]

So King's "mighty army of love" marched toward "the blessed community." Gone from King's version of the Negro mission was the elder Powell's belief that the black man needs the white man's competitiveness and business acumen as much as the white needs the black's ability to love. Competitiveness is a cancer to be cut away if society is to be transformed into community. That King learned Kelsey's lesson well was reflected in his speeches and sermons. "Segregation," he told his congregation in 1956, "is a blatant denial of the unity which we all have in Christ. It substitutes an 'I-it' relationship for the 'I-thou' relationship. Segregation relegates the segregated to the status of a thing rather than elevates him to the status of a person." Pursuing his subject further in the vein of Kelsey's antihumanism, he told his people to beware of self-denial, self-sacrifice and generosity. If not infused with love these will be simply egoism and spiritual pride. He clearly agreed with his old teacher in defining man as "existence-in-love."[41]

Lest it be thought that King was on the verge of a headlong plunge into the irrational, it must be emphasized that there were strong bonds holding him back. After Morehouse and Crozer The-

---

40 *Ibid.*, p. 77.

41 Martin Luther King, Jr., "Paul's Letter to American Christians," sermon, Dexter Avenue Baptist Church, Montgomery, Alabama, November 4, 1956, King papers, Boston University Library.

ological Seminary, King went on to study with a group of rationalist theologians at Boston University. Two men, in particular, L. Harold DeWolf, King's faculty adviser, and Edgar S. Brightman, were fighting what was perhaps a delaying action against those who would banish reason from religion. These two influenced King thoroughly, as his dissertation for the Doctor of Philosophy degree—a sustained argument based on their premises—attests. Both these men were supporters of "Theistic personalism," both were waging a vigorous counterattack against the "crisis theologians" in defense of reason.[42]

During two world wars Europe underwent a horror so total and devastating that all the old assumptions about man's reasonableness and cilization's progress toward higher forms suddenly, for many, seemed superficial. Obviously man's nature is rooted in evil, how else can such man-made horror be explained? And, where was God during those evil days? Hiding his face? Religion in Europe was shaken to its roots. There was begun a critical reexamination of Christianity by men like Karl Barth and Emil Brunner. Their critique was steeped in Soren Kierkegaard's 19th-century sweeping rejection of rational religion. Kierkegaard taught that reason disjoins the thinker from the thing he is thinking about by turning it into an object. Reason splits man away from God by attempting to make of Him an object. Following the wars, during which God seemed hidden from man, this kind of thinking made sense. Then, there was the crucial problem of evil: how does one reconcile the existence of such evil with the belief of a God who might, if he could, stop evil from materializing? Reason cannot reconcile evil with the idea of an omnipotent God. The conclusion of the "crisis theologians" was that God is "totally other," that he cannot be approached by human reason, that the problem of the existence of God and evil is not the province of reason. Man must cast aside reason and accept the absurd, must make a leap of faith. Neither DeWolf nor Brightman would accept such a conclusion. They were defending a God that man could know and love as a person as well as revere as a "totally other" being. DeWolf approached the question of evil by saying that a rational and good

---

[42] For King's account of the influence of DeWolf and Brightman on his thinking, see, Martin Luther King, Jr., *Stride Toward Freedom: The Montgomery Story* (New York: Harper and Brothers, 1958), p. 100.

God must have a plan in which evil plays its part. Reason may not be able to comprehend this plan in its totality, but it must make the attempt. For his part Brightman rested his defense on the position taken by William James, a position that made God finite and not responsible for the evil in the world but hoped that God and man, working together might eradicate man-made evil. Brightman thought of God not as the infinite creator of the "crisis theologians" but as a finite builder, building purpose and values as he toils.[43]

What both Brightman and DeWolf were defending was the idea of a universe governed according to a rational plan in which man, through reason, might work for a better existence. One might be led to think that King, confronted with the centuries of devastation wrought upon the Negro in America, would incline toward the crisis theology and its acceptance of the irrational. That he did not is probably explained by the Negro Baptist church's traditional belief in a personal God and by the circumstance of his having studied under two personalist theologians. But, beyond these two things, King believed in the Christ-like Negro and the mission ideology with its implication that God does have a rational plan for the Negro in America—a plan which explains the evil white America has done. As King explained it in a 1956 sermon, "Evil is with us as a stark, grim, and colossal reality." But the story of the captive Jews in Egypt "symbolizes something basic about the universe. . . . This story, at bottom, symbolizes the death of evil. It was the death of inhuman oppression and ungodly exploitation." He went on to tell his listeners of his faith in the "moral foundation" of the universe. In a real sense King's continued faith in man's reason and his belief in the Negro mission as part of the divine plan were indissolubly linked.[44]

One of King's biographers claims that King did not become a Gandhian until the Montgomery bus boycott of 1956 was well under way and a white woman suggested the similarity of his methods with those of the great Indian. This claim, whether true or not, serves to point up the fact that the paths along which the

---

[43] L. Harold DeWolf, *The Religious Revolt against Reason* (New York: Harper & Bros., 1949), pp. 129–30; Edgar Sheffield Brightman, *A Philosophy of Religion* (Inglewood Cliffs, N.J.: Princeton-Hall, Inc., 1946), p. 216.

[44] Martin Luther King, Jr. "The Death of Evil upon the Shore," sermon, Cathedral of St. John the Divine, New York City, May 17, 1956, King papers, Boston University Library.

civil rights movement was to follow in the 1960's had been long since laid out in Negro thought and tradition. If King was not a Gandhian his instincts told him to act like one. The Christ-like mythology dovetails well with the idea of nonviolent love. The specific channels through which these ideas passed to ultimately meet and give direction to the 1960 to 1963 protests are complex but discernible.

It is hard to say exactly when and where the seed of nonviolent suffering was planted in the Negro mind. It may have been Howard Thurman who first planted it there. Thurman, another graduate of Morehouse, listened to Gandhi himself tell it on a visit to India in 1935. When Gandhi was through Thurman told him that the Negro American was ready for it. He traveled back to Howard University, where President Mordecai Johnson had asked him to come as a teacher of religion and philosophy, carrying his new doctrine with him. "To each of us," he said, "[Christ's] death reveals redemptive suffering as the grand potential of human life and human suffering." Perhaps it was Thurman who planted the seed in President Mordecai Johnson's mind; if so, he had found fertile ground, for Johnson, too, preached that doctrine. Speaking of St. Paul in a 1924 sermon, Johnson said: "He discovered that the way to happiness is the way of the cross. That suffering man is the man who lays hold of the realities of life, and that the one who runs from the cross runs from life." Johnson made his pilgrimage to see Gandhi in 1950. When he returned it was with the message of redemptive love on his lips. The young Martin Luther King, at that time studying for his B.D. at Crozer Theological Seminary in Chester, Pennsylvania, journeyed to Philadelphia in order to hear Johnson lecture on Gandhi. So impressed was he that by his own account he quickly read a half-dozen books about the Indian. One source for the ideas of nonviolence and redemptive love, then, was a small group of highly educated Baptist clergymen who began their intellectual journeys at Morehouse College in Atlanta, Georgia.[45]

A second center for this kind of thought was a student group led

---

45 Quoted in Elizabeth Yates, *Howard Thurman: Portrait of a Practical Dreamer* (New York: The John Day Co., 1946), p. 233; Mordecai W. Johnson, "The Blindness of Obsession," sermon, First Baptist Church, Charleston, W.Va., July 13, 1924, Moorland Collection, Howard University Library; King, *Stride Toward Freedom*, *op. cit.*, p. 97.

by James M. Lawson in Nashville, Tennessee, during the years 1959 to 1962. Lawson, a divinity student at Vanderbilt University, spread the philosophy of nonviolence and redemptive love among a group of Fisk University students. John Lewis, one of the affected students, and later chairman of SNCC, said that the fermenting force of the early days of the movement that became SNCC was Lawson and his nonviolent philosophy: "Lawson didn't talk much about demonstration. But he philosophized about keeping in harmony with the Christian faith until Christ's example wasn't something remote anymore. Your flesh could suffer like Christ's out of love." "The Movement" which got under way with the Greensboro "sit-ins" in February, 1960, quickly led to a meeting of interested students from across the country. The meeting at Raleigh, North Carolina, in April of 1960, turned out to be SNCC's founding convention, and it was again Lawson who set the tone and temper. Speaking to the group, he asked that the Negro, through Christian nonviolence, and acting for God, work for the "redeemed community." With Lawson's help the idea had become worked into the fabric of the student movement. It was echoed in SNCC's original statement of philosophy and purpose: "Through nonviolence . . . The redemptive community supercedes immoral social systems."[46]

The third center for the philosophy of nonviolence was the Fellowship of Reconciliation headed by A. J. Muste, pacifist. These were the professionals—practical men who relied more upon organization than emotion. Though they were idealists working for a better society, nonviolence, for them, tended to be a tactic rather than an ideology. A. J. Muste, who had introduced nonviolence into labor disputes years before most of the SNCC youngsters were born, was, by the time he started serving as executive director of FOR, the leading pacifist in the country. It was a speech that Muste made at Vanderbilt University that brought Lawson around to the nonviolent philosophy. It was from Muste that the Quaker pacifist Bayard Rustin learned the Gandhian approach. It

---

46 Quoted in Paul Good, "Odyssey of a Man—And a Movement," *New York Times Magazine,* June 25, 1967, 5 ff.; James M. Lawson, "We Are Trying to Raise the 'Moral Issue,'" Francis L. Broderick and August Meier (eds.), *Negro Protest Thought in the Twentieth Century* (Indianapolis, Ind., Bobbs-Merrill Co., Inc., 1965), pp. 274–81; SNCC release, May, 1960, in SNCC folder, King papers, Boston University Library.

was within FOR that the idea of nonviolence was first brought to bear on the racial problem, an idea, first formulated by James Farmer in 1942, which led to the organization of the Congress of Racial Equality. CORE, with the aid and support of Muste and FOR, began sit-ins in 1942 and freedom rides in 1947. By the time the Montgomery bus boycott catapulted King into national prominence in 1956, Bayard Rustin, James Farmer, and others of CORE were old hands at the business of nonviolent protest. Rustin helped King organize the bus boycott and later the Southern Christian Leadership Conference. When the sit-ins began in Greensboro, CORE representatives were quickly on the spot to give guidance in nonviolent techniques.

Men like Bayard Rustin and James Farmer were not, however, charismatic moral leaders like King and Lawson, nor were they moralists. They relate back to the sociological imagination of the social scientists who, during the 1930's, called for fundamental social and economic structural reorganization but were not concerned with either moral revolution or a redeemed community. They led sit-ins, freedom rides, and nonviolent protests; they were jailed and beaten, and, in the case of Farmer, almost lynched. But they never departed from the sociological ideal of the integrated society. Standing at the watershed of the protest movement in 1965, with the old discriminatory legal structure in ruins, but with the black masses seemingly no nearer equality, Rustin wrote what may be said to be the classic statement of the sociological mentality: "But in any case, hearts are not relevant to the issue; neither racial affinities nor racial hostilities are rooted there. It is institutions—social, political, and economic institutions—which are the ultimate molders of collective sentiments." Reconstruct those institutions—reconstruct them immediately—then let the processes of history transform the psychology of the people. The idea of redeeming men's hearts was, for Rustin, irrelevant. The problem was, for him, as for Farmer, a matter of power.[47]

Rustin wrote the above statement at the beginning of 1965, a time when the protest movement had come to a worried halt. By that time a Negro might eat at a Howard Johnson restaurant or

---

[47] Bayard Rustin, "From Protest to Politics," Broderick and Meier (eds.), *Negro Protest Thought in the Twentieth Century*, (Indianapolis, Ind.: Bobbs-Merrill Co., Inc., 1965) p. 413.

sleep at a Holiday Inn, but he could not get a job, or decent housing, or an adequate education. In these fundamental areas he was slipping back. As Rustin pointed out in his statement, two of three of the unemployed were Negroes; there were more Negro dropouts from high school than there were unskilled or semiskilled jobs opening up for them—the chance for a black youth in the ghetto was less than it had been a decade before, and the ghettos were rapidly growing. It would be a little more than a year before "Black Power" would emerge as a slogan, but already Rustin and Farmer were working out programs that would provide it with a framework. Social forces were forcing the shift in direction. What, Rustin asked, is the good of having access to motels and restaurants without having the money to make use of them. Then, in a sentence, he revealed the essence of the shift: "A conscious bid for *political power* is being made, and in the course of that effort a tactical shift is being effected: direct-action techniques are being subordinated to a strategy calling for the building of community institutions or power bases." If political power was to become a reality, community organization was a necessity. The massive economic aid needed for the ghetto had no chance of materializing under existing political power relations.[48]

So the nonmoralistic sociological imagination mapped out the strategy that was to be appropriated by a highly moralistic movement—"Black Power." It was stated purely in terms of power, and based on the proposition that men are rationally motivated by economic self-interest. The fact that the anti-rationalist, highly moralistic black power advocates could pick it up and use it as the formal framework for their demands proves a point—the point that the black power segment of the protest movement had given up on the white man, was no longer concerned with the white man's moral awakening. On the level of society immoral power would always control; on the social level the Negro would emulate the white man. But emulation would not mean assimilation— it would not mean becoming like the white man. The Negro's true humanity would be preserved on the level of community—the mystical black community—which no white man could ever enter.

In May of 1966, "Black Power" erupted from the SNCC Nash-

---

[48] *Ibid.*, p. 407.

ville retreat in the form of Stokely Carmichael and his adherents. Suddenly there emerged such figures as H. "Rap" Brown, Floyd McKissick, and a host of others, to turn both SNCC and CORE into organizations totally different from what they had been during the balmy days when redemption had seemed just around the corner. John Lewis, chairman of SNCC from June, 1963, and James Farmer, national director of CORE since February, 1961, either stepped (Farmer was in poor health) or were pushed aside. Their belief systems—in Lewis' case the mission ideology and in Farmer's the sociological imagination—which had been militant enough for them to sound very dangerous in 1965, could not be stretched to the point demanded by the new doctrines. For the March on Washington in the summer of 1963, John Lewis had prepared a statement which read, in part, "In the struggle we must seek more than mere civil rights; we must work for the community of love, peace, and true brotherhood. Our minds, souls, and hearts cannot rest until freedom and justice exist for *all the people*." "All the people" was soon to become too inclusive for the community envisioned by the workers of SNCC.[49]

The foundations for "black power" had been laid long since. The sociological imagination had created the formal program— political power and community organization. The literary imagination had shown the way to the ideal of community based on the black man's unique genius. The ghetto lore provided the transvaluation of values in the con man ideal. All that was required was hurt—white society provided the hurt.

On August 7, 1964, James Chaney's funeral and memorial service took place in Meridian, Mississippi. The remains of the civil rights worker's body had recently been dug out of a dirt dam near Philadelphia, Mississippi. David Dennis of CORE, the assistant director for the Mississippi Summer Project, spoke at the service. "I am not here," he said, "to pay tribute—I am too sick and tired. Do YOU hear me, I am S-I-C-K and T-I-R-E-D." He had watched too many die, had attended too many funerals. The names he named were by then familiar to a whole nation—Mack Parker, Medgar Evers, Herbert Lee, Lewis Allen, Emmet Till, four little

---

49 Quoted in Howard Zinn, *SNCC: The New Abolitionists* (Boston: Beacon Press, 1964), p. 217.

girls bombed in a Birmingham church. To his listeners he addressed a message born of heartache and frustration: it was *their* sons and daughters who were dying ". . . and you have done nothing about it, and if you don't do anything NOW baby, I say God Damn Your Souls."[50]

James Chaney, along with Michael Schwerner and Andrew Goodman, had been murdered for their civil rights activities in Philadelphia, Mississippi, on June 21. While dragging the Mississippi River for their bodies the corpses of two unidentified Negroes were found—one cut in half and one without a head—a discovery that gave point to another incident that occurred during that same search when it shifted to Neshoba County's swamp: from among a group of whites jeering at the searching sailors one was heard to shout, "We throw two or three niggers in every year, to feed the fish."[51]

For SNCC and CORE workers like Dennis the stages in the struggle were punctuated by death. Take, for example, the death of Herbert Lee. Back in July of 1961, SNCC worker Robert Moses decided, quite on his own, that what was needed was not so much integrated lunch counters as to get out the vote. In his quest for the vote only the toughest and most backward area of Mississippi would do. This was Amite County, where the sheriff's father was the local Klan leader, where only one of the country's 5,500 blacks was registered to vote, where the 1962 school expenditures per pupil was $70.46 for whites, $2.24 for blacks. On August 28, Moses got a voter registration school going in a local church; Herbert Lee was one of those who attended. On September 25, Herbert Lee, 52-year-old father of nine, was murdered by a member of the state legislature. Prosecution was made impossible when the one witness who volunteered to testify was murdered.

By the summer of 1964, Moses and his SNCC group in Mississippi had a large political movement going. An "underground election," held the previous year, had collected 82,000 votes for drugstore owner Aaron Henry (whose home and store were bombed in the process). It seemed, by 1964, with 9,100 Negroes

---

[50] Quoted in letter from Meridian, Miss., August 11, 1964, in Elizabeth Sutherland (ed.), *Letters from Mississippi* (New York: McGraw-Hill Book Co., 1965), p. 192.

[51] Quoted in William McCord, *Mississippi: The Long, Hot Summer* (New York: W. W. Norton and Co., Inc., 1965), p. 81.

added to the state's registered voters, and with the Democratic national convention approaching, the time for an attempted overthrow of the state's political machinery. The Mississippi Freedom Democratic party was to be organized for this purpose by SNCC and CORE regulars with the help of the summer volunteers due to arrive for the Summer Project. Besides nominating Henry for governor, the group supported for Congress a most remarkable woman. In 1962, Mrs. Fannie Lou Hamer had tried to register to vote. She and 17 others rode a bus to the place of registration, but police turned them back because, as they said, the bus was the wrong color. Her audacity cost her her plantation job. She began working for the civil rights groups. This caused her arrest in June, 1963. A Negro man was forced by police to beat her unmercifully. The beating was repeated on August 11, 1964. The Freedom Democratic party was banned by the state as a menace to society. It was officially charged with being a Communist organization. But the bombings, the beatings, the bannings were not enough. Throughout the state in August, 1964, precinct and county meetings were conducted by the new party. Between 60,000 and 80,000 blacks signed the "freedom ballot" (police confiscated many), so that by the time of the Democratic national convention, August 23, a full-fledged political party had been born. Hopes were dashed when the President refused to recognize it as the legitimate Democratic party of Mississippi.[52]

The Mississippi Freedom Democratic party was one of the high points of a summer that saw hundreds of volunteers from across the country invade Mississippi for the Summer Project. The volunteer were very much like the original nonviolent protestors of the 1960 to 1963 period—wholesome, idealistic, well-adjusted middle-class types. In striking contrast were the SNCC and CORE regulars—stoical, unsmiling, with a "premature air of cynicism." These had been beaten, jailed, and, in many cases, shot at. One of the veterans, trying hard to explain the situation to the new arrivals, pointed to his friend, Jimmy Travis: "He has six slugs in him, man, and the last one went right through the back of his neck when he was driving a car outside Greenwood. Ask Jesse

---

[52] This account of Robert Moses in Amite County is taken largely from Newfield, *A Prophetic Minority, op. cit.,* pp. 75–81; the political process is recorded in McCord, *Mississippi: The Long, Hot Summer, op. cit.,* pp. 114–115.

here—he has been beaten so that we couldn't recognize him time and time and time and time again." The difference between those veterans and the first two years of the protest movement was the difference between them and the Summer Project volunteers. And for the veterans a new leader was emerging. During the week of indoctrination for the Summer Project a debate was held between James Lawson, who had so much influenced the early SNCC movement, and Stokely Carmichael. In the mind of one observer Lawson came out second best. It gets to the point, said Carmichael, ". . . when you get tired of being beaten and going back the next day for your beating for 5 days in a row. You get tired of ending up on the floor of the police station screaming at the top of your lungs that yes, you are a nigger, boss." Love and nonviolence have little relevance when one is confronted by brutes. The observer felt that Carmichael's views were those of SNCC in Mississippi that summer of 1964.[53]

The emergent leader was Stokely Carmichael, and his was a new kind of nonviolence. In July, during the 1964 Summer Project, the authorities at Greenwood, Mississippi, had incarcerated some 50 demonstrators in the county penal farm. The 50, under Carmichael's inspiration, had given the farm authorities fits. They had stopped up the drains and flooded one floor; they had started several fires; they had torn boards off of the walls and thrown them out the windows; and, final indignity, against the protests of the guards they had persisted in singing their freedom songs. Carmichael proved himself utterly unafraid of and utterly scornful toward the forces of southern law.[54]

President Johnson's attempted compromise with the Mississippi Freedom Democratic party during the Atlantic City national convention brought from Carmichael the cynical comment that there was no difference between the liberals and the followers of Goldwater. The observation, according to one familiar with SNCC workers, was well received. Carmichael went over to Lowndes County, Alabama, in January, 1965 to organize an all-black party where not one of 12,435 Negroes were registered to vote. After the federal Voting Rights Act of 1965 was passed Lowndes County

---

[53] *Ibid.*, p. 51; quoted in letter of June 19, 1964, in Sutherland, *Letters from Mississippi, op. cit.*, p. 6; quoted in undated letter, in *ibid.*, p. 30.

[54] Described in letter of July 22, in *ibid.*, p. 177.

Democrats raised the qualifying fees for the county 900 percent in order to make it impossible for the destitute Negroes of the area to run for office. A separate black party, then, seemed not only logical, it was a necessity. It was logical because the liberals in the national Democratic party seemed unwilling or unable to support true civil libertarians over the segregationist power structure of the South. It was necessary because it was the only way Negroes might attain public office at all.[55]

When Negroes reached the stage of building their own political party the 1965 words of Bayard Rustin became particularly relevant. In order to build political power a community base must first be organized. "Traditionally," Carmichael told a Howard University audience in late 1966, "for each new ethnic group the route to social and political integration into America's pluralistic society, has been through the organization of their own institutions with which to represent their communal needs within the larger society. This is simply stated what the advocates of black power are saying." In that 1966 speech Carmichael made what had become the basic assumption of the protest movement: that society and community are separate entities. But he went beyond the assumptions of King to those of LeRoi Jones to say that it is only the Negroes who form the community. Negroes, as Carmichael believed, want nothing to do with integrating into a white society well on its way to totalitarianism. What the black man does want and need, Carmichael argued, is political and economic control over his own community. Such control is only possible if he is able to make his potential power felt on the national level, and only if the total social, political and economic power structure of the country is profoundly transformed.[56]

By the time of their respective annual conventions in 1967, both CORE and SNCC were in the process of reading their white members out of the movement. The rationale for this move was spelled out in a position paper drawn up by SNCC workers in Atlanta, Georgia. The basic assumption was that the black community had

---

[55] Bruce Payne, "SNCC: An Overview Two Years Later," Mitchell Cohen and Dennis Hale (eds.), *The New Student Left* (Boston: Beacon Press, 1967), p. 87; SNCC, *"What Would It Profit a Man . . .* , A Report on Alabama," c. 1966.

[56] Stokely Carmichael, speech to Howard Law School, Supplement to *The Barrister*, Vol. 3 (October 14, 1966).

produced a culture, a soul or value system—the paper covered these concepts with the term "nitty-gritty"—to which the white members could not relate. Implied was that whites, no matter how committed to the cause, did not have soul, or, at least, not *the* soul. They could not, said the paper, relate to chitterlings, hog's head cheese, pig's feet, ham hocks, slavery, or the black man's religious experience. "Black people," said the paper, "are not willing to align themselves with a western culture that daily emasculates our beauty, our pride, and our manhood." And, finally, "Whites are the ones who must try to raise themselves to our humanistic level."[57]

Black Power, as the paper just quoted indicates, was not unlike King's Christ-like mythology except in one vital respect—it had lost its concern for the white man. "We can build a community of love," wrote Carmichael, "only where we have the ability and power to do so; among blacks."[58]

If building a community on the concept of the "nitty-gritty," and on the closely related concept of "funk" must have disturbed Martin Luther King and those who followed the Southern Christian Leadership Conference, it would have appalled W. E. B. Du Bois. The idea of eating hog's head cheese would have turned his New England stomach. And the sight described by Jack Newfield of the SNCC worker he saw on the 1965 Selma to Montgomery march in sunglasses, goatee, and overalls, singing, "Do What the Spirit Say Do," was best not seen by Du Bois in *his* goatee, kid gloves, and cane. Both men believed equally in the Negro spirit, but the vision each held put them in different ages. For Du Bois the spirit was always to be guided by the mind and the direction was always toward individual excellence. Yet the vision that guided the Selma marcher was always latent in Du Bois. There was the sense of isolation, and the unspoken need for a sense of community; there was the suspicion that the rationalist approach does not after all get at the core of the human spirit; there was, above all, the anger. The logic, always present in the Du Bois vision, was toward separatism, and toward an irrational, emotional

57 "The Vine City Project Paper on 'Whites in the Movement,'" Cohen and Hale (eds.), *The New Student Left, op. cit.*, pp. 97–108.

58 Stokely Carmichael, "What We Want," Cohen and Hale (eds.), *The New Student Left, op. cit.*, p. 119.

approach to the world and to the understanding of man. The evolution from the Du Bois vision toward that held by the Selma marcher, while perhaps not inevitable in any abstract sense, was made so by white society's unyielding resistance to reason.

Selected bibliography

Robert A. Bone, *The Negro Novel in America*. New Haven, Conn.: Yale University Press, 1958. Literary criticism of a high order covering the full range of Negro literature.

Francis L. Broderick, *W. E. B. Du Bois: Negro Leader in a Time of Crisis*. Stanford, Calif.: Stanford University Press, 1959. The best biography of Du Bois. It combines insight and thorough scholarship based on access to the now closed Du Bois papers.

Sterling A. Brown, *The Negro in American Fiction*. Washington, D.C.: Associates in Negro Folk Education, 1937. The best literary study of the Negro Renaissance, made by an active participant.

E. David Cronon, *Black Moses: The Story of Marcus Garvey and the Universal Negro Improvement Association*. Madison, Wis.: University of Wisconsin Press, 1955. Essential for an understanding of the early stages of black nationalism.

Harold Cruse, *The Crisis of the Negro Intellectual*. New York: William Morrow & Co., Inc. 1967. A critical discussion of the struggle for cultural supremacy between the black nationalists and the Marxists in Harlem literary circles. Cruse blames the Marxists for the Negro's inability to develop a cultural consciousness.

E. Franklin Frazier, *Black Bourgeoisie: The Rise of a New Middle Class in the United States*. New York: The Free Press, 1957. A brilliant sociological essay on the black middle class written with pen dipped in acid. Few books have had more influence on Negro thought.

Thomas F. Gossett, *Race: The History of an Idea in America*. Dallas: Southern Methodist University Press, 1963. It is difficult to realize the respectability that the idea of race has had among scholars as well as among apologists for racism. Gossett shows not only the development and decline of the idea but how deeply it was until recently woven into the fabric of American social theory.

Hugh Hawkins, ed., *Booker T. Washington and His Critics: The Problem of Negro Leadership.* Boston: D. C Heath & Co., 1962. Interpretive articles shedding light on the all-important Washington-Du Bois controversy, one of the formative episodes in the development of Negro thought.

Malcolm X and A. Haley, *The Autobiography of Malcolm X.* New York: Grove Press, Inc., 1965. As a sociological study, a treatise on black nationalism, and a human document, this stands at the top. It can be supplemented by C. Eric Lincoln's, *The Black Muslims in America,* Boston: Beacon Press, 1961, and by E. U. Essien-Udom, *Black Nationalism: The Search for an Identity in America.* Chicago: University of Chicago Press, 1962.

Benjamin Mays, *The Negro's God, As Reflected in His Literature.* Boston: Chapman & Grimes, Inc., 1938. An excellent and insightful study in a field where little scholarly work has been done. For an entirely different approach to the study of Negro religion see Arthur Huff Fauset, *Black Gods of the Metropolis: Negro Religious Cults of the Urban North,* Philadelphia, University of Pennsylvania Press, 1944. Fauset's study is an essay in the art of swindle.

August Meier, *Negro Thought in America, 1880–1915.* Ann Arbor, Mich.: University of Michigan Press, 1963. A great amount of scholarly research went into this book. Its main concern is the Washington-Du Bois controversy which it handles in the conventional way but with great skill. See also August Meier and Francis L. Broderick's compilation, *Negro Protest Thought in the Twentieth Century,* Indianapolis: Bobbs-Merrill Co., Inc., 1965.

Jack Newfield, *A Prophetic Minority.* New York: New American Library, 1966. The best interpretive account of the civil rights movement in the 1960's as it pertains to the evolution from nonviolence to "black power" in the South. It can be supplemented with Howard Zinn's *SNCC: The New Abolitionists,* Boston, Beacon Press, 1964, and William McCord's, *Mississippi: The Long Hot Summer,* New York: W. W. Norton & Co., Inc., 1965.

Robert A. Parker, *The Incredible Messiah: The Deification of Father Divine.* Boston: Little, Brown & Co., 1937. The tendency is to ignore what can't be understood. An understanding of Father Divine and his appeal, however, would be the key to unlocking the history and sociology of the black ghetto. Unfortunately, this book is descriptive rather than analytical.

J. Saunders Redding, *To Make a Poet Black*. Chapel Hill, N. C.: University of North Carolina Press, 1939. A first-rate argument of a thesis thoroughly at odds with the one presented in this study.

Samuel R. Spencer, *Booker T. Washington and the Negro's Place in American Life*. Boston, Little, Brown & Co., 1955. A balanced account of Washington which reflects the recent trend of handling him kindly. The carefully documented, insightful account of Washington's life is yet to be written.

C. Vann Woodward, *The Strange Career of Jim Crow*. New York, Oxford University Press, 1955. Traces the post-Reconstruction rise of racism in the South. The thesis is the now hotly debated one that racism in the South is a recent thing, having risen on the shoulders of the post-Reconstruction struggle for political power.

Whitney M. Young, *To Be Equal*. New York: McGraw-Hill Book Co., 1964. An excellent introduction to the socio-economic problems that confront the Negro and the country. To be supplemented by the thoughtful Charles E. Silberman study, *Crisis in Black and White*, New York: Random House, Inc., 1965.

Index

This book has been set in 11 and 10 point Baskerville, leaded 2 points. Chapter numbers and titles are in 48 and 24 point Bodoni Bold. The size of the type page is 26 × 43⅔ picas.